COMPLETE WINE SELECTOR

How to choose the right wine every time

Published by Firefly Books Ltd. 2013

First printing

Publisher Cataloging-in-Publication Data (U.S.)

A CIP record for this title is available from the Library of Congress

Library and Archives Canada Cataloguing in Publication

Cole, Katherine, author
Complete wine selector : how to choose the right wine every time / Katherine Cole ; Neil Beckett, editor.
Includes index.
ISBN 978-1-77085-225-9 (pbk.)
1. Wine and wine making. I. Beckett, Neil, editor II. Title.
TP548.C635 2013 641.2'2 C2013-902052-7

Published in the United States by
Firefly Books (U.S.) Inc.
P.O. Box 1338, Ellicott Station
Buffalo, New York 14205

Published in Canada by
Firefly Books Ltd.
50 Staples Avenue, Unit 1
Richmond Hill, Ontario L4B 0A7

Printed in China

Fine Wine Editions

Publisher Johanna Wilson; Editor Neil Beckett; Art Director Bob Morley; Design Consultant Peter Dawson, Grade Design Consultants; Designer Simon Murrel, Sands Editorial Solutions; Picture Researcher Kazumi Suzuki; Production Manager Nikki Ingram

COMPLETE WINE SELECTOR

How to choose the right wine every time

Katherine Cole

FIREFLY BOOKS

CONTENTS

FOREWORD

Every ten years—or is it every five, or every two?—a new book appears that claims to banish the cobwebs, cut the pomposity, shed new light and simplify the whole archaic business of wine. My publisher made the claim for me in 1966. Many of us make the attempt, but the stubborn fact remains: Wine is a complicated subject, inherently and irredeemably complicated. It's not alone. The World Cup, The World Series, Formula One, Horse Racing and, for that matter, pop music are all complicated if you are into more than the headlines. The dilemma with wine? It's meant to be jolly fun, delicious, go well with food, give you the holiday feeling. Surely all this can be done without anything as heavy as facts.

Well, no. Not if you want more than just a cheerful swallow and a light head. True, there is industrial wine, which is as simple as it is boring and unsatisfying. But the authentic stuff, made by individuals in their own vineyards with such inconveniences as the weather to deal with, is as various and as variable as, well, individuals, vineyards and weather.

It was when I was just finishing the huge research project that was my *Wine Companion*, back in 1983, that I looked around for a shortcut for readers through the thousands of entries. I divided wine into 10 different styles. I grouped light aromatic whites...through to rich sweet reds. It was helpful then, I think, even as a sketch of an idea. It has taken 30 years, it seems, to find a writer to adopt it wholeheartedly and breathe life into it.

Wherever she found the idea, Katherine Cole has done precisely this—thoroughly, graphically, and I think extremely helpfully. But she has gone much further. She builds a whole wine primer around the structure of wine flavors and weights, relates them to food and mood, and gives specific examples ranging from deluxe to budget. As you read, learn from her practical experience and reach her masterclasses, where you will suddenly find the complexities fascinating after all. The cobwebs have gone. The glass in your hand shines brighter and more enticingly than ever.

INTRODUCTION

"So I grew up in New York, in a working-class home. Then I was a hippie, living in Iowa City, getting my PhD in Creative Writing. Finally I ended up in L.A., a young guy of about 30. My agent, Georges, who was the most sophisticated gentleman in the world, was flying into town and coming over to dinner and I thought, 'I'd better get something good.' I didn't know anything about wine, but I went to a shop and spent *wayyyy* more than I could afford on a bottle of red and a bottle of white, both from California. Meanwhile, Georges and his wife, Anne, rented a car at the airport and stopped at a wine shop along the way to my place. They, too, bought one bottle of red and another bottle of white, French wines, which were not nearly as expensive as what I had bought. But you know what? Their wines were one thousand times better than mine."

I heard this story recently from the American novelist T. Coraghessan Boyle. Boyle is a distinguished professor of English and the much-lauded author of more than 23 works of fiction. His books have been translated into more than two dozen foreign languages. He's the sort of guy who is fêted with glamorous dinner parties wherever he goes, on every continent.

But T.C. Boyle is just as tentative as you or I about selecting and purchasing wine. He might write eloquently about a Riesling from Piesport (in *Talk Talk*, 2006), but when he walks into a bottle shop—even today—he gravitates toward the two or three labels he knows he can rely on. For example: Byron, which produces some of his favorite Pinot Noirs and Chardonnays in the Santa Maria Valley, very near his Santa Barbara home.

WHY THIS BOOK IS BETTER THAN A PSYCHIATRIST

Like most of us, Boyle possesses a deep, dark secret: While he loves wine, he does not love the process of selecting wine. That's why he keeps going back to his old standbys. "You find something you like and it can be pretty consistent, year to year," Boyle told me. "With Byron, you know what you are getting. As far as I'm concerned, once I find something I like, I tend to stick with it."

Boyle's experience is universally relatable. We might be eminently successful in business or medicine, design or literature, but when we duck into a wine shop or pick up a thick restaurant wine list, we feel as though we've stepped into that recurring nightmare—you know the one—in which we're standing in a college lecture hall, stark naked, for a final exam in a subject we've never studied.

Perplexed, nonplussed, panicked, we might decide that the best course of action will be to overpay, just as the young T.C. Boyle did when he wanted to impress his urbane French literary agent. Surely the most expensive wine will be the best?

Or, with time and increased wisdom, we return, like Boyle does today, to the one or two reliably familiar labels that are readily available in restaurants and wine shops.

But here's the rub: If you're overpaying for wine, or tasting the same release week after week, you're cheating yourself. Imagine paying twice the usual price for a music download that just isn't that sweet. Imagine watching the same episode of *Girls* every week for the rest of your life. How foolish would that be?

Consider *Complete Wine Selector* your therapy. Read this book and you'll overcome your paralyzing fear of the world of wine. And you'll open yourself up to new sensory experiences. Because wine is like anything else we consume culturally: The more we allow ourselves to engage intellectually with it, the more likely it is to blow our minds.

CURIOSITY TRUMPS POMPOSITY

With a subtle-yet-somehow-menacing bow, the sommelier hands you a biblically proportioned tome at Le Restaurant Snob Français. And you suddenly wish you were the kind of tiresome know-it-all who can handle a wine list (or at least bluff his way through it).

When you enter L'Enoteca Confusione, the bell at the front door clangs like a siren, and suddenly the shopkeeper is there, breathing down your neck as you scan those shelves stacked sky-high with alien-looking bottles and labels. And now you're wishing you were a National Lottery winner, so you could throw your credit card down at that shop and declare, "A case of your best!"

For too long, wine appreciation has been the hegemony of those with quiz-show memories. But we are here to tell you: You need not be Rain Man to navigate the vinous world. Clear your mind of all concerns related to village, vintage or *Vitis vinifera. Complete Wine Selector* dispenses with the irrational manner in which most wine shops and wine lists are organized—by geographical region—instead guiding you through the 10 most common styles.

And for too long, wine collection has been the domain of those with thick wallets. But today, you need not be a wizard of finance to have a world of fine wine at your fingertips. Some of the most delicious alcoholic beverages on the planet, my friends, are priced about the same as a sandwich and cup of coffee at your neighborhood diner.

By reading this book, you'll join the new wave of wine enthusiasts. These are the travelers who embrace the unfamiliar, always curious about those out-of-the-way viticultural regions no one's ever heard of. They're the foodies with a keen sense for when to go for a lower-alcohol option and when to embrace fruity opulence. They're the savvy economists who know that the word "reserve" isn't usually worth the extra expense. And they're the confident consumers who know that the priciest bottle isn't necessarily the best.

In the pages of *Complete Wine Selector*, you'll meet the world's top sommeliers, tour the planet's best restaurants and wine shops, spy on a vineyard and winery at work, and learn how to store and serve wine in your own home.

And we'll do our best to use the simplest language possible. Where wine books of ages past sounded as baroque as a harpsichord concerto, we'll aim for plainsong. Aided by lots of user-friendly charts and symbols (not, we assure you, cymbals).

We are here to debunk the belief that you've got to be a disgustingly wealthy winner of the world blind-tasting championships to truly appreciate wine. All you need is a sense of adventure. And a copy of *Complete Wine Selector* on your coffee table.

Alongside a copy of T.C. Boyle's latest novel, of course. Cheers!

SECTION 1
WINE STYLES

1 CRISP, LEAN WHITES

1 CRISP, LEAN WHITES

Cue "The Girl from Ipanema" and imagine yourself at a casual beachside café on a sunny afternoon, snacking on some salted almonds or *pommes frites*, and maybe a simple salad. Now, what to drink?

It's got to slake your thirst as well as being mouthwateringly tasty. And you don't want to have to think too much about it, or pay very much for it. A crisp and lean white should be all of these things. It should also share the common denominators of acidity, minerality and, often, spritz—three terms that we'll explore in depth later. It's a wine style that should be drunk immediately and inexpensively, so it shouldn't spend time in costly oak barrels. Most important, the best lean white wines are like expertly mixed margaritas: salty, thirst-quenching, brimming with delicious acidity and simply... fun.

Speaking of margaritas, if there's any flavor component shared by all crisp and clean white wines, it's citrus. Think of what that final garnish of lemon zest does for a plate of herbaceous pasta, or how a squeeze of fresh orange and a drizzle of Ligurian olive oil transform raw scallops into delectable *carpaccio*. This is how the citrus note in a crisp white wine transforms the food on your plate.

Chardonnay that's been vinified in stainless steel instead of oak barrels can be crisp and lean. So can Sauvignon Blanc from Bordeaux, or Chenin Blanc from Saumur. But these varieties take on rich, aromatic characteristics elsewhere. So, for this section, we'll focus on grapes that are known first and foremost for their fierce freshness. Many of these varieties may be unfamiliar to you. Look to cooler climates and the influence of the ocean: northern Italy, Portugal and Spain; mountainous Austria or Savoie; or seaside regions like the Greek islands or France's Bay of Biscay, where the air is briny and the cuisine is herbaceous.

Soon, you'll be in the mood to ice down some oysters and chill a bottle of Muscadet, or plop a bottle of Vinho Verde in an ice bucket and put together a *bossa nova*-heavy playlist of Astrud and João Gilberto, Elis Regina and Stan Getz. Whatever the weather's doing, you can always feel those warm sea breezes and smell that salt air when you've got a glass of crisp, lean white wine in hand.

YOU'LL ENJOY THESE WINES IF...

- You love citrusy beverages, such as lemonade or gin-and-tonic
- You are on a budget
- You enjoy light fare, such as shellfish and salads

WHAT THE EXPERTS SAY

"We do several first courses of seafood with citrus. Calamari with avocado, for example, or, in Argentina, we do a lot of ceviche—raw fish with lime, really spicy. I always recommend something dry and crisp with medium-to-high acidity and a more mineral aspect, like a Rueda Verdejo. Soave from Italy is interesting with salads. With arugula with goat cheese, Verdicchio is a really good choice because it's more green and racy. These wines are not complex, but they don't usually have oak and they always have good acidity."

Paz Levinson, Sommelier, Nectarine, Buenos Aires, Argentina

GOOD TO DRINK WITH

KEY

$	UNDER $15	$$$$	$50–100
$$	$15–30	$$$$$	$100+
$$$	$30–50		

THE NAMES TO LOOK FOR

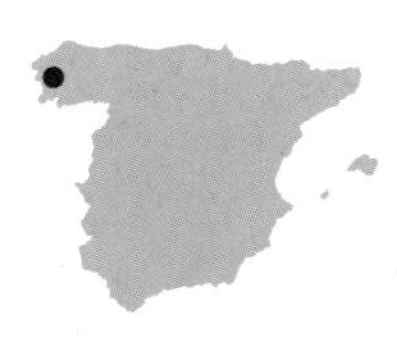

ALBARIÑO RIAS BAIXAS, SPAIN

Like Verdejo from Rueda, Albariño was virtually unknown outside Spain until recently. Smooth, lemony and (mostly) affordable, it's poised today to displace Pinot Grigio as the go-to, by-the-glass option for restaurants. Minerality and tropical fruit and floral notes make this a wine that can outlast cocktail hour and hang with the main course.

[**PRICE RANGE: $-$$$**]

[**ABV: 11-13.5%**]

[**DRINK IT: 1-5 YEARS AFTER THE VINTAGE**]

CHOICE

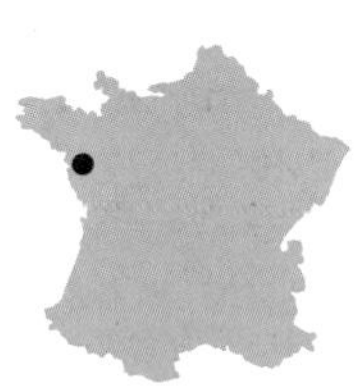

MELON DE BOURGOGNE LOIRE VALLEY, FRANCE

Think maritime breezes, ocean brine and seashells, bottled, and you've got a good sense of Muscadet, the Loire Valley's coastally influenced white. Its searing acidity is counterbalanced by the popular *sur lie* winemaking, which brings creaminess to the mouthfeel. Inexpensive yet essential, for clam bakes, crab boils, *moules frites* and, of course, oysters on the half-shell.

[**PRICE RANGE: $-$$**]

[**ABV: 10.5-12%**]

[**DRINK IT: 1-3 YEARS AFTER THE VINTAGE**]

RODITIS PELOPONNESE, GREECE

This delicate grape is actually pink-skinned, but the wine is pale, crisp and fragrant with citrus and floral notes, especially when produced in the sub-appellation of Patras. It's ideal for washing down *mezedes*—Greek-style tapas—so serve it with cucumbers, feta, yogurt, wild greens, squid, octopus and lamb, and don't skimp on the lemon and fresh herbs.

[**PRICE RANGE: $-$$**]

[**ABV: 11.5-13%**]

[**DRINK IT: IMMEDIATELY**]

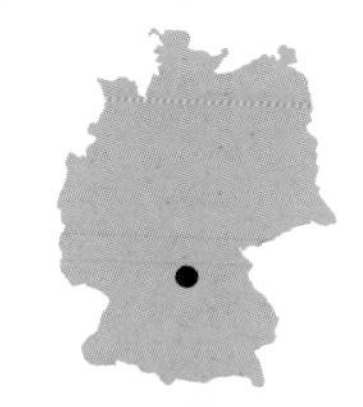

SILVANER FRANKEN, GERMANY

Say what? If you've never heard of Silvaner, you're not alone. But this crisp, fennel-scented white is appearing on more and more wine lists, and I'd argue that it's ready to have a moment. (In Alsace, France, where it's spelled "Sylvaner," it's beginning to break out of blends and fly solo.) If you aren't on board with the sweetness of some German Riesling, give herbaceous, woodsy Silvaner a try.

[**PRICE RANGE: $-$$**]

[**ABV: 11-13%**]

[**DRINK IT: 1-3 YEARS AFTER THE VINTAGE**]

SOAVE VENETO, ITALY

Italy might be famous for long-lived reds like Barolo, but look to northerly zones like Alto Adige, Friuli, Liguria, Marches, Piedmont, Trentino and the Veneto for minerally, food-loving whites that would be delicious with tonight's risotto or pasta. Almond-scented Soave, made from the indigenous Garganega grape, has a lovely, soothing, chamomile-tea quality.

[**PRICE RANGE: $-$$**]

[**ABV: 11-13.5%**]

[**DRINK IT: 1-5 YEARS AFTER THE VINTAGE**]

VINHO VERDE MINHO, PORTUGAL

The "green wine" of verdant northwest Portugal's Costa Verde fizzes with spritz, refreshes at 11.5% alcohol or less, and is always dirt-cheap by comparison with most other wines. Appealing notes of citrus, stone-fruits, almonds, sand and flowers come from any of 25 different grape varieties, including Alvarinho (the same thing as the Spanish Albariño).

[**PRICE RANGE: $**]

[**ABV: 8-11.5%**]

[**DRINK IT: IMMEDIATELY**]

TAKE ONE WINE: BURGÁNS RÍAS BAIXAS ALBARIÑO

THE BASICS

GRAPE VARIETY: Albariño

REGION: Val do Salnés, Rías Baixas, Galicia, Spain

ALCOHOL LEVEL: 12.5%

PRICE: $–$$

AVAILABILITY: Widely available

APPEARANCE: Bright, translucent, greenish-straw.

TASTING NOTE: Lemon verbena; tarragon; tropical fruits and flowers; lemon chiffon; brine; white pepper; refreshing acidity.

FOOD MATCH: Salty snacks, seafood or light rice dishes.

DRINK OR KEEP: Drink this pick-me-up as soon as it's chilled.

WHY DOES IT TASTE THAT WAY?

Rías Baixas (pronounced REE-AHSS BYE-SHAHSS) is the leading *Denominación de Origen*, (DO) or official Spanish winegrowing region in Galicia, northwestern Spain. Albariño is the name of the game here: More than 99 percent of the wine produced is white; and Albariño represents 90 percent of that.

Due to the cool, damp, coastal climate here, the vines are trained—often on trellises supported by granite posts, to withstand maritime winds—for maximum sunlight exposure and minimal chance of rot. The bunches are picked by hand, then transported to the winery as quickly as possible to avoid oxidation. While higher end bottlings might be more voluptuous thanks to barrel aging, this fresh style of Albariño is fermented in stainless steel for the classic snappy style that Galicia is known for. And yet, it's luscious too, thanks to maceration *sur lie* and malolactic fermentation. (You'll learn about these terms soon, in our Masterclass on acidity and minerality.)

WHO MADE IT?

This wine is a group effort. In 1986, as Albariño was just beginning to be exported outside Spain, 50 Galician growers joined forces to form a winemaking cooperative, naming it after Martín Códax, an influential Galician poet and composer in the Middle Ages.

Today Bodegas Martín Códax is a major economic force for the region, attracting tourists to its contemporary tasting room (the famous Camino de Santiago, or pilgrimage route to the Cathedral of Santiago de Compostela, is close by) and counting 600 local families among its members. Lead winemaker Luciano Amoedo led the movement to have Rías Baixas designated a *Denominación de Origen*, or official winegrowing region, in 1988. Katia Álverez oversees Albariño production, and an American importer, Eric Solomon, selects the blend that will become Burgáns.

CRACKING THE CODE
BURGÁNS
BURGÁNS
ALBARIÑO
Exclusivamente elaborado con uvas de Albariño procedentes de parcelas seleccionadas do Val do Salnés.
RIAS BAIXAS
DENOMINACION DE ORIXE
75 cl. / 12,5% Vol.
CLOSURE
The screwcap is an indicator that this wine isn't meant to age.
WINE NAME
"Burgáns" is the Celtic name for the slope where the winery is located. The original inhabitants of Galicia were actually Celts; the Celtic triskele symbol on the label is a reference to this little historical tidbit. Burgáns is also the proprietary name for a distinctive style of Albariño produced by the cooperative winery Bodegas Martín Códax.
REGION
Rías Baixas means "lower fiords." If you look at a map of the northwest coast of Spain, you'll see fingers of land that are surrounded by water on three sides.
OFFICIAL STAMP
You'll find a special seal on the back of the bottle with the official stamp of Rías Baixas. This certifies that the grapes and wine have passed inspection with the consejo regulador and gives the bottle's serial number.
SUBREGION
Val do Salnés, the oldest subregion of Rías Baixas, is said to be the birthplace of Albariño. Some of the best-known Albariño producers are located here. "Salnés" is Galician for "drinks." Just thought you'd get a kick out of that.
ALCOHOL
Look for the tiny number on the bottom or side of label to find out the wine's alcohol content. Seeing that this wine is a relatively low 12.5%, we can guess that it will be crisp and lean.

BURGÁNS RÍAS BAIXAS ALBARIÑO

WHY THAT PRICE?

Crisp, lean white wines tend to be inexpensive because the grapes aren't overly costly to grow, and the winemaking doesn't involve aging in French oak barrels. In addition, these wines are released young, so they don't take up valuable space in the winery. And they tend to be packaged in basic, lightweight bottles topped with simple corks or screwcaps, so the materials and shipping costs are lower.

It's also important to note that Bodegas Martín Códax is a cooperative winery. Once upon a time—back when almost every rural home was part of a small farmstead, raising everything from olives to sheep—most European villages had their own unofficial cooperatives. Local farmers would bring their grapes to these centrally located barns and collaboratively make rustic wines, on communally owned equipment, for everyone to enjoy. Although some of the old cooperatives still exist, an increasing number of today's co-ops are sophisticated businesses that create value by pooling their resources. Perhaps the most famous winemaking cooperative is Cantina Sociale dei Produttori del Barbaresco, which produces quite serious red wines from the Nebbiolo grape, in northwestern Italy.

WHAT FOOD DOES IT GO WITH?

The culinary tradition in Galicia is all about seafood, so any fish or shellfish dish will work with the Burgáns. The wine's fresh acidity and fruit are delicious counterpoints to salt, and the creamy texture works with similarly smooth sauces.

So try *Bacalao* (salt cod) with *aioli* (garlic mayonnaise); *fritto misto* (deep-fried vegetables with lemon mayonnaise); *tom yung gai* (lemongrass, coconut and kaffir lime soup); or a *salade Niçoise* topped with hard-boiled eggs. And don't forget the garnishes: Crisp white wines like this one love a squeeze of lime or a pinch of chopped fresh cilantro or parsley.

Left: Part of the patchwork of small vineyards that make up the Rías Baixas DO on Galicia's southwest coast; one of the rías (fiords) that give the region its name is in the background.

TOP FOOD MATCH:
Risotto with scallops and spring vegetables

SALADS

LIGHT PASTAS

SEAFOOD

10 OF THE BEST

COOL RÍAS BAIXAS ALBARIÑOS

BENITO SANTOS	\$–\$\$\$
LA CANA	\$–\$\$
DO FERREIRO	\$–\$\$\$
FORJAS DEL SALNÈS	\$–\$\$\$
MORGADÍO	\$–\$\$
PACO & LOLA	\$–\$\$
PALACIO DE FEFIÑANES	\$\$
PAZO SEÑORANS	\$–\$\$\$\$
PEDRALONGA	\$\$
LA VAL	\$

AROUND THE WORLD

WINES IN A SIMILAR STYLE FROM DIFFERENT COUNTRIES

Abacela, Estate Grown, Albariño,
Umpqua Valley, Oregon, U.S. \$\$

Bouza, Albariño,
Las Violetas, Uruguay \$\$

Quinta do Soalheiro,
Vinho Verde Alvarinho,
Monção e Melgaço, Portugal \$–\$\$

CHOICE MADE SIMPLE

EXPERT'S PERSONAL FAVORITES

Recommended by Matteo Ghiringhelli, Sommelier, Il Vino, Paris, France

MATTIA BARZAGHI, IMPRONTA VERNACCIA, VERNACCIA DI SAN GIMIGNANO TUSCANY, ITALY $

LAGAR DE BESADA, EX LIBRIS ALBARIÑO RÍAS BAIXAS, GALICIA, SPAIN $

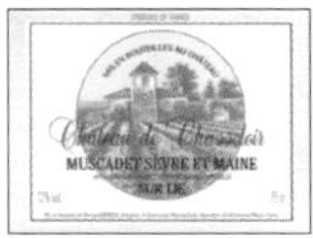

CHÂTEAU DE CHASSELOIR, MUSCADET SÈVRE ET MAINE (MELON DE BOURGOGNE) MUSCADET, LOIRE, FRANCE $

DOMAINE CHIROULET, TERRES BLANCHES (GROS MANSENG / SAUVIGNON BLANC / UGNI BLANC) GASCONY, FRANCE $

CONTINI, TYRSOS (VERMENTINO) SARDINIA, ITALY $

GRACI, ETNA BIANCO (CATARRATTO / CARRICANTE) ETNA, SICILY, ITALY $$

KIENTZLER, RIBEAUVILLÉ SYLVANER (SYLVANER) ALSACE, FRANCE $

CAVE LA MADELEINE, PAÏEN D'ARDON (SAVAGNIN BLANC) ARDON, VALAIS, SWITZERLAND $$

RAPARIGA DA QUINTA, BRANCO, (ANTÃO VAZ / ARINTO) ALENTEJO, PORTUGAL $

FATTORIA SAN LORENZO, VIGNA DELLE OCHE, VERDICCHIO DEI CASTELLI DI JESI (CLASSICO SUPERIORE) MARCHE, ITALY $–$$

WORLD OF FINE WINE RECOMMENDATIONS

RAFAEL PALACIOS, AS SORTES (GODELLO) VALDEORRAS, GALICIA, SPAIN $$$

BODEGAS GERARDO MÉNDEZ, DO FERREIRO CEPAS VELLAS (ALBARIÑO) RÍAS BAIXAS, GALICIA, SPAIN $$$

DOMAINE A & P DE VILLAINE, ALIGOTÉ DE BOUZERON (ALIGOTÉ) BOUZERON, BURGUNDY $$

DOMAINE PONSOT, MOREY-ST-DENIS PREMIER CRU CLOS DES MONTS LUISANTS (ALIGOTÉ) BURGUNDY, FRANCE $$$$

CLOS DU TUE-BOEUF, TOURAINE, BRIN DE CHEVRE (MENU PINEAU) LOIRE, FRANCE $$

WEINGUT HORST SAUER, ESCHERNDORFER LUMP SILVANER GROSSES GEWÄCHS (SILVANER) FRANKEN, GERMANY $$

WEINGUT WELTNER KÜCHENMEISTER SYLVANER GROSSES GEWÄCHS (SILVANER) FRANKEN, GERMANY $$

CANTINA TERLAN, VORBERG RESERVA PINOT BIANCO (PINOT BLANC) ALTO ADIGE, ITALY $$

LA GIUSTINIANA, GAVI DI GAVI LUGARARA (GAVI) PIEMONTE, ITALY $$

VILLA BUCCI, VERDICCHIO DEI CASTELLI DI JESI CLASSICO SUPERIORE (VERDICCHIO) MARCHE, ITALY $$

(Grape Varieties in Brackets)

VERSATILE FOOD WINES

DOMAINE DE BÉGROLLES, MUSCADET SÈVRE ET MAINE (MELON DE BOURGOGNE) MUSCADET, LOIRE, FRANCE $

DURIN, PIGATO (PIGATO) RIVIERA LIGURE DI PONENTE, LIGURIA, ITALY $$

CASA VINICOLA BRUNO GIACOSA, ROERO ARNEIS (ARNEIS) PIEDMONT, ITALY $$

PIEROPAN, LA ROCCA SOAVE (CLASSICO SUPERIORE) (GARGANEGA) VENETO, ITALY, $$

JULIUSSPITAL, SILVANER TROCKEN (SILVANER) FRANKEN, GERMANY $–$$

FATTORIA LAILA, VERDICCHIO DEI CASTELLI DI JESI (VERDICCHIO) CASTELLI DI JESI (CLASSICO SUPERIORE), MARCHE, ITALY $–$$

DOMAINE SIGALAS, ASSYRTIKO ATHIRI (ASSYRTIKO / ATHIRI) SANTORINI, GREECE $–$$

TETRAMYTHOS, RODITIS PATRAS (RODITIS) PATRAS, PELOPONNESE, GREECE $–$$

VALDESIL, GODELLO SOBRE LÍAS (GODELLO) VALDEORRAS, GALICIA, SPAIN $$

HERMANOS DE VILLAR, IPSUM (VERDEJO / VIURA) CASTILLA Y RION, RUEDA, SPAIN $–$$

BEST ON A BUDGET

MICHEL DELHOMMEAU, CUVÉE ST. VINCENT MUSCADET SÈVRE ET MAINE (MELON DE BOURGOGNE) MUSCADET, LOIRE, FRANCE $

GIRAURDON, BOURGOGNE ALIGOTÉ (ALIGOTÉ) BURGUNDY, FRANCE $

DOMAINE LABBÉ, ABYMES (JACQUÈRE) SAVOIE, FRANCE $

CASA FERREIRINHA PLANALTO WHITE (MALVASIA FINA / VIOSINHO / GOUVEIO / CODEGA) DOURO, PORTUGAL $

INAMA, VIN SOAVE (GARGANEGA) SOAVE (CLASSICO SUPERIORE), VENETO, ITALY $

QUINTA DA AVELEDA, VINHO VERDE (LOUREIRO / TRAJADURA / ALVARINHO) VINHO VERDE, MINHO, PORTUGAL $

CASA SANTOS LIMA, FERNÃO PIRES (FERNÃO PIRES [MARIA GOMES]) ESTREMADURA, PORTUGAL $

DOMAINE REINE JULIETTE, TERRES ROUGES (PICPOUL DE PINET) COTEAUX DU LANGUEDOC, FRANCE $

DOMAINE DU TARIQUET, CLASSIC (UGNI BLANC / COLOMBARD / SAUVIGNON BLANC / GROS MANSENG) GASCONY, FRANCE $

DOMAINE DES TERRISSES, BLANC SEC (LEN DE L'EHL / MAUZAC) GAILLAC, FRANCE $

MASTERCLASS: ACIDITY AND MINERALITY

We tend to think of wine in terms of aromas and flavors: fruit, flowers, smoke, leather. But the two most important building blocks in a great wine don't necessarily call upon your sense of smell or taste; they are more closely related to texture. They are **acidity** and **minerality**.

Acidity is most obvious in crisp white wines. Here's why: Suck on a slice of lemon, then take a sip of milk or sprinkle a spoonful of sugar on your tongue, and you'll notice that the sensation of acidity is immediately dampened. So, in very fruity wines, or wines that have gone through **malolactic fermentation**—in which sharp malic acids are converted into the same smooth lactic acids that are in dairy products—we don't notice acidity as much. Lean, dry white wines that aren't sweet and haven't gone through "malo" are acidity's most transparent conductors.

Acidity might sound off-putting, but in fact, it's far more unpleasant to sip a wine that's "flabby," or low in acid, especially if you're sitting down to a meal. A dash of vinegar over fish and chips, a squeeze of lemon over veal cutlets, a dressing on a salad, tomatoes on pizza, soy sauce on stir-fry or even olive oil on bread—these are all agents of acidity that please our palates. In the same way, a briskly acidic wine makes a delicious foil for food.

If you want to put your tolerance for acidity to the test, try an Aligoté (a white varietal wine) from Burgundy. I like to call this the "alligator wine" because of its sharp snap.

Ideally, the weather during the growing season would be balmy during the day, to ripen the fruit, and chilly at night, to preserve acidity. But in cool growing regions, vintners might be forced to **de-acidify** their wines in particularly cold years to make them more pleasant on the palate. Likewise, too much warm weather might force winemakers to **acidify**, to avoid the dreaded "flabbiness."

Although I'm a fervent embracer of acidity, I have my limits if I have to taste through hundreds of Rieslings in a day. Some professional wine tasters even gargle with baking soda and brush with special toothpastes to prevent the acidity from all that wine stripping the enamel off their teeth. But happily you won't have any such problems.

As for minerality, it's much more difficult to define. Wine lovers claim that minerality is an integral part of **terroir**—the notion that you can taste the place where the vines were grown. You'll hear oenophiles referring to a "chalky Chablis," or "gravelly" Cabernet Sauvignon, for example. But geologists tell us that minerality is a myth: Plants, they say, can't conduct flavor from the substrata. Nonetheless, minerality is something we *perceive* in wine, regardless of its origin, and like acidity, it's most noticeable in light, crisp whites.

HOW TO IDENTIFY THESE ELEMENTS

1: Suck on a lemon slice or sip a teaspoonful of vinegar and you'll get a sense of what acidity feels like in your mouth. It isn't so much a flavor—although it tends to accompany citrusy notes of tartness or sourness—as a sensation. You'll feel a pleasant sting at the top of your tongue; the sides of your mouth will water; and your lips will pucker pleasantly.

2: To try to wrap your mind around the idea of minerality, wash—thoroughly!—a pebble. While it's still damp, smell the aroma of wet stone. Then, pop the pebble in your mouth. You might detect a faint flavor of dirt, and a matte, paperlike texture. You might, too, feel dryness along the sides of your tongue.

3: Acidity and minerality make the most impact not in tasting the wine, but in the aftereffect, or the **finish**. After you've put that lemon slice aside, the acidity lingers, continuing to produce a waterfall of juiciness in your mouth. The stone, too, might leave your mouth feeling and tasting a bit chalky, in an oddly pleasant way. A fine wine will linger in your mouth similarly.

CRACKING THE CODE

Common descriptors for Muscadet are "briny minerality" and "oyster shells." Could these aroma and flavor components come from sea breezes, blowing in from the Bay of Biscay and down the Loire River or, perhaps, the distinctive soils of the Muscadet region? A geologist or biologist might say no, but a believer in terroir would say yes.

Crisp and refreshing Muscadet serves the same purpose as a squeeze of lemon or a drizzle of mignonette. The acidity in all three of these accompaniments complements flavors from the ocean and brings a prickly, lively feeling to your tongue that contrasts with the slippery sensation of a raw oyster.

LEES AGING
The sea-green bottle is a signature of Muscadet. Like most of the best examples, this wine was aged *sur lie*, meaning that it sat on its lees, or spent yeast cells, prior to bottling. This imparts a creamy texture that complements the elements of acidity and minerality.

APPELLATION
Muscadet's proximity to the Atlantic Ocean makes it the coolest and wettest growing region in the Loire Valley. That makes for wines of naturally high acidity and low alcohol. Sèvre et Maine is the most important sub-appellation of the Muscadet wine region.

ALCOHOL
Muscadet is made from a fairly neutral white grape called Melon de Bourgogne. Because this is a light wine, at 12% ABV, we're better able to perceive its bright acidity. If it were higher in alcohol and sugar, the acidity would be less noticeable.

SUBSOIL
Who says there is no such thing as minerality? In France's Loire Valley winegrowing region of Muscadet, vigneron Guy Bossard farms Domaine de L'Ecu, an estate composed of three different subsoils: gneiss, orthogneiss and granite. He separately vinifies the grapes from these three different parcels following identical regimes, yet ends up with three wines that taste markedly different from one another. And so each of the three wine labels shows the rock of that vineyard parcel's respective underlying soil.

ROCK TYPE
What does gneiss taste like? I'm not sure, but this wine does have a distinctly flinty flavor to it.

MASTERCLASS: SIX WINES TO BUY

In the category of crisp whites, the element of acidity is about as subtle as a piano falling on your head from a second-story window. Minerality is more challenging to identify. See if you can detect subtle notes of beach sand in Vinho Verde from Portugal and in Txakoli from Spain's Basque country. Or, try to make out the cool limestone characteristic in the Cortese grape, from Piedmont's Gavi region, or the slate in Riesling from Germany's Mosel River Valley. In France's Loire Valley, Sancerre is said to have notes of "gunflint," while Muscadet (on the preceding page), smells like oyster shells. Finally, the celebrated chardonnays of Chablis, in Burgundy, are famously "chalky."

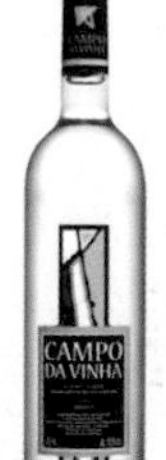

CAMPO DA VINHA
VINHO VERDE BRANCO
(Loureiro / Trajadura)
Vinho Verde, Minho, Portugal $

ALTERNATIVE CHOICES

ALIANÇA VINHO VERDE BRANCO
(Azal / Pedernã / Trajadura / Loureiro)
Vinho Verde, Minho, Portugal $

CASA DE VILA VINHO VERDE BRANCO
(Trajadura / Loureiro)
Vinho Verde, Minho, Portugal $

GURRUTXAGA
TXAKOLI
(Hondarrabi Zuri / Mune Mahatsa / Txori Mahatsa)
Bizkaiko Txakolina, Spain $$

ALTERNATIVE CHOICES

AMEZTOI TXAKOLI
(Hondarrabi Zuri) Getariako Txakolina, Spain $$

TXOMIN ETXANIZ GETARIA WHITE
(Hondarrabi Zuri) Getariako Txakolina, Spain $–$$

VILLA SPARINA
GAVI DI GAVI
(Cortese) Gavi, Piedmont, Italy $–$$

ALTERNATIVE CHOICES

CASTELVERO CORTESE
(Cortese) Monferrato, Piedmont, Italy $

SAROTTO AURORA TENUTA MANENTI
(Cortese) Gavi, Piedmont, Italy $–$$

SCHLOSS LIESER*
BRAUNEBERGER JUFFER SONNENUHR TROCKEN
(Riesling) Mosel, Germany $$

ALTERNATIVE CHOICES

DR. LOOSEN BLUE SLATE KABINETT
(Riesling) Mosel, Germany $–$$

STEIN BLAUSCHIEFER TROCKEN
(Riesling) Mosel, Germany $$

* Matteo Ghiringhelli's pick

GÉRARD & PIERRE MORIN
SANCERRE VIEILLES VIGNES
(Sauvignon Blanc) Sancerre, Loire, France $$

ALTERNATIVE CHOICES

PATIENT COTTAT SANCERRE VIEILLES VIGNES
(Sauvignon Blanc) Sancerre, Loire, France $$

LUCIEN CROCHET SANCERRE
(Sauvignon Blanc) Sancerre, Loire, France $$

DOMAINE FRANÇOIS RAVENEAU
CHABLIS PREMIER CRU FORÊT
(Chardonnay) Chablis, Burgundy, France $$$$–$$$$$

ALTERNATIVE CHOICES

FRÉDÉRIC GEUGUEN, DOMAINE DES CHENEVIÈRES GRANDES VIGNES
(Chardonnay) Chablis, Burgundy, France $$

FRANCINE ET OLIVIER SAVARY SÉLECTION VIEILLES VIGNES
(Chardonnay) Chablis, Burgundy, France $$

HOW TO SERVE IT

The freshest, lightest whites, like Txakoli or Vinho Verde, taste best ice-cold. Wines with a bit more fragrance and depth, such as Riesling, Gavi, Sancerre or Chablis, are most enjoyable when they're cool but not totally chilled, so let them sit on the counter for 15 minutes or so after removing them from the refrigerator and before serving them. No need for fancy stemware with these; a small, simple wine glass is just fine.

HOW TO TALK ABOUT IT

Acidity is a sensation, rather than a flavor. So try to separate the two ideas in your mind. Acidity is not lemony—although the two often go hand-in-hand in a light white wine—it's "crisp," "bright," "racy" or "zippy," energizing the surface of your tongue in the same way that a splash of cold water invigorates the nerves in your face. Minerality, confusingly, is something you can both smell and feel. So you might find "chalky minerality on the nose" or "chalky minerality on the finish."

AROMATIC AND SENSORY CLUES

Any wine—white, red, sweet and fortified alike—can be brisk with acidity, so as mentioned above, don't, assume that acidity will always accompany citrus aromas and flavors. Feel for that mouthwatering sensation and that stimulating sting at the top of your tongue. More generally, acidity refreshes your palate while making you thirst for another sip. Minerality, too, can be present in any style of wine. It smells like stones and feels like paper.

FOOD MATCHES

Serve these white wines as aperitifs, with green olives and salted almonds. Or, with seafood: think steamed clams or mussels, cold crab or shrimp salad. They make ideal matches for mouth-coating foods such as *chèvre* or leek-and potato soup, cutting through pasty textures with their crisp acidity. And don't be afraid to match them up with lighter meats: Roasted chicken and fried pork chops absolutely scream to be paired with a perky, fruity Riesling or smooth, minerally Chablis.

MASTERCLASS: WHAT'S TRENDING?
REDUCTIVE + OXIDATIVE WINES

SPRITZ INTO ACTION

You might think "spritz" is what you do with a lemon wedge over a pan of sautéing green beans. But in vinous vocabulary, the word "spritz" has its own definition. Oenophiles use this tasting term to describe a wine that's slightly *pétillant*, as the French would say it, or, if you like the German better, *spritzig*. It doesn't imply the big, ubiquitous bubbles of seltzer water, so don't equate a "spritzy" wine in your mind with a lime spritzer; you may not see any bubbles at all, in fact, when a "spritzy" wine is in your glass. But in your mouth, you'll feel pleasant pinpricks—evidence of the presence of a bit of carbon dioxide trapped in the liquid. Winemakers don't add this CO_2 on purpose; they just capture what's already there naturally.

We exhale carbon dioxide. So does wine, in its own way, because the byproducts of fermentation are alcohol and CO_2. In warm wineries, this gas dissipates naturally. But in chilly cellars, the wine often doesn't exhale, and the CO_2 can be trapped in the liquid. While spritz is desirable in a light, crisp white wine, it isn't in heavier whites and reds. To avoid this problem, the vintner might bubble a bit of neutral nitrogen or argon gas into the wine during bottling, expelling any excess CO_2. If you open a bottle of red and find it to be a bit spritzy, it's possible that the wine came from a cold cellar, and the vintner was hurrying to bottle it, not realizing that secondary, or malolactic, fermentation hadn't quite completed. Just allow the wine to warm up in its glass for a while, and that unwelcome spritz might dissipate.

REDUCTIVE WINEMAKING

An intentionally spritzy white is made by the reductive method: The wine stays in cool, compressed steel tanks until it's bottled, to shield it from oxygen as much as possible. This traps the carbon dioxide (CO_2) from fermentation inside the wine, although some wineries also inject it. (An interesting aside: Because CO_2 is an antioxidant that enhances acidity, wines bottled with it tend to require lower levels of sulfites at bottling. In addition, fresh, spritzy whites tend to be relatively low in alcohol. So, if someone you know gets headaches from drinking wine, he or she might have more tolerance for wines with a bit of spritz.) Unfortunately, spritz isn't something that's noted on wine labels, so ask your sommelier or wine merchant for guidance.

WHITES WITH SPRITZ

Here are a few of the many whites that are sometimes (or always) made in a spritzy style. If you've just completed our Masterclass on acidity and minerality, you'll notice that, in the realm of light white wines, spritz and acidity tend to go hand in hand.

ABYMES (JACQUÈRE)
GRÜNER VELTLINER
MUSCADET
PINOT BIANCO
PINOT GRIGIO
RIESLING
SOAVE
TXAKOLI
VINHO VERDE

CASE STUDY: SPRITZ

BROADBENT VINHO VERDE Vinho Verde, Portugal $

Vinho Verde is a winemaking region in northwestern Portugal known for spritzy, low-alcohol whites that should be drunk young. The grape content—in this case, the Portuguese varieties Loureiro, Trajadura and Pedernã (a.k.a. Arinto)—isn't as important as the crisp, bright regional style. At just 9% alcohol by volume, this is a wine for a warm-weather lunch, with lively notes of citrus rind, white peaches and freesia. Blender and importer Bartholomew Broadbent ships his Vinho Verde in refrigerated containers to keep it as fresh as possible. "People who like cold American beer tend to like Vinho Verde, too," he says.

INTRODUCING: OXYGEN!

If there's a counterpoint to reductive winemaking, it's oxidative winemaking. And if the fresh, spritzy white has an opposite, it's the smooth, luscious, oxygen-rich white. A century ago, it wasn't possible to produce the crisp white wines we enjoy today thanks to the invention of closed-top steel tanks, temperature control and inert gases. Back then, whites were made in a style similar to reds. And often, they were dreadful.

Modern winemaking has embraced the technological innovation and sterility of reductive winemaking, but open-air oenology has also increased in popularity in recent years, as traditionalist vintners have rediscovered the art of fermenting their whites in open containers.

Before going any further, we should note that the terms "reductive" and "oxidative" can be, confusingly, associated with wine flaws. An overly "reductive" wine might stink of onions, rubber or rotten eggs; an unintentionally "oxidized" wine looks yellow and smells strongly like Sherry or vinegar. We'll investigate these flaws in Section 3 of this book; we'll also address extreme styles of oxidized wines (such as Vin Jaune and Sherry) later in Section 1. For now, let's just consider white wines that are supposed to be slightly oxidized.

How do you know you're tasting an intentionally oxidative white, rather than a spoiled one? It might have a golden hue, a silky texture, pleasing spicy notes on the palate and delicately nutty aromas. These wines are an acquired taste, so don't feel like a failure if you try one and don't like it.

WHY OXIDATIVE WHITES MATTER

Intentionally oxidative whites are all the rage nowadays thanks to the emergence of the natural wine movement, which espouses a return to the traditional methods of centuries past. But according to wine importer Bartholomew Broadbent, this style of winemaking is no fad. Contrary to what you might expect, "Whites are the longest-lived wines in the world," he tells me. Broadbent once tasted a white dating back to 1670: "The color looked as if it was no more than ten years old; it was very fresh; and at just 6% alcohol, in perfect condition," he recalls. So: How can a nearly 350-year-old, low-alcohol white wine taste just fine, when a two-year-old wine can spoil just sitting on your kitchen counter for a day or two?

A wine made by reductive methods can go into shock when it's exposed to oxygen. But white wine that has been allowed to breathe in the cellar builds up a tolerance for air. "The best way to prevent a house from burning down is to char the beams, because it is very difficult to reignite a burned piece of wood," Broadbent explains. Likewise, "A wine that has been lightly oxidized in a cask, over time, is very difficult to spoil." Ironically, an intentionally oxidized wine actually *needs* air to be properly enjoyed; it's not uncommon to decant a "natural"-style white wine for hours, or even *days*, before drinking it. "Because when a wine has been in cask for a long time and then you bottle it, you've basically cut off the supply of oxygen it has been living on. You resuscitate it when you decant it," says Broadbent.

CASE STUDY: OXYGEN

CHATEAU MUSAR WHITE Bekaa Valley, Lebanon $$

"In the U.S., wineries are allowed to add something like 50 different additives to wines. At Château Musar in Lebanon, they do not add anything at all," says Bartholomew Broadbent, who imports this very traditional white made from indigenous varieties Obaideh (similar to Chardonnay) and Merwah (similar to Semillon). Château Musar waits seven years before releasing this oxygen-loving white; once open, it will stay fresh for a week or more, and tastes best served at room temperature. "We sell vintages going back to 1954," Broadbent reports. In short, it's the opposite, vinously speaking, of Vinho Verde.

2 LIVELY, AROMATIC WHITES

2 LIVELY, AROMATIC WHITES

We contemplate art; we listen to music. We lick ice cream cones. We pet our dogs and cats, snuggle with our babies, and kiss our significant others. But how often do we take the time to indulge our olfactory organs? If you're the kind of person who regularly stops to sniff at the door of a coffee shop or bakery, if you have been known to pause midstride to bury your nose in a cloud of lilacs, or if you're the sort who noses melons you aren't even planning to purchase, you need to get to know the rolodex of aromatic whites.

Because there are always exceptions to the rules, you'll find some awfully aromatic wines in preceding and following sections, respectively, of this book. For this category, we'll limit our scope to those whites that combine fragrance with energy, sophistication with flouncy flair. If crisp and lean whites are Arial Narrow, and rich and full whites are Gill Sans Ultra Bold, then the lively aromatic whites are written in French Script (or, at the very least, something with a serif). Or, if you prefer architectural terms, they aren't Mid-Century Modern, nor are they Baroque. Rather, they're Postmodern: Built on clean lines, they tend to go off the rails in strangely delicious and unexpected directions.

Aromatic wines go with other aromatics. Whether you're puffing on a clove cigarette (who *does* that anymore?) or browsing a recipe that calls for fresh fennel, rosemary, lemongrass, thyme or mint, an aromatic white should be clutched in your available paw. At the same time, these personality-driven whites perk up neutral foods, like pork, or chicken and dumplings. Can't smell phooey in your tofu? Then get a whiff of what's in your glass. You'll dig the lychee in that Gewurztraminer, the kumquat in Pinot Blanc, the kiwi in Grüner Veltliner, the passionfruit in Muscat, the green apple in Riesling, or the white peaches in Pinot Gris. You get the idea: These are wines for the senses—above all for our sense of smell.

YOU'LL ENJOY THESE WINES IF...

- You love the scent of fresh-cut flowers
- You hanker for herbaceous foods
- You're a sucker for spiced cider

WHAT THE EXPERTS SAY

"Aromatic whites are the perfect entryway into an evening of wine: You're eating passed food and drinking Sauvignon Blanc from Sancerre, or munching on crudo *with bone-dry Riesling from Alsace. And a green-chile-and-chicken taco with Riesling? Incredible. (You can sip a sweet Riesling if you want to dampen the heat from the chiles, or a dry Riesling if you want to emphasize it.) Or you know what's really good? Alsatian Muscat with asparagus and butter. And Pinot Gris with veal with cream sauce, and..."*

Michael Madrigale, Head Sommelier / Wine Buyer for Bar Boulud, Épicerie Boulud & Boulud Sud, New York City, U.S.

GOOD TO DRINK WITH

LOBSTER
PORK OR VEAL TERRINE
WHITE FISH
FRESH HERB SALAD
GOAT CHEESE
STIR FRY

KEY

$	UNDER $15	$$$$	$50–100
$$	$15–30	$$$$$	$100+
$$$	$30–50		

THE NAMES TO LOOK FOR

SAUVIGNON BLANC MARLBOROUGH, NEW ZEALAND

Nettles, grapefruit pith, gooseberries and sweat. You're either into in-your-face aromas like these, or you aren't. Unless, that is, you've taken the time to revisit New Zealand Sauvignon Blanc, and discovered the new crop of softer, mellower wines. They aren't exactly the minerals-and-sweet-hay Sauv Blancs of Sancerre, but they're gentler and more interesting than they used to be.

[PRICE RANGE: $-$$]

[ABV: 12.5–14%]

[DRINK IT: 1-3 YEARS AFTER THE VINTAGE]

CHOICE

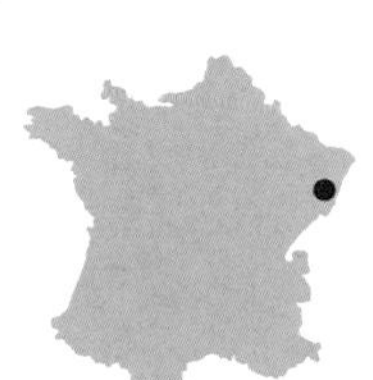

GEWURZTRAMINER ALSACE, FRANCE

Gewurztraminer (add the umlaut if you're in Germany) can be a perplexing wine—so unctuous!—until you get a good one. And then it's like you've stuck your finger in an electrical outlet. Marzipan! Lychee! Rosewater! Honey! Ginger! Who knew a dry wine could smell or taste this way? Well, now you do. I'll call an ambulance.

[PRICE RANGE: $-$$$$]

[ABV: 13–14%]

[DRINK IT: 1-15 YEARS AFTER THE VINTAGE]

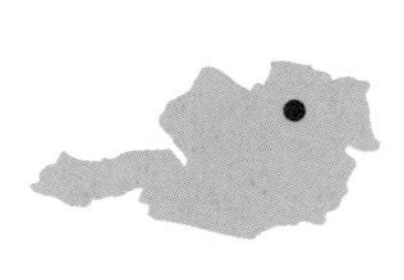

GRÜNER VELTLINER WACHAU, AUSTRIA

Faster than you could say *"prädikatswein,"* the green-bottled white from the land of the Blue Danube became the darling of restaurant wine lists. How did this happen? Because sommeliers realized that a reasonably priced wine that smells and tastes like aloe, white pepper and gardenias will sell like wildfire. And you know what rhymes with Gru Ve? Groovy.

[PRICE RANGE: $-$$]

[ABV: 12.5–13.5%]

[DRINK IT: 1-3 YEARS AFTER THE VINTAGE]

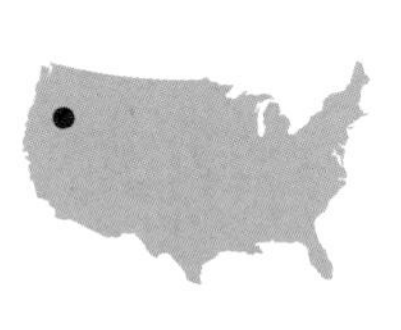

PINOT GRIS OREGON, UNITED STATES

In Italy, it is lemony Pinot Grigio. In Oregon and France, it is Pinot Gris. The "gray" grape has a pink skin, and when it hasn't had a Donatella Versace done on it, it's all wacky spice and beautiful, wrinkly peaches. And when it's allowed to express its voluptuous, fruity self, I dare you to name a cuisine it won't pair with. But East Asian food rules supreme.

[PRICE RANGE: $-$$]

[ABV: 12.5–13.5%]

[DRINK IT: 1-3 YEARS AFTER THE VINTAGE]

RIESLING MOSEL, GERMANY

Not only is this grape gaining ground in New World winemaking regions, but geeky German Rieslings, with their wordy labels and complex classification system, are all the rage right now. So don't think: Just try one. Wherever it falls on the sweetness spectrum, its citrus-and-apple notes and zingy acidity will kill with whatever you're eating.

[PRICE RANGE: $-$$$$]

[ABV: 8–13%]

[DRINK IT: 1-50 YEARS AFTER THE VINTAGE]

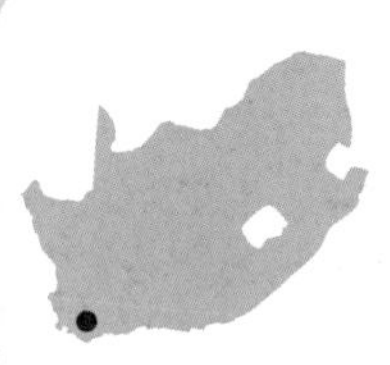

CHENIN BLANC STELLENBOSCH, SOUTH AFRICA

As France's Loire Valley has shown, Chenin is the Pink Panther of grapes, availing itself of a variety of guises. South African vintners once churned it out as "steen," a flimsy, fruity quaffer; but today, they're taking advantage of their proliferation of old plantings and coaxing this chameleon into everything from floral aperitifs to after-dinner treats.

[PRICE RANGE: $-$$$$]

[ABV: 12–14%]

[DRINK IT: 1-3 YEARS AFTER THE VINTAGE]

TAKE ONE WINE:
MAHI MARLBOROUGH SAUVIGNON BLANC

THE BASICS

GRAPE VARIETY: Sauvignon Blanc

REGION: Marlborough, New Zealand

ALCOHOL LEVEL: 13.5%

PRICE: $$

AVAILABILITY: Widely available

APPEARANCE: Pale straw

TASTING NOTE: A meadow in a spring breeze; candied lemon; gooseberries; lime chiffon; white pepper; fresh ginger.

FOOD MATCH: Forgive me for this one, but grilled mahi-mahi, served with a *salsa verde ajo*. Or: creamy linguini with fresh spring peas; a gooey Panini with fontina and pan-fried ramps, fiddleheads or garlic scapes; parmesan cheese straws; smoked trout on crackers with cream cheese and dill; herbed lemon-chicken skewers; or crisp salad topped with warm chèvre.

DRINK OR KEEP: A wine that is made to show off its vibrant, youthful fruit flavors, it is at its best in the first year or two after vintage.

WHY DOES IT TASTE THAT WAY?

Once upon a time, aspiring sommeliers loved New Zealand Sauvignon Blanc. Not because it smelled like fresh-cut grass, grapefruit pith, gooseberries and feline urine, mind you, but rather because it was so simple to identify blind in examinations.

But times have changed. As new vineyard sites have come online in New Zealand and vine tending and winemaking techniques have changed, styles have shifted. Today's spectrum of NZSBs includes more ripe tropical-fruit notes and, in wines like this one, the rounded mouthfeel that results from partial aging in neutral (i.e., not overtly woody) barrels.

While wineries like Mahi aren't trying to emulate the originals—those chalky, flinty and softly herbaceous Sauv Blancs from France's Loire Valley—they're molding serious whites that are grounded in texture rather than the cartoonish "cat pee" notes of decades past. Sorry, junior somms.

WHO MADE IT?

Brian Bicknell interspersed his New Zealand winemaking career with stints in Hungary, France and Chile before returning to Marlborough to work as winemaker and general manager at Seresin Estate. In 2001, Brian and his wife Nicola launched Mahi in order to explore the diversity and depth of the Marlborough region. They bottle single-vineyard wines as well as blends like this one, always working with properties that are farmed organically, biodynamically or sustainably. They only vinify the free-run juice, or the purest juice that spills out of the wine press first, selling the secondary pressed juice to other wineries. Drawing from his years of experience, Brian breaks from the Marlborough mold of all stainless-steel fermentation by setting aside a portion of his Sauvignon Blanc and allowing it to go through spontaneous fermentation in neutral (older) oak barrels. This brings a soft texture and nuanced character to the finished blend.

CRACKING THE CODE
CLOSURE
The majority of New Zealand Sauvignon Blanc producers top their bottles with screwcaps, which seal in this white's fresh flavors.
WINE NAME
Mahi is a Maori word meaning "our craft."
GRAPE ORIGIN
While Mahi also bottles Sauv Blancs from single vineyards, this is a blend that represents a variety of sites throughout the Marlborough region, mostly in the cooler western end of the Wairau Valley.
ALCOHOL
At 13.5% ABV, this is a fragrant white that demands to be noticed.
BOTTLE
A wider bottle with a dark tint hints that this is more than a simple quaffer; it's a wine for the dinner table.
LOGO
The logo is an adaptation of the Maori koru, a design based on the shape of a baby fern frond. It symbolizes new life and growth, as well as, in this case, the patience necessary to see a snail-paced wine all the way through from grape to bottle.
Mahi
Marlborough
SAUVIGNON BLANC
MARLBOROUGH NEW ZEALAND

MAHI MARLBOROUGH SAUVIGNON BLANC

WHY THAT PRICE?

New Zealand has managed to hit a pricing sweet spot. The Sauvignon Blanc prices here are comparable to those of the Loire Valley, leaving New World competitors like Chile and South Africa to fill in the value end of the market. But just because most Kiwi Sauvignon Blancs fall in the $15-to-$30 range doesn't mean they're all worth that much. Ask your wine merchant: How many tons per hectare of fruit did the vineyard produce? (The average is approximately 13, but Mahi sources from vineyards that only get 10.) Was the wine vinified in stainless-steel tanks, or did a portion of it go into neutral oak barrels? Does the winery produce 4,000 cases annually, or 400,000? In short, don't pay $20 for a wine that's riding the coattails of a national reputation for quality. Instead, seek out producers, like Mahi, that work with sustainably farmed vineyards and put time and care into their winemaking.

WHAT FOOD DOES IT GO WITH?

Sauvignon Blanc is an outlier. Its unique combination of sail-ripping acidity and chlorophyll notes (think ferns, herbs, grass) make it a wine that can't just cozy up to whatever you're serving tonight. It works as an apéritif, however, and it's a winner with foods that are both creamy and herbaceous. So start with an emollient base—whether it's mayo, goat cheese, soufflé or a buttermilk dressing—and pile on the greens. Fennel, endive, celery, parsley, radicchio or raw cabbage all fit the bill. Salad with Green Goddess dressing? Yes. Coleslaw on a fish taco? Yep. Goat cheese with a stripe of smoked paprika and a dill crust? Oh, yeah. A lobster roll with a chopped celery garnish? Now you're talking.

Left: A vineyard in Marlborough, New Zealand's largest wine region, which produces aromatic, brisk wines.

TOP FOOD MATCH:
Flaky tartlette of leeks with crème fraîche

CREAM SAUCES

FRESH HERBS

SEAFOOD

10 OF THE BEST

NEW ZEALAND SAUVIGNON BLANCS, FROM ZESTY TO MELLOW

CLOUDY BAY	$$
DRYLANDS	$–$$
MAN O' WAR	$–$$
MILLS REEF	$
NAUTILUS	$–$$
PALLISER ESTATE	$–$$
SAINT CLAIR	$–$$
SERESIN	$–$$
WHITEHAVEN	$–$$
WOOLLASTON	$–$$

AROUND THE WORLD

WINES IN A SIMILAR STYLE FROM DIFFERENT COUNTRIES

Didier Dagueneau, Silex
Pouilly-Fumé, Loire, France $$$$–$$$$$

Efesté, I Feral
Columbia Valley, Washington, U.S. $$

Miguel Torres, Las Mulas Reserve
Central Valley, Chile $

CHOICE MADE SIMPLE

EXPERT'S PERSONAL FAVORITES

Recommended by Dawn Davies, Wine and Spirits Buyer, The Wonder Bar, Selfridges, London, U.K.

DOMAINE GÉRARD BOULAY, SANCERRE, MONTS DAMNÉS,
(SAUVIGNON BLANC)
LOIRE, FRANCE $$$

CHAPEL DOWN, BACCHUS
KENT, ENGLAND, UNITED KINGDOM $

KEN FORRESTER, THE FMC (FORRESTER MEINERT CHENIN)
(CHENIN BLANC) STELLENBOSCH, SOUTH AFRICA $$–$$$

FRANZ HIRTZBERGER, HONIVOGL SMARAGD GRÜNER VELTLINER
WACHAU, AUSTRIA $$$$

DOMAINE HUËT, VOUVRAY LE HAUT LIEU SEC
(CHENIN BLANC)
LOIRE VALLEY, FRANCE $$

EGON MÜLLER SCHARZHOFBERGER, SCHARZHOF
(RIESLING) MOSEL, GERMANY $$

RONCÚS, PINOT BIANCO
COLLIO ORIENTALI, FRIULI-VENEZIA GIULIA, ITALY $$

CLOS DU ROUGE GORGE, BLANC
(MACABEO) VIN DE PAYS DES CÔTES CATALANES, LANGUEDOC-ROUSSILLON, FRANCE $$–$$$

TINPOT HUT, PINOT GRIS
MARLBOROUGH, NEW ZEALAND $

DOMAINE WEINBACH, CUVÉE THÉO GEWURZTRAMINER
ALSACE, FRANCE $$–$$$

WORLD OF FINE WINE RECOMMENDATIONS

DOMAINE DIDIER DAGUENEAU, BLANC FUMÉ DE POUILLY SILEX
(SAUVIGNON BLANC)
LOIRE, FRANCE $$$$$

LUCIEN CROCHET, SANCERRE LE CHÊNE
(SAUVIGNON BLANC)
LOIRE, FRANCE $$$

DOG POINT, VINEYARD SECTION 94 SAUVIGNON BLANC
MARLBOROUGH, NEW ZEALAND $$$

JJ PRÜM WEHLENER SONNENUHR RIESLING KABINETT
MOSEL, GERMANY $$$

A CHRISTMANN KONIGSBACHER IDIG GROSSES GEWÄCHS RIESLING
PFALZ, GERMANY $$$$

WEINGUT CLEMENS BUSCH MARIENBERG FELSTERRASSE RIESLING
MOSEL, GERMANY $$$

DOMAINE PAUL BLANCK SCHLOSSBERG RIESLING
ALSACE, FRANCE $$$

WEINGUT SCHLOSS GOBELSBURG, LAMM GRÜNER VELTLINER RESERVE
KAMPTAL, AUSTRIA $$$$

DOMAINE ZIND HUMBRECHT HENGST GEWURZTRAMINER
ALSACE, FRANCE $$$$

VERGELEGEN WHITE BLEND
(SAUVIGNON BLANC / SEMILLON)
STELLENBOSCH, SOUTH AFRICA $$$

(Grape Varieties in Brackets)

ORGANIC, BIODYNAMIC OR NATURAL

BINNER, LES SAVEURS
(RIESLING / SYLVANER / AUXERROIS / GEWURZTRAMINER / PINOT GRIS)
ALSACE, FRANCE $$

FRANÇOIS CHIDAINE, MONTLOUIS, CLOS DU BREUIL (CHENIN BLANC)
LOIRE VALLEY, FRANCE $$

DOMAINE MARCEL DEISS, GEWURZTRAMINER
ALSACE, FRANCE $$

PASCAL JOLIVET, SANCERRE
(SAUVIGNON BLANC)
LOIRE, FRANCE $$

COULÉE DE SERRANT, CLOS DE LA COULÉE DE SERRANT, SAVENNIÈRES
(CHENIN BLANC)
LOIRE, FRANCE $$$$

KING ESTATE, SIGNATURE COLLECTION, PINOT GRIS
OREGON, U.S. $$

MANINCOR, MOSCATO GIALLO,
ALTO ADIGE, ITALY $$

NIKOLAIHOF, HEFEABZUG, GRÜNER VELTLINER
WACHAU, AUSTRIA $$

PACIFIC RIM, WALLULA VINEYARD RIESLING HORSE HEAVEN HILLS, COLUMBIA VALLEY, WASHINGTON, U.S. $$$

KARL SCHAEFER, DÜRKHEIMER SPEILBERG, RIESLING
PFALZ, GERMANY $$

BEST ON A BUDGET

BONTERRA VINEYARDS, SAUVIGNON BLANC
LAKE COUNTY, MENDOCINO COUNTY, CALIFORNIA, U.S. $

CLOUDLINE, PINOT GRIS
WILLAMETTE VALLEY, OREGON, U.S. $

ERSTE & NEUE, WEISSBURGUNDER PRUNAR
(PINOT BIANCO)
ALTO ADIGE/SÜDTIROL, ITALY $

FUENTE SECA
(MACABEO / SAUVIGNON BLANC)
UTIEL-REQUENA, SPAIN $

ALOIS LAGEDER, MÜLLER-THURGAU
ALTO ADIGE, ITALY $

LOIMER, LOIS, GRÜNER-VELTLINER
KAMPTAL, AUSTRIA $

MEYER-FONNÉ, GENTIL EDELZWICKER (BLEND)
ALSACE, FRANCE $

PEÑALOLÉN, SAUVIGNON BLANC
LIMARÍ VALLEY, CASABLANCA VALLEY, CHILE $

CHATEAU STE. MICHELLE, DRY RIESLING COLUMBIA VALLEY, WASHINGTON, U.S. $

JL WOLF, VILLA WOLF, GEWURZTRAMINER
PFALZ, GERMANY $

MASTERCLASS: SLEUTHING FOR SWEETNESS

It has happened to all of us: We buy a bottle of white wine, open it and find that it tastes sweeter—or drier—than we thought. Especially when we are dealing with aromatic grape varieties, like Riesling, Gewurztraminer, Muscat, Pinot Gris or Chenin Blanc, sweetness levels can vary, depending on when the grapes were harvested and how the winemaker vinified them. So how can you know if your wine will taste fruity, sweet, fruity *and* sweet or simply dry?

The simplest course of action is to ask a wine merchant or sommelier—if one is available—for help. But you might be surprised to hear that among themselves, even wine experts complain about the lack of transparency in labeling of wines that are somewhere on the nebulous sweetness spectrum.

In recognition of this fact, the International Riesling Foundation has developed a Riesling Taste Profile, which is now printed on the back labels of a small but increasing number of Riesling bottles, alerting consumers as to whether the wine inside is dry, medium dry, medium sweet or sweet.

But this doesn't help with aromatic whites that aren't Rieslings, or those wineries that have not yet adopted the scale. This is where a tech sheet—a page of technical data and detailed descriptions—can be helpful. If you've visited a winery tasting room or explored a few winery web sites, you may have come across one. And you've probably thought, "Oh, that isn't for me. That's for professionals." But if the winery is sharing the information, why not use it?

Unfortunately, if you can get your hands on a tech sheet, the sugar number alone won't tell you much. Amounts vary wildly, from less than one gram to—in rare cases—more than 400 grams per liter. And then there's the additional problem that a wine with a relatively high level of residual sugar might not taste sweet at all if that sugar is balanced out by lots of acidity, while a wine with a moderate sugar level will taste sweet if the acidity is low and the alcohol is relatively high.

According to the International Riesling Foundation's Riesling Taste Profile, sugar levels are lower than, or equal to, acidity levels in a **Dry** wine. A **Medium Dry** wine can have up to twice as much sugar as acidity. In a **Medium Sweet** wine, the sugar level might be from two to four times the acidity level. And a **Sweet** wine will have more than four times as much sugar as acidity.

Keep in mind that these are general guidelines that don't take alcohol or pH levels into account. But they can still be quite helpful for those wishing to delve deeper into the mysteries of sweetness. We'll look opposite at the technical detail that can help us decode the sweetness level of a white wine.

HOW TO IDENTIFY THESE ELEMENTS

1: Don't assume that a single grape variety will always taste a certain way. In the Loire Valley, Vouvray produces fruity and faintly sweet Chenin Blanc, while Savennières Chenin Blanc is dry. And Chenin from South Africa tends to be zippy and crisp. Don't worry—you don't have to memorize this. Just don't be afraid to ask: "Is this sweet, or dry or in-between?"

2: On the sweetest end of the spectrum, here are some terms that you'll find on *dessert-style* wine labels: **late harvest, ice wine,** ***vendange tardive, moelleux, liquoreux, recioto, sélection de grains nobles.*** (And there are plenty more, but we'll dig deep into German, Austrian, Hungarian and Loire Valley ripeness classifications in our section on Lusciously Sweet Wines.)

3: If you are interested in delving deeper, peek at the **tech** or **data** sheets available on many winery websites and in tasting rooms. These sheets contains clues to help you decipher how the wine will taste. But remember that grams per liter of sugar is a relative, and not an absolute, number. We'll decode a tech sheet together on the facing page.

MASTERING THE TECH SHEET

VINIFICATION
Hmmm.... We may have tasted Riesling, and maybe Gewurztraminer, previously. But we might not be familiar with Auxerrois. Let's look for clues as to how this wine might taste. For starters, we know that it was vinified in stainless steel—a tip-off that this wine won't be oaky or buttery.

WINE NAME
All we know from looking at the label (reproduced here) is that this is a wine from Alsace. "Fleur de Lotus" is a proprietary, or unique, name given to this particular blend by the winery. It sounds enticing, but doesn't tell us much about how the wine will taste. We'll need to investigate the tech sheet to deduce more about this wine.

VINS D'ALSACE JOSMEYER

Wine made from organically and biodynamically grown grapes

JOSMEYER
ALSACE
Fleur de Lotus

A.O.C. ALSACE FLEUR DE LOTUS 2009

THE RANGE

Range: Blend
Typically made from 60–65% Auxerrois (for body), 30–35% Gewurztraminer (for spice and fat) and 5% Riesling (for acidity and increasing length), this blend is vinified exclusively in stainless steel.

VINES

Terroir: Between Wintzenheim and Turckheim these flat alluvian deposits of the Fecht are rich in clay (22%). The soil is predominantly of sand, shingle and silt with a high incidence of pebbles and frequent plates of loess. From the vineyard come wines which are soft and sensual.

Age of vines: 35 years on average

Grape Variety: Pinots, Gewurztraminer, Muscat and Riesling

THE WINE

Sugar Level: 8g/liter
Alcohol Level: 12.5% volume
Acidity Level: 4.5g/liter (tartaric acidity)
Yields: 65 hl/ha
Wine Tasting: The nose is open and aromatic on floral aromas and notes of coriander. The mouth, pulpy and structured, is on spicy notes and has a final freshness. Wine with a beautiful balance.

SUGAR LEVEL
8 grams per liter looks like a lot of sugar. After all, many wines have less than 1 gram per liter. Could this be a semi-sweet wine?

TASTING NOTE
Hmmm.... The tasting note describes this blend as floral and spicy, but sweetness isn't mentioned. Time to look at the numbers.

GRAPE VARIETIES
Oh, no! Now we're really confused about the grape variety. It's common in Alsace to refer to Auxerrois as one of the "Pinots," but we didn't see any mention of Muscat above. (Winemakers are so busy making wine, they don't always have time to proofread their tech sheets!) Our best bet is to go by the description and the numbers.

ACIDITY
Now we can really use our sleuthing skills. If we divide 8 g/l of sugar by 4.5 g/l of acidity, we get 1.8... and that tells us that this is a Medium Dry, or just barely sweet, wine.

MASTERCLASS: SIX WINES TO BUY

Think that Riesling is always sweet? Think again. Different growing regions and winemaking techniques produce a wide spectrum of wines from the same grape variety. To give you a general sense of the different vinification styles of a range of aromatic whites all over the world, here's a selection of wines to try with your friends. If you look up the technical data, you might be surprised by what you find. Keep in mind that alcohol is also an important factor: The glycerin that comes with higher alcohol levels greatly emphasizes the sensation of sweetness.

PIERRE SPARR RÉSERVE
(Pinot Gris) Alsace, France $$

ALTERNATIVE CHOICES
DOMAINE SCHLUMBERGER
LES PRINCES ABBÉS
(Pinot Gris) Alsace, France $–$$

HUGEL TRADITION
(Pinot Gris) Alsace, France $

MEDIUM SWEET

DOMAINE HUËT
VOUVRAY CLOS DU BOURG SEC
(Chenin Blanc) Loire Valley, France $$–$$$

ALTERNATIVE CHOICES
DOMAINE DES AUBUISIÈRES CUVÉE DE SILEX
(Chenin Blanc) Vouvray, Loire Valley, France $–$$

FRANÇOIS PINON LES TROIS ARGILES
(Chenin Blanc) Vouvray, Loire Valley, France $$

MEDIUM DRY / MEDIUM SWEET

J HOFSTÄTTER
JOSEPH WEISSBURGUNDER
(Pinot Bianco) Alto Adige, Italy $–$$

ALTERNATIVE CHOICES
KELLEREI-CANTINA ANDRIAN
(Pinot Bianco) Alto Adige, Italy $

SCHIOPETTO COLLIO
(Pinot Bianco) Friuli-Venezia Giulia, Italy $$

DRY

PIKES TRADITIONALE
(Riesling) Clare Valley, Australia $$

ALTERNATIVE CHOICES
BETHANY
(Riesling) Eden Valley, Australia $$

ELDREDGE VINEYARDS
(Riesling) Clare Valley, Australia $$

DRY

TEDDY HALL SYBRAND MANKADAN
(Chenin Blanc) Stellenbosch, South Africa $

ALTERNATIVE CHOICES
MULLINEUX KLOOF STREET
(Chenin Blanc) Swartland, South Africa $–$$

PAINTED WOLF THE DEN
(Chenin Blanc) Western Cape, South Africa $

DRY

PONZI PINOT GRIS
Willamette Valley, Oregon, U.S. $$

ALTERNATIVE CHOICES
ADELSHEIM PINOT GRIS
Willamette Valley, Oregon, U.S. $$

CHEHALEM 3 VINEYARD
(Pinot Gris) Willamette Valley, Oregon, U.S.

DRY

HOW TO SERVE IT

Temperature is important when you're trying to perceive sweetness, since a warmer wine will taste more sugary. So be sure to chill all the wines to an equal temperature—cool but not ice-cold—and pull them all out of the refrigerator at once. If possible, see if you can round up enough glasses so that you can taste all of the wines side-by-side (perhaps each of your guests can bring his or her own six glasses). Then, have your friends line up their glasses from dry to sweet. How do your lineups compare?

HOW TO TALK ABOUT IT

At a tasting, you might hear, "What's the **RS** on this?" RS refers to **residual sugar**. In Germany, a wine with 0 to 9 grams/liter of residual sugar is dry. But it's also important to keep in mind that German wines tend to be high in acidity, which counterbalances the sugar. So, "What's the **TA** on this?" is another good question. If the TA, or **total acidity**, is greater than or roughly equal to the RS, the wine will taste dry.

AROMATIC AND SENSORY CLUES

Alcohol is a major player. A Riesling from Germany with nearly 80 grams per liter of residual sugar might taste simply fruity if it has copious acidity and low alcohol. And a Pinot Gris from Alsace might taste sweet if the alcohol level is, say, 13.5% or higher. You'll know you're tasting a wine with a higher alcohol level if it slides slowly down the sides of your glass, has an oily texture, and creates a burning sensation on your tongue.

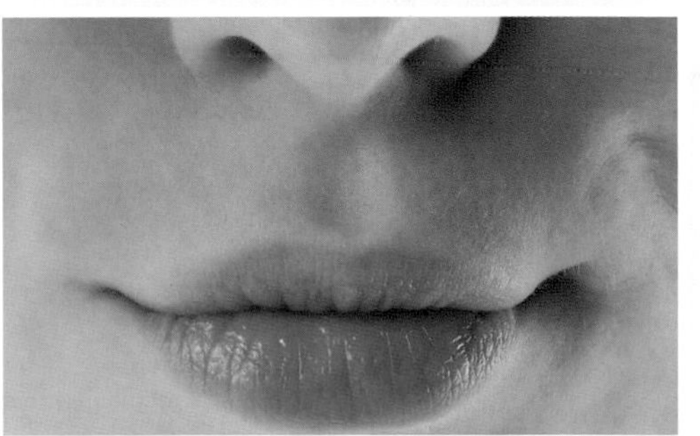

FOOD MATCHES

Order a platter of sushi that includes a variety of rolls, and be sure to ask for extra pickled ginger and wasabi. These garnishes will be interesting to try alone with each wine. Does the sweetest or the most alcoholic wine lessen the fiery impact of the wasabi? Which fares best with ginger? Which works with a spicy tuna roll, and which with an avocado roll?

MASTERCLASS: WHAT'S TRENDING?

WRAPPING OUR MINDS AROUND SWEET AND FRUIT

FROM BN TO GG IN GERMANY

It all started with this Blue Nun. If you were of drinking age anytime between the 1950s and the mid-1980s, you know whom I'm talking about. She was *liebfraumilch*, or—and you just don't want to think too hard about this translation—"milk of the beloved lady," a blend of aromatic white wines based on a Riesling cross-breed called Müller Thurgau. This slender blue-bottled beverage was bland, pallid and softly sweet, and went well with a wide variety of foods. And because she was so wildly popular for so long, she's been a headache for German winemakers for decades. Despite the fact that she's drier and more subtle in her current form, she has created a whole generation of drinkers who say, "Oh, I don't drink Riesling. It's too sweet for me."

Alas, for many Baby Boomers, all Riesling is German, and therefore, all German wines are cloying. Of course, if you're familiar with Riesling from Australia or Alsace, "sweet" isn't the first word this varietal brings to mind. And the deeper you explore the searing acidity and minerality of Germany's finest Rieslings, the further your mind travels from saccharine. Yes, many of Germany's best Rieslings are high in residual sugar. But they're also balanced. Fortunately, times are changing. The children of the Blue Nun generation are coming up, and they're geeking out on German Rieslings. The new term to know is *Grosses Gewächs*, or "GG," as the cool kids say it. This designation goes on the best single-vineyard wines, and the hottest category here are the *trocken*, or bone-dry, bottlings. Try one if you can—you'll be surprised by its savory minerality.

SWEET-TALKING GERMAN LEGEND

Whatever you do, don't bring up the word "sweet" with Ernst Loosen. This powerhouse producer has brought his family's Weingut Dr. Loosen to the forefront of the wine world with its ethereal single-vineyard bottlings and affordable "Dr. L" Riesling; he also owns the J.L. Wolf winery, where he explores the drier side of German Riesling and Pinot Noir. He collaborates with Chateau Ste. Michelle in Washington State, where he founded the international Riesling Rendezvous, and he co-owns the J. Christopher winery in Oregon. But despite all his accomplishments, Loosen still has trouble getting his message across. "To be frank, nobody wants to talk sweet. That is the problem," Loosen says. "If we say 'sweet,' we think about dessert wines."

Loosen struggles with describing his nation's complex *Prädikats*, or wine classifications, to winery visitors. In Germany, a **Kabinett** is a reserve-quality Riesling; a **Spätlese** is a late-harvest Riesling; and an **Auslese** is made from the most raisined bunches selected from the late harvest. "In the New World, in Australia, Canada or the United States, when people talk about 'late harvest,' they are always referring to sweet dessert-style wines," Loosen points out. "But Spätlese in Germany is a completely different category for us. It's just a later harvest date. If I were to talk about sweet wine, people would think about dessert wine. They think about Port, Sauternes or Vin Santo. But here in Germany, even Auslese is not that sweet. So I can't talk about sweet. It just leads to a misunderstanding. Therefore, we say 'fruity.'"

LOOSEN ON TASTING RIESLING

- Don't trust your nose. "A dry wine can smell sweet if it has a lot of glycerin and alcohol."
- Don't dwell on the RS alone. "A wine can taste very sweet if there is no acidity. But I can show you wines with 50 grams of residual sugar that taste medium-dry because they have 12 grams of acidity."
- "The higher the alcohol, the sweeter the impression of the wine—1 gram of glycerin tastes 10 times sweeter than 1 gram of sugar. Sauternes often has very low acidity and high alcohol. So it tastes sweeter."
- "I avoid the word 'sweet' for my *Kabinett* and *Spätlese* Rieslings. Instead, I talk about 'mouthwatering juiciness.' These are wines that taste like biting into a fresh apple, or a white peach, with clean fruit flavors."

THE EVOLUTION OF FRUIT IN NEW ZEALAND SAUV BLANC

When we think of "fruit" in wines, we tend to imagine that stereotypical cornucopia, overflowing with peaches and plums, apples and oranges, cherries and berries. But in New Zealand Sauvignon Blanc, the "straight-up fresh and fruity style," as winemaker Brian Bicknell calls it, is all gooseberries, lime, fresh-mown grass and grapefruit pith. And, maybe, that infamous aforementioned cat pee. It's a style that's either irresistible or repellant. And it's a puzzle to winemakers like Bicknell, who have been taking this flavor profile apart and trying to put it back together again. "It comes down to your personal taste," says Bicknell. "But the straight-up fresh-and-fruity style isn't one I particularly like to drink."

"When I started making wine, in 1989, most New Zealand wineries were up in Auckland," Bicknell recalls. At harvest, the fruit would be dumped into the backs of refrigerated trucks for the 16-hour journey to the winery. Inevitably, the skins would split, and the flavors that resulted from this inadvertent, lengthy maceration on the skins, were intense and, as Bicknell puts it, "obvious." Over time, wineries began opening in the heart of Marlborough wine country, eliminating this problem of unintentional maceration-by-transportation. The next big step toward a style shift came when vine tenders learned to selectively prune leaves so as to expose the fruit bunches to sunlight. This careful leaf pulling creates riper, more tropical fruit flavors and cuts down on those green, grassy notes in the finished wine, Bicknell says.

SHIFTING WINERY PRACTICES IN MIDDLE EARTH

New Zealand vintners have discovered that Sauvignon Blanc is a grape that tends to express that cat pee or sweaty aroma. So vine tenders have begun looking carefully at how much nitrogen they add to the vines prior to harvest, and winemakers are considering how to cut back on the YAN, or yeast-assimilable nitrogen additions, used to stabilize fermenting wines, Bicknell tells me. Because nitrogen fertilizers are ammonia, and ammonia is a component of urine and sweat. (Sorry about that.) Bicknell sees organic farming as a way around this problem in the vineyard, where he uses a seaweed-based fertilizer, and in the winery, where he uses an organic, amino-acid-based yeast supplement.

Bicknell's other method for smoothing out his Sauv Blanc is allowing a portion of it to ferment spontaneously in barrel. Allowing natural or "wild" yeasts to start fermentation is all the rage among natural wine aficionados (see WHAT'S TRENDING in our section on Light, Refreshing Reds). But it also has practical applications for Bicknell, who has found that wild-yeast fermentations create more complex flavors. The typical Marlborough Sauv Blanc goes through a reductive winemaking regime, in chilled, stainless-steel tanks, which preserves those fresh-fruit flavors that practically jump out of your glass (as you'll recall from our previous WHAT'S TRENDING). Oxidative winemaking, in neutral oak barrels that are allowed to warm up, creates wines with mellower aromas and smoother textures. "It's like making gazpacho versus tomato sauce," Bicknell explains.

TASTING THE DIFFERENCE

To wrap your mind around these different styles, taste two NZSBs that have been produced by the two different methods. So let's look at Greywacke, the label from Kevin Judd, who was the founding winemaker of the world-famous Cloudy Bay. Tasting Judd's two Sauv Blancs—one reductive and fruity, the other oxidative and contemplative, both excellent—side-by-side is like listening to two renditions of "Islands in the Stream" back to back. Start with the Dolly Parton–Kenny Rogers version. Admit it: You love this toe-tapper. It's so catchy! Now listen to the version that Feist recorded with fellow Canadian indie rockers Constantines. It is so raw, so real, and so mournful that you'll be asking yourself existential questions. OK, now you're ready to taste...

Greywacke, Sauvignon Blanc, Marlborough, New Zealand $$

Sassy and grassy. Green and zesty. Grapefruit rind, lime peel and pungent gooseberry. Freshly sliced fennel. Dolly wears a sequined gown, her cleavage is obvious. Kenny is in a tux, his hair luxuriant. Lights are flashing, the place is bumping. The crowd goes wild.

Greywacke, Wild Sauvignon, Marlborough, New Zealand $$–$$$

Released with a couple more years' age on it. Smooth, creamy, viscous. Spicy, smoky. Ginger. A slow, creeping acidity. Feist, with messy hair and no makeup, wears a Nordic ski sweater. The guys wear black jeans and tight T-shirts and sweat over their instruments. Swaying, and quietly weeping, the crowd goes wild.

3 RICH, FULL-BODIED WHITES

3 RICH, FULL-BODIED WHITES

There is the great white shark. And then there is the great white, Chard. Planted in more places on the planet than any other grape, it is the most prolific white variety. Wherever you go—whether it's a three-star Michelin restaurant or a gas-station convenience store—you can be certain to find a Chardonnay. Why is Chardonnay so popular? Because it's white—it doesn't stain your teeth purple or tear up the inside of your mouth. Because it's a rich and decadent indulgence. And because it's easy to find and simple to say.

For the past few years, cork dorks have, rather impractically, been turning up their noses at big whites like chard. (Because, of course, it's just not cool if everyone likes it.) But this is about as productive as a game of Whac-A-Mole: No matter how many times you try to beat the great white down, it will keep popping up in other spots. Like Chile. Or Israel, or Mexico. And did I mention India? All places, by the way, where a certain cold-blooded man-eater can be found in coastal waters. Coincidence? I don't think so.

There are Chardonnays from Burgundy that are so soothing and delicate that they might make you consider seeing a loan shark, if only you could drink them every day. But Burgundies are the whale sharks of this chapter: They have a lifespan of 70 years, and, even though they swim alongside the carnivores, they're gentle-hearted souls.

Other ferocious big whites include menacing Marsanne, viperous Viognier, that siren Sémillon, torrential Torrontés, fortress-like Fiano, and formidable Falanghina. These wines tend to be higher in alcoholic heft, giving them a slick texture, and can shoulder some oak, under which a lighter grape would wilt. These wines have teeth.

Do not shy away from the great whites, and do not listen to those who counsel you to hide from them. Instead, face them boldly. But for goodness' sake, don't serve them without food. Hunger and great whites? Baaaad combination.

YOU'LL ENJOY THESE WINES IF...

- You consider yourself a "red wine drinker"
- You are a sucker for silky sweets like crème brûlée
- You lean toward savory mid-weight foods, like creamy pasta, hearty soups or roasted poultry

WHAT THE EXPERTS SAY

"Rich white wines are great to pair with dishes that normally call for a lighter red, like game birds and certain pork preparations. I especially like mineral-driven California Chardonnay during Dungeness crab season, or an old-vine Sémillon for richer fishes like sturgeon and scallops. These wines comprise a key part of the food-pairing spectrum. One of their primary characteristics is their heartiness, which increases their appeal when the weather turns colder."

Kelli White, Sommelier, Press, St. Helena, Napa Valley, California, U.S.

KEY

$	UNDER $15	$$$$	$50–100
$$	$15–30	$$$$$	$100+
$$$	$30–50		

THE NAMES TO LOOK FOR

CHARDONNAY MARGARET RIVER, AUSTRALIA

If you think Chardonnay is the sole domain of Burgundy or California, think again. And if you think Australian Chardonnay is all pineapple, oak and buttered popcorn, you're not paying attention. Australian vintners, along with other New World producers, are exploring texture and nuance in the world's most popular white grape.

[**PRICE RANGE: $-$$$$$**]

[**ABV: 12.5–15%**]

[**DRINK IT: 1-5 YEARS AFTER THE VINTAGE**]

CHOICE

FALANGHINA CAMPANIA, ITALY

Campania, in the ankle of Italy's boot, was a thriving wine-producing region in classical times. Its timeless grape varieties include sturdy, herbaceous whites like Fiano, Greco di Tufo and Falanghina, the last of these loved by the Ancient Romans for its appealing, nutty, briny and ripe-fruit notes. Though typically vinified in stainless steel, this is a wine with gravitas.

[**PRICE RANGE: $-$$**]

[**ABV: 13–14%**]

[**DRINK IT: 1-10 YEARS AFTER THE VINTAGE**]

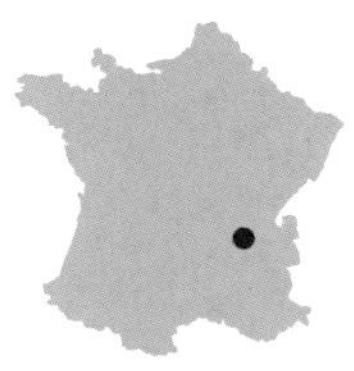

MARSANNE RHÔNE, FRANCE

Collectors pay big bucks for Hermitage Blanc, a Marsanne-based, barrel-aged white redolent of spice, quince, nuts and ginger, growing golden, waxy, and honeyed with age. Its exotic aromatic profile invites pairing with spiced ethnic cuisines, and its silky mouthfeel can soften the heat of chili peppers.

[**PRICE RANGE: $-$$$$$**]

[**ABV: 13–16.5%**]

[**2-20 YEARS AFTER THE VINTAGE**]

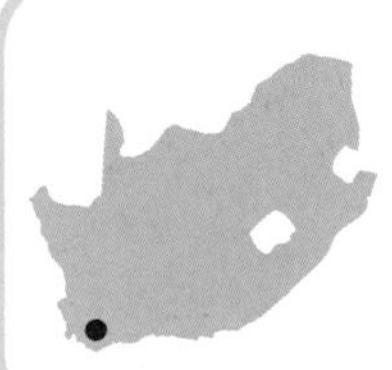

SÉMILLON SOUTH AFRICA

Sémillon was once South Africa's signature grape, accounting for nearly all of the vineyards planted in that nation. Today, it's a footnote—but those vines that remain are old and full of character. The wines are often oaked to achieve a creamy, nutty richness. Other hot spots for Sémillon: Bordeaux, Australia and Washington in the U.S.

[**PRICE RANGE: $$**]

[**ABV: 13–14.5%**]

[**DRINK IT: 1-10 YEARS AFTER THE VINTAGE**]

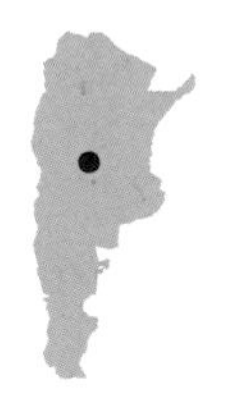

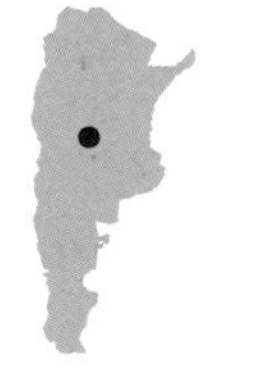

TORRONTÉS SALTA, ARGENTINA

Torrontés is a singularly South American grape, thriving in windblown foothills of the Andes at elevations unheard of in other parts of the world. But while life at 3,000 to 6,000 feet of altitude might make us short of breath, it breathes a sexy perfume of tropical fruits and flowers into Torrontés.

[**PRICE RANGE: $-$$**]

[**ABV: 12.5–14.5%**]

[**DRINK IT: 1-3 YEARS AFTER THE VINTAGE**]

VIOGNIER CALIFORNIA, U.S.

Heady Viognier is the fragrant, floral force powering Condrieu, from France's Northern Rhône, and giving Chardonnay a run for its money up and down the west coast of the U.S.; it's also strong in Australia, Argentina, South Africa and Chile. Often high in alcohol, its trademark is its seductive nose of white flowers and stone fruits.

[**PRICE RANGE: $-$$**]

[**ABV: 13–14%**]

[**DRINK IT: 1-3 YEARS AFTER THE VINTAGE**]

TAKE ONE WINE: LEEUWIN ESTATE PRELUDE VINEYARDS MARGARET RIVER CHARDONNAY

THE BASICS

GRAPE VARIETY: Chardonnay

REGION: Margaret River, Western Australia, Australia

ALCOHOL LEVEL: 14%

PRICE: $$–$$$

AVAILABILITY: Widely available

APPEARANCE: Pale gold

TASTING NOTE: Cool minerality on the nose; uplifting notes of pear, crème brûlée and lemon verbena on the palate, finishing with a punch of fresh ginger and a wave of mouthwatering acidity. Silky, luxuriant mouthfeel.

FOOD MATCH: Grilled monkfish; oven-roasted broccoli or cauliflower; cheese and chorizo panini with fig compote; Moroccan vegetable stew.

DRINK OR KEEP: Drink upon release (two years after the vintage date), or keep for up to eight years.

WHY DOES IT TASTE THAT WAY?

Just a stone's throw from the Indian Ocean on the southwestern tip of Australia, Leeuwin Estate enjoys a coastal Mediterranean-type climate, with temperatures that never get too hot or too cold. Crop yields are naturally low because the soil is lean and gravelly, and the region doesn't experience cold snaps, which promote flowering and thus fruit production. In addition, the Chardonnay clone (cultivar) planted here is the Gin Gin, also called the Mendoza clone, which is highly prone to *millerandage*, or the tendency to produce grapes of different sizes—"hens and chicks"—on the same bunch. All of these factors add up to fruit that's forceful and flavorful.

In decades past, Aussie winemakers had a tendency to pump up the volume on their Chards by harvesting overripe fruit, aging in toasty new-oak barrels, and allowing for full malolactic fermentation (a secondary fermentation common to barrel-aged white wines), for that buttered-popcorn effect. But a new style is emerging here, as it is in other New World Chardonnay-producing regions. Winemaker Paul Atwood captures fresher flavor by picking a bit earlier than he used to, and he only uses malolactic fermentation in years when the acidity is particularly high. He ferments and ages this wine in mellow air-dried barrels and regularly stirs the lees for a smooth mouthfeel. The resulting wine is silky and subtle.

WHO MADE IT?

Denis and Tricia Horgan were looking to diversify their cattle ranch when, in 1972, the legendary Californian vintner Robert Mondavi appeared on their doorstep and offered to buy it. Mondavi had identified Margaret River as a highly promising wine region and determined that Leeuwin Estate offered the best terroir in the area. The Horgans demurred, but a friendship formed, and Mondavi advised the couple as they cleared land and planted vines in their ancient, gravelly soil. Today, Leeuwin Estate is also well known for its headliner concerts, but I prefer its less-splashy side, as evidenced by the Prelude Vineyards bottling.

CRACKING THE CODE
BOTTLE SHAPE
The sloping shoulders of the green Burgundy-style bottle signal that this is Chardonnay.
GRAPE ORIGIN
"Prelude Vineyards" doesn't actually refer to a single specific place. It's a proprietary name. All the grapes are, however, from Leeuwin Estate's vineyards.
ALCOHOL
This is a weighty wine, at 14% ABV.
CLOSURE
Most Australian Chardonnays nowadays are topped with screwcap, to preserve the fresh tropical-fruit notes of these wines.
PRODUCER
Leeuwin Estate is about 10 miles south of the Leeuwin-Naturaliste National Park, which follows a stretch of north-south coastline and defines the parameters of the Leeuwin-Naturaliste Ridge, an ancient granite landmass which protects vineyards from ferocious maritime winds.
REGION
Margaret River is a peninsula in southwestern Western Australia.
LEEUWIN ESTATE
PRELUDE VINEYARDS
MARGARET RIVER
CHARDONNAY
2010
WINE OF AUSTRALIA
750mL

LEEUWIN ESTATE PRELUDE VINEYARDS MARGARET RIVER CHARDONNAY

WHY THAT PRICE?

One of Australia's most renowned producers, Leeuwin Estate can command steep prices for its Art Series Chardonnay ($$$$). The fruit for the Prelude Vineyards bottling comes from younger vineyard blocks, where the grapes have more youthful, fruit-forward flavors. It gets less new oak than the Art Series bottling and is made in a drink-now style. All these factors add up to a relative value.

WHAT FOOD DOES IT GO WITH?

A pillowy-soft Chardonnay adores foods that share its plush texture, like rich sauces or whipped potatoes. The bright fruit and ginger notes in the Prelude accent dishes that incorporate sweet and spice, such as a Middle Eastern chickpea-and-apricot stew. And its faintly toasty notes complement toasty flavors such as browned nuts or smoked salmon. Caramelized winter vegetables tend to push all the right buttons, and don't forget to punch them up with a bit of spice.

TOP FOOD MATCH:
Butternut squash ravioli with nutmeg, toasted hazelnuts and crispy sage

POULTRY

SWEET POTATOES

SPICES

Left: A vineyard in the temperate coastal region south of Perth, Australia, typical of those that provide fruit for Leeuwin Estate's Prelude Vineyards Chardonnay.

10 OF THE BEST

EYE-OPENING AUSSIE CHARDONNAYS

BINDI	$$$$
CULLEN	$$$$
FIRST DROP	$$
GIANT STEPS	$$$
HEGGIES VINEYARD	$$
HILL-SMITH ESTATE	$$
ROBERT OATLEY	$–$$
PLANTAGENET	$$
WOLF BLASS	$
THE YARD	$$–$$$

AROUND THE WORLD

SIMILAR STYLE WINES FROM DIFFERENT COUNTRIES

Bergström, Sigrid
Willamette Valley, Oregon, U.S. $$$

Domaine Philippe Colin, Chassagne-Montrachet 1er Cru Les Chenevottes
Burgundy, France $$$$

Elena Walch, Cardellino
Alto Adige, Italy $$

CHOICE MADE SIMPLE

EXPERT'S PERSONAL FAVORITES

Recommended by Franck Moreau, MS, Group Sommelier, Merivale, Australia

BONNY DOON, LE CIGARE BLANC (GRENACHE BLANC / ROUSSANNE) MONTEREY COUNTY, CALIFORNIA, U.S. $

ARNALDO CAPRAI, GRECANTE GRECHETTO DEI COLLI MARTANI UMBRIA, ITALY $–$$

ÁLVARO CASTRO (QUINTA DA PELLADA), BRANCO RESERVA (ENCRUZADO / CERCIAL) DÃO PORTUGAL $–$$

YVES CUILLERON, LES CHAILLETS, CONDRIEU (VIOGNIER) NORTHERN RHÔNE, FRANCE $$$–$$$$

R LÓPEZ DE HEREDIA, VIÑA GRAVONIA BLANCO RESERVA RIOJA, SPAIN $$

KUMEU RIVER, MATÉ'S VINEYARD CHARDONNAY AUCKLAND, NEW ZEALAND $$$

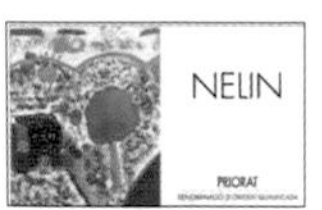

CLOS MOGADOR, NELIN (GARNACHA BLANCA BLEND) PRIORAT, CATALONIA, SPAIN $$$

PLANETA, LA COMETA (FIANO) SICILY, ITALY $$

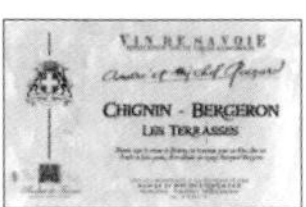

DOMAINE ANDRÉ ET MICHEL QUENARD, CHIGNIN BERGERON (ROUSSANNE) SAVOIE, FRANCE $–$$

TYRRELL'S WINES VAT 1 SEMILLON HUNTER VALLEY, NEW SOUTH WALES, AUSTRALIA $$$–$$$$

WORLD OF FINE WINE RECOMMENDATIONS

LAROCHE, CHABLIS GRAND CRU LES BLANCHOTS RÉSERVE DE L'OBÉDIENCE (CHARDONNAY) BURGUNDY, FRANCE $$$$

WILLIAM FÈVRE, CHABLIS GRAND CRU LES CLOS (CHARDONNAY) BURGUNDY, FRANCE $$$$

ALBERT GRIVAULT, MEURSAULT PREMIER CRU CLOS DES PERRIÈRES (CHARDONNAY) BURGUNDY, FRANCE $$$$

DOMAINE LEFLAIVE, PULIGNY-MONTRACHET PREMIER CRU LES PUCELLES (CHARDONNAY) BURGUNDY, FRANCE $$$$$

RAMEY HYDE VINEYARD CHARDONNAY CARNEROS, NAPA VALLEY, CALIFORNIA, U.S. $$$$

MOUNTADAM VINEYARDS, HIGH EDEN CHARDONNAY EDEN VALLEY, SOUTH AUSTRALIA $$$

PENFOLDS, YATTARNA BIN 144 CHARDONNAY AUSTRALIA $$$$

M CHAPOUTIER, ERMITAGE BLANC DE L'ORÉE (MARSANNE) NORTHERN RHÔNE, FRANCE $$$$$

DOMAINE DE CHEVALIER BLANC (SAUVIGNON BLANC / SEMILLON) GRAVES, BORDEAUX, FRANCE $$$$

SADIE FAMILY, PALLADIUS (VIOGNIER / CHARDONNAY / CHENIN BLANC / GRENACHE BLANC) SOUTH AFRICA $$$$

(*Grape Varieties in Brackets*)

LEFT-FIELD ALTERNATIVES

BOUTARI, WHITE
(ASSYRTIKO)
SANTORINI, GREECE $-$$

CIAVOLICH, ARIES
(PECORINO)
COLLINE PESCARESI, ABRUZZO, ITALY $$

DOMAINE BRU-BACHÉ, JURANÇON SEC
(GROS MANSENG)
JURANÇON, SOUTHWEST FRANCE $$

DOMAINE JEAN-LOUIS CHAVÉ, HERMITAGE BLANC (MARSANNE / ROUSSANNE) HERMITAGE, NORTHERN RHÔNE, FRANCE $$$$$

DONKEY & GOAT, UNTENDED CHARDONNAY
ANDERSON VALLEY, CALIFORNIA, U.S. $$-$$$

BOEKENHOUTSKLOOF, SÉMILLON
FRANSCHHOEK VALLEY, WESTERN CAPE, SOUTH AFRICA $$

LA MIRANDA DE SECASTILLA
(GARNACHA BLANCA)
SOMONTANO, ARAGON, SPAIN $-$$

ANDREW RICH VINTNER, CIEL DU CHEVAL VINEYARD ROUSSANNE
COLUMBIA VALLEY, WASHINGTON, U.S. $$

CHÂTEAU LA ROQUE, CLOS DES BÉNÉDICTINS BLANC (ROLLE [VERMENTINO] / MARSANNE / ROUSSANNE) LANGUEDOC, FRANCE $$

CHÂTEAU TOUR DES GENDRES, CUVÉE DES CONTI SEC
(SÉMILLON / SAUVIGNON BLANC / MUSCADELLE) SOUTHWEST FRANCE $-$$

BEST ON A BUDGET

CRIOS DE SUSANA BALBO, TORRONTÉS
CAFAYATE VALLEY, ARGENTINA $

DOMAINE GRAND VENEUR CÔTES DU RHÔNE BLANC
(ROUSSANNE / VIOGNIER / CLAIRETTE)
RHÔNE, FRANCE $

CHÂTEAU GRAND VILLAGE BLANC
(SÉMILLON / SAUVIGNON BLANC)
BORDEAUX, FRANCE $

FEUDI DI SAN GREGORIO, FALANGHINA
SANNIO, CAMPANIA, ITALY $

MAS CARLOT, CLAIRETTE DE BELLEGARDE
(CLAIRETTE)
RHÔNE, FRANCE $

MIL PIEDRAS, VIOGNIER
UCO VALLEY, MENDOZA, ARGENTINA $

NITÍDA, SÉMILLON
DURBANVILLE, SOUTH AFRICA $-$$

PALAZZONE, ORVIETO CLASSICO
(PROCANICO / VERDELLO / GRECHETTO / DRUPEGGIO / MALVASIA) UMBRIA, ITALY $

HENRI PERRUSSET, MÂCON-VILLAGES
(CHARDONNAY)
BURGUNDY, FRANCE, $-$$

RESSÒ, GARNACHA BLANCA
CATALUNYA, SPAIN $

MASTERCLASS: THAT'S HOT. OR NOT.

Someone really needs to come up with some new terms to take the heat off of "hot." Because it just has way too many lexicon-related responsibilities. Just think of all the word associations: oven, sun, Buster Poindexter, radiator, desert, Paul Whiteman and His Orchestra, campfire, Timbuktu, Chile peppers, the Red Hot Chili Peppers, the spilled tea that burned my hand yesterday, radioactivity, Paris Hilton, swine flu, menopause, high-occupancy tolls, Nelly, the Hawaii Opera Theatre, thieves, electric stoves, and don't get me started on hot-swapping, hotboxes, hotbeds, hot dogs, hot springs, hot tubs, hot-air balloons, hot zones, Hot Wheels, hotspots and "getting the hots."

And now, please make space in your brain for one more application for the most overused three letters in our vocabulary. Because it's time to immerse ourselves in hot, the oenogeek definition.

When a wine is overly alcoholic—or, simply feels that way on your palate—you may refer to it as "hot," because it creates a burning sensation in your mouth. It's onomatopoetic: If you take a sip of higher alcohol wine, then open your mouth wide and whisper "haaaahhhhhhtt"—the same way you might if you'd just had a spoonful of scalding soup—you can actually feel the alcohol fumes radiating off your tongue and throat like waves of heat rising from the pavement in Yuma.

Another concept that it's quite important to learn in conjunction with heat is **balance.** A wine with a moderate alcohol level of 13% might go down like lighter fluid, while a wine at 14.5% might be smooth as silk if it has plentiful **fruit**, **acidity** and **tannins** to balance out the high alcohol.

Why is heat more noticeable in white wines than in reds? Consider this: Most of us (i.e., non-Russians) prefer to drink vodka as part of a cocktail, rather than swigging it straight. Yet we don't mind sipping bourbon neat or on the rocks. This is because vodka is a neutral spirit, with no flavor to speak of. Bourbon, on the other hand, tastes of caramel and spice thanks to the charred-oak barrels it ages in. The alcohol isn't as off-putting in bourbon, because our palates are kept busy processing those additional flavor components.

White wines have a vodka-like purity: They tend to be pressed off their skins and aged in stainless-steel vats or neutral (old) barrels, so they lack the tannins, toast, texture and concentrated fruit that red wines have. Red wines macerate in their pungent, tannic skins, then, like bourbon, age in toasted oak barrels. With so much going on in the glass, the alcohol is less noticeable. And now you know one reason why rich, full whites tend to see new-oak barrels more often than their lower alcohol brethren do.

If you do have a hot white wine in your hand, I've got a good food-pairing rule of thumb for you: Just play the word-association game. Hot dogs and—contrary to popular opinion, hot chilis—pair quite well with these heavies. As for the Red Hot Chili Peppers, that's a personal choice.

HOW TO IDENTIFY THESE ELEMENTS

1: Swirl a hot wine and it will show its **legs**: Instead of spilling straight to the bottom of your glass, it will glide slowly down the sides in visible rivulets.

2: If you sniff a hot wine, you might get a whiff of alcohol or feel that burning sensation in the back of your throat, even before you've tasted it.

3: High-alcohol wines feel viscous in your mouth. In oeno-speak, this texture is described as **fat, heavy** or **oily**.

IN THE VINEYARD

DIURNAL SHIFT
Some of the world's greatest wine regions have wide **diurnal temperature variations**, or warm days counterbalanced by chilly nights. A large **diurnal shift** allows the grapes to ripen while maintaining their acidity, resulting in balanced wines.

SUGAR LEVELS
Contrary to what you may have heard, the harvest date is not determined by the sugar levels (**brix**) in the fruit. Instead, the vine tender must wait for flavors to reach maturity. If the brix shoots up before physiological ripeness is achieved, the resulting wine will taste "hot."

CLIMATE
A "hot" wine is born in a hot vineyard—either in a generally warm growing region or, alternately, in a cool-climate region that has experienced an unusually warm summer.

ALCOHOL
The planet is heating up, and so is wine. Back in the 1960s, '70s and early '80s, most dry table wines fell somewhere between 11% and 13% ABV. Modern farming and winemaking techniques, a fashion for "big" wine styles and global climate change have all contributed to increasingly higher alcohol levels in wines in recent years.

IRRIGATION
Heat stress can cause grapes to **shut down**, ceasing sugar production. Irrigation keeps the grapes in business, extending hangtime (the period of time the cluster remains on the vine prior to harvest) and continuing the ripening process through the hottest days of summer. But this can result in unnaturally high sugar levels, requiring the winemaker to reduce the alcohol and add acid once the wine is in the cellar.

MASTERCLASS: SIX WINES TO BUY

Depending on where the vineyard is located and the whims of the winemaker, it's possible to vinify the same grape many different ways, resulting in a wide range of wines. Chardonnay, for example, can be big, brassy and hot, or light, understated and even thin. The following six wines exemplify this. I've selected some examples of each of three **varietals** (wines made from a single grape)—Chardonnay, Sémillon and Viognier—and listed more delicate interpretations first, then fuller, riper styles second. Taste them **blind** and try to guess which wines come from the same grapes, and which wines have the higher alcohol levels.

LES HÉRITIERS DU COMTE LAFON MÂCON-VILLAGES BLANC
(Chardonnay) Mâconnais, Burgundy, France $$

ALTERNATIVE CHOICES

EVESHAM WOOD CHARDONNAY
Willamette Valley, Oregon, U.S. $$

LIOCO CHARDONNAY
Russian River Valley, Sonoma, California, U.S. $$

MARCASSIN MARCASSIN VINEYARD
(Chardonnay) Sonoma Coast, California, U.S. $$$$$

ALTERNATIVE CHOICES

EL MOLINO CHARDONNAY
Rutherford, Napa Valley, California, U.S. $$$–$$$$

GUNDLACH BUNDSCHU CHARDONNAY
Sonoma County, California, U.S. $$

BROKENWOOD ILR RESERVE
(Sémillon) Hunter Valley, New South Wales, Australia $$$

ALTERNATIVE CHOICES

MOUNT PLEASANT ELIZABETH
(Sémillon) Hunter Valley, New South Wales, Australia $

VASSE FELIX ESTATE
(Sémillon) Margaret River, Western Australia, Australia $$

L'ECOLE NO. 41 SEVEN HILLS VINEYARD ESTATE
(Semillon) Walla Walla, Washington, U.S. $$

ALTERNATIVE CHOICES

FIDÉLITAS SEMILLON
Columbia Valley, Washington, U.S. $$

CADARETTA SBS
(Sémillon / Sauvignon Blanc) Columbia Valley, Washington, U.S. $$

YALUMBA THE Y SERIES
(Viognier) South Australia, Australia ABV $

ALTERNATIVE CHOICES

ILLAHE VIOGNIER
Willamette Valley, Oregon, U.S. $

PINE RIDGE VINEYARDS
(Chenin Blanc / Viognier) Clarksburg, California, U.S. $

ANDRÉ PERRET CONDRIEU
(Viognier) Northern Rhône, France $$$$

ALTERNATIVE CHOICES

DOMAINE GEORGES VERNAY COTEAU DE VERNON, CONDRIEU
(Viognier) Northern Rhône, France $$$$$

CUILLERON VERTIGE, CONDRIEU
(Viognier) Northern Rhône, France $$$$

HOW TO SERVE IT

You might know a consummate party host—the kind who keeps vodka and gin bottles in the freezer to make the smoothest, silkiest cocktails. Similarly, full-bodied wines are smoother on the palate at colder temperatures, because you don't notice the alcohol as much. However, chilling also deadens their aromatics and flavors. So be sure not to serve these wines cool but not cold. About 45 minutes in the refrigerator should suffice (depending on your refrigerator's settings); remove all of the bottles at the same time for temperature consistency.

HOW TO TASTE IT

This is a fun tasting to do blind with friends. Mix up the order of the wines, number them 1 through 6, and note the region, grape variety and alcohol level of each wine. Wrap each bottle in paper, write the corresponding number on each one, and taste through. See if you and your friends can guess which wines are higher in alcohol, and try to match up the three pairs of the same grape variety. No cheating!

HOW TO TALK ABOUT IT

A wine with a noticeable but pleasing amount of **heat** is **full-bodied**; a full-bodied wine that lacks acidity is **flabby**. And a wine that lacks alcoholic oomph is **thin** or **watery**. The best wines taste complete no matter what the alcohol number on the label says; these are **balanced**. You might be surprised to find that some wines taste balanced even at 15% ABV.

FOOD MATCHES

There's no better foil for comparing white wines of varying degrees of alcohol than cheese. Select an assortment that includes an earthy raw sheep's milk cheese, a Camembert, a Fontina and a Stilton, then focus on sensation rather than flavor as you taste with the wines. With the mouth-coating texture of cheese, do you prefer the complementary viscosity of a full-bodied white or the crisp acidity of a lighter wine?

MASTERCLASS: WHAT'S TRENDING?
SOMMS STAND UP FOR BIG WHITE WINES

CALIFORNIA CHARDONNAY: BACKLASH TO THE BACKLASH

Forget about hot—California Chardonnay used to be cool. Its moment in the sun may have dawned in 1982, when Kendall-Jackson released its Vintners Reserve bottling. The pre-foodie generation rejoiced: Just as they were turning away from Daiquiris and beef Stroganoff in favor of California cuisine, here was a characterful, high-quality, American-made white wine to wash down the sudden surge of grilled portobellos and sun-dried tomato pesto. Soft, a touch sweet, and rounded by inoffensive oak, K-J was easy to find in shops and restaurants, and affordable (at $7.50, it was half the price of Sonoma-Cutrer), but much posher than the plonk that was sold by the jug in supermarkets. Then along came insipid Pinot Grigio from Italy, and sushi, and before you could say "flash-in-the-pan," you couldn't get into a cocktail party without knowing the code: "ABC," as in, "I'll drink anything but Chardonnay." Vintners reacted by vinifying the wine in stainless steel rather than oak, producing a beverage that tasted like... Pinot Grigio from Italy. Sommeliers, too, were running in the opposite direction, back into the slender, elegant arms of Burgundy—Chablis, Corton-Charlemagne, Meursault and Montrachet were just so genteel and refined in comparison with their loud, boisterous American counterparts. But no one can resist California's charms for long. And today, hipster oenophiles unburdened by history are showing up with bottles of old-school Cali Chard or asking for "anything Burgundy...or California."

KELLI WHITE'S FAVE CALI CHARDS

"Living and working in Napa Valley, I think about alcohol levels a lot," says Kelli White, Sommelier at Press in St. Helena, California. "Often that abrasive heat that is so offensive and easily criticized is the result of the winemaker imposing a style on the grape," she explains. "But there are many examples of full-bodied California Chardonnays that achieve their heft naturally and wear their weight with grace." Here, White shares with us three of her favorites for pairing with the menu at Press. "All three wines possess the intense fruit concentration, the natural acidity and the mineral complexity that can support a higher alcohol level," she says. "These same qualities make the wine more attractive for food pairing."

Hyde de Villaine, Hyde Vineyard (Chardonnay), Napa Valley, California $$$$
Food match: Roasted oysters with creamy leeks, bacon, arugula and parmesan

Kongsgaard, The Judge (Chardonnay) Napa Valley, California $$$$$
Food match: Grilled Bandera quail with French lentils, lacinato kale, Nueske bacon and figs

Rudd, Edge Hill Bacigalupi Vineyard (Chardonnay) Russian River Valley, Sonoma County, California $$$$*
Food match: Grilled walu with roasted baby artichoke, fennel, turnips, rosemary and arugula hazelnut salsa verde

**For the sake of transparency, it should be noted that Press is owned by Rudd Winery owner Leslie Rudd.*

MORE CLASSIC CALI CHARDS

Byron, Central Coast $$

Grgich Hills, Napa Valley $$$

Hanzell, Sonoma County $$$–$$$$$

Heitz Cellar, Napa Valley $$

Kosta Browne, Sonoma County $$$$

Littorai, Sonoma County $$$$

Mayacamas, Napa Valley $$$

Chateau Montelena, Napa Valley $$$

Neyers, Napa Valley $$–$$$

Pahlmeyer, Napa Valley $$$–$$$$

Peay, Sonoma County $$–$$$$

Rochioli, Sonoma County $$$–$$$$

Rombauer, Napa Valley $$$

Schug, Sonoma County $$–$$$

Sea Smoke, Central Coast $$$$

Williams Selyem, Sonoma County $$$$

A SOMMELIER'S PERSPECTIVE ON PAIRING BIG WHITES

"I think it's a mistake for sommeliers not to look at full-bodied white wines," says François Chartier. "We have a problem in that we are always looking at wine on its own. But we drink wine while we are eating." To that end, Chartier, a Canadian sommelier-turned-food-pairing sleuth, has been collaborating with scientists and famous chefs like Ferran Adrià of elBulli to determine the best wine-and-food matches. "When you put foods together that share the same aromatic compounds, we call it **aromatic synergy**; the result is bigger than the sum of each of the compounds. I think there is a time, a place, and a kind of food for every wine on the planet. And full-bodied whites are great to match with food."

NEW ATTITUDES TO OAK, SPICES AND HOT PEPPERS

According to Chartier, aging white wines in oak barrels, on the lees, increases their **glutamic acid** compounds, which—just like monosodium glutamate, once so popular in Asian restaurants—are extremely receptive to **umami**, that elusive flavor that's something like savory. Which foods are rich in umami? Soy sauce, of course. Also: "Aged parmesan cheese, crabs and seaweed," says Chartier. And, he adds, cured meats, lobster, mushrooms, tomato paste, poultry and pork. In addition, **malolactic fermentation**, which converts tart malic acids into softer lactic acids, makes whites more amenable to scallops, sesame seeds, wild rice, caramelized onion and coconut. "Soft spices like coriander, clove, ginger, turmeric and saffron go fabulously with oak-aged whites because they have the same aromatic compounds," Chartier adds. Now: How about heavy spices, like chili peppers? "Everybody always says that with very spicy food, we need to drink very light, very cold white wine. I don't agree with that at all," says Chartier. Nor does he think the old standby, beer, is a good match: "The spicy compounds in chilis, called **capsaicins**, burn your palate when in the presence of beer or water." Instead, Chartier points to the **Scoville Scale**, the way in which pungency is measured: Incremental amounts of a sugar solution are added to a pepper extract until tasters can't detect the spice. If sugar is the dampening agent, argues Chartier, we should be drinking fruity, ripe wines with fiery foods. "Full-bodied white wines at around 14% ABV are fabulous with spicy Asian and Mexican food," he says.

RECOMMENDED READING

In *Taste Buds and Molecules: The Art and Science of Food, Wine, and Flavor,* François Chartier reveals the molecular compositions of our foods and wines, suggesting new and surprising pairings. For example: saffron, carrots, yellow apples and rosé wines are all rich in carotenoids—so consider serving any or all of those things together. Oh, and Muscat? According to Chartier, this underappreciated grape variety is freakishly versatile on the table. A punchy design with flow charts enlivens the browsing experience.

"*In the course of my research...I noticed that foods could be divided into large aromatic families so as to provide greater precision when looking for harmonious wine and food pairings.*"

4 LUSCIOUSLY SWEET WHITES

4 LUSCIOUSLY SWEET WHITES

You think this part isn't for you. You, after all, don't drink sweet wines. I know you. You've steadfastly refused to attend your girlfriend's yoga class, despite your long-festering lower-back pain. You insist on ordering steak when your cholesterol levels are screaming for you to choose salmon. You turn your nose up at the *oeuvre* of Woody Allen in favor of thrillers, battle scenes and Westerns. You don't read fiction or, God forbid, poetry. There is no Adele in your playlist.

Well, I've got news for you, buddy. Remember the only piece of poetry you ever enjoyed, *The Iliad*? Did Hector, Nestor or Odysseus swig Scotch out of hip flasks before hitting the battlefield? Oh, no. They sipped a juicy sweet wine, further sweetened with honey, before slaying their enemies. Alexander the Great? Hannibal? They guzzled the same stuff. Julius Caesar, Napoléon and the most badass of them all, Queen Elizabeth I of England, were all sweet-wine devotees.

So it's time to man up and explore the most exciting and underappreciated corner of the wine world. And slow down there, fella: You don't get to tackle Port, Sherry or other fortified beverages in this unit. Nope. Instead, we're going to focus all of our attention on their supposedly simpering, lower-alcohol sisters. Which you don't drink.

Here's the good news: We've already met many of the sweet-wine grape varieties in our unit on aromatic whites. They're just vinified differently to make the dessert-worthy styles. And here's the bad news: Luscious late-harvest grapes require careful picking and processing, so this category doesn't come cheap. The price ranges given throughout this unit are misleading because, for the most part, they refer to half-bottle sizes. But are you really the type who would suck down a full bottle of dessert wine? Probably not... unless you're the sort who can pull on a full suit of armor, mount a chariot and throw bronze-tipped spears at people, all before lunchtime (chest bumps with other helmeted chariot dudes are totally optional).

Yeah, maybe this part *isn't* for you. Or is it?

YOU'LL ENJOY THESE WINES IF...

- You would eat dessert first if you could
- You're looking for something lighter than fortified wines and spirits
- You enjoy salty cheeses and savory foie gras

WHAT THE EXPERTS SAY

"More than 40 percent of our tables go for a sweet wine; we offer it to every table. Tokaji Aszú goes beautifully with spices, like cinnamon, even in Christmas breads. Canadian Icewine has such exuberance and brightness; it goes with fruit-based desserts, maybe with a little chamomile ice cream. And when you don't really know what to do, you can always pair dessert wines with citrus. I love the flavor of orange with sweet wine."

Adrien Falcon, Wine Director, Bouley, New York City, U.S.

GOOD TO DRINK WITH

KEY

$	UNDER $15	$$$$	$50–100
$$	$15–30	$$$$$	$100+
$$$	$30–50		

THE NAMES TO LOOK FOR

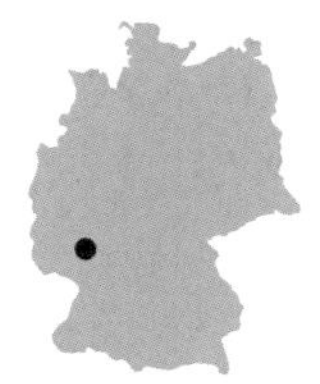

AUSLESE RIESLING RHEINHESSEN, GERMANY

"I don't drink sweet wine." Oh, really? Then you haven't tried Auslese. It's the dessert drink that can be drunk at dinner: Rich but never cloying, it's an accompaniment to roasted pork, a response to a chili-flecked stir-fry, and a foil for raw cow's milk cheeses. Who said anything about dessert? Although an apple pie will do nicely.

[**PRICE RANGE:** $-$$$$$]

[**ABV:** 8–13%]

[**DRINK IT:** 2–50 YEARS AFTER THE VINTAGE]

CHOICE

MOSCATO ITALY

The irony is delicious: One of the planet's most serious wine regions, Piedmont, produces a frothy, fun, low-alcohol sweet wine that begs to be drunk with breakfast (or, at least, brunch). *Frizzante*—Italian for "fizzy"—Moscato d'Asti has the fragrance of spring blossoms and white peaches, plus a lemon-curd lushness. What's not to love?

[**PRICE RANGE:** $-$$]

[**ABV:** 5–7%]

[**DRINK IT:** IMMEDIATELY]

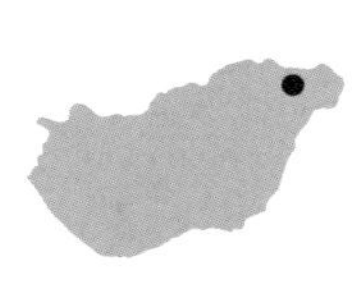

TOKAJ ASZÚ HUNGARY

In Hungary, the Furmint grape variety, among others, is prone to a delicious contradiction called noble rot. Vintners have a unique method of turning their nobly rotten fruit into a one-of-a-kind wine, which ranges in intensity from a honeyed tropical-fruit parfait to a molasses-like miracle. Hallelujah.

[**PRICE RANGE:** $$-$$$$$]

[**ABV:** 2–14%]

[**DRINK IT:** 5–300 YEARS AFTER THE VINTAGE]

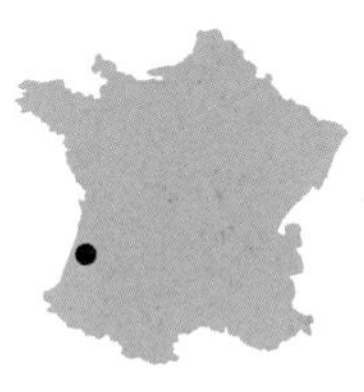

SAUTERNES BORDEAUX, FRANCE

Who would pay $200,000 for a half-bottle? A collector bidding on a 1787 Château d'Yquem, that's who. Yquem is Sauternes, and Sauternes is a honeyed blend of Sémillon and Sauvignon Blanc with the acidity and alcohol to stand up to anything from oysters to foie gras. Also: It ages better than a cryogenically frozen billionaire.

[**PRICE RANGE:** $-$$$$$]

[**ABV:** 8–13%]

[**DRINK IT:** 2–50 YEARS AFTER THE VINTAGE]

VIN SANTO TUSCANY, ITALY

Raisins are vinified throughout Italy; but in Tuscany, they taste like a gift from God. While Vin Santo can be dry, sweet or even rosé, it's most divine in its caramel-colored after-dinner form, redolent of roasted nuts and butterscotch. Forget speaking in tongues. In this state of ecstasy, your tongue speaks to you: "More, *per favore*!"

[**PRICE RANGE:** $$-$$$$$]

[**ABV:** 14–18%]

[**DRINK IT:** 4–10 YEARS AFTER THE VINTAGE]

VIDAL ICEWINE ONTARIO, CANADA

In German, it's Eiswein; in Canuck, it's Icewine, all one word. The Great White North produces enough Icewine from Riesling to fund a few NHL teams, but also, surprisingly, from Vidal, a hardy, thick-skinned cross-breed that thrives in subzero conditions. Its high acidity and sugar levels make Vidal Icewine stand out, so grab it if you see it.

[**PRICE RANGE:** $]

[**ABV:** 8–11.5%]

[**DRINK IT:** IMMEDIATELY]

TAKE ONE WINE: REICHSGRAF VON KESSELSTATT SCHARZHOFBERGER AUSLESE RIESLING

THE BASICS

GRAPE VARIETY: Riesling

REGION: Saar, Mosel, Germany

ALCOHOL LEVEL: 8%

PRICE: $$$–$$$$ (for a full-sized, 750ml bottle)

AVAILABILITY: Widely available

APPEARANCE: Buttery, sunflower gold

TASTING NOTE: Silky mouthfeel with prickly energy. Honey, chamomile, cinnamon, apricot and marmalade, then tart notes of kumquat and quinine, finishing with gingersnap, cardamom and allspice. Petrol notes with cellar age. Invigorating enough for dinner yet also luscious enough for dessert.

FOOD MATCH: Salty, hard cheeses, or semisoft, pungent, cow's-milk cheeses such as Reblochon. Snickerdoodles, meringue or *muhallabia*, the Moroccan rice pudding made with almonds, pistachios and rose water. Also: Hot dogs.

DRINK OR KEEP: This wine will continue to evolve for two decades after the vintage date, but is best enjoyed at between five and 15 years of age.

WHY DOES IT TASTE THAT WAY?

Germany's top winegrowing area, known simply as "the Mosel," actually consists of three smaller subregions, named after the **Mosel River** and its tributaries, the **Saar** and the **Ruwer**. South-facing Scharzhofberg is the top **Erste Lage**, or premium-quality, vineyard in the chilly Saar, with the steep slopes and rocky slate soil for which this region is famous. In the best vintages, such as 1999, the vineyard develops **botrytis**, or **noble rot**, which raisins the grapes, resulting in honeyed, preserve-like—not rotten!—aromas and flavors. Workers walk through the steep vineyard multiple times throughout the harvest season, waiting until the last possible minute to pick the Auslese bunches at the peak of ripeness. In the winery, cellar hands sort out the shriveled, nobly rotten late-harvest fruit for the unctuous ***goldkapsel*** bottling.

WHO MADE IT?

Reichsgraf von Kesselstatt has been in the winegrowing business for more than 660 years. (Historical aside: A certain Friedrich von Kesselstatt put his viniferous knowledge to work in the late 14th century when he was appointed "court sommelier.") The family's savvy moves over the years included converting almost all of their plantings to Riesling in the 18th century, and purchasing four defunct monasteries, along with their impressive vineyard holdings, in the 19th century. Today, Annegret Reh-Gartner runs the sprawling estate, overseeing 89 acres (36 hectares) of prime vineyard sites, equally split between the Mosel, Saar and Ruwer. (Contemporary aside: Annegret is married to German star chef Gerhard Gartner.) R von K is known as an old-school producer, favoring native-yeast fermentations and using large wooden tanks (*fuders*) whenever appropriate. This approach to Riesling production is coming back into vogue today among the young guns, who look to R von K as a standard-bearer of tradition.

CRACKING THE CODE
CAPSULE
The gold foil, or **goldkapsel**, is a sign that this is a reserve-quality Auslese, sourced from the grapes affected by **botrytis** (**noble rot**).
BOTTLE
The traditional long, slender, green bottle in the **hock** shape is used all over the world today for Riesling.
QUALITY LEVEL
If you take a peek at the back label, you'll note that the alcohol is a mere 8%, and you'll see the words **Qualitätswein mit Prädikat** (**QMP** for short), indicating that this is a top-quality wine.
PRODUCER
Reichsgraf means "rich earl." Germans love to brag about their formal titles, and you'll often find them on winery labels. There's an especially strong tradition of PhD-holding "Doktors" purchasing vineyards, then naming them after themselves. (There's also an old wives' tale that rural Germans used to pay their medical bills by leaving parcels of land to their doctors.)
LABEL
This is a mercifully minimalistic label, considering that this family winery dates back to 1349. Some German labels lay on the umlauts and Gothic calligraphy so thick that it's impossible to make any sense out of what might be in the bottle.
LATE HARVEST
Riesling is the name of the grape. This wine was made from **Auslese**—"select"— late-harvest grapes, set aside from the rest of the vintage for their quality.
VINEYARD
"Scharzhofberger" means "from the Scharzhofberg Vineyard."
REICHSGRAF VON KESSELSTATT
2005 SCHARZHOFBERGER
RIESLING AUSLESE FUDER 10

REICHSGRAF VON KESSELSTATT SCHARZHOFBERGER AUSLESE RIESLING

WHY THAT PRICE?

If you think you might be turning into a German Riesling buff, I am very sorry, because this category was undervalued…until five minutes ago. Suddenly, every sommelier and bottle-shop owner in every major metropolitan area is stocking up on Riesling, and its once shockingly low prices are rising accordingly. In addition, because Auslese requires such careful hand-picking and sorting, it is a costly wine to produce. That said, this is a more affordable bottling than, say, R von K's top vineyard site (Josephöfer, in Mosel proper); and if you consider that the price I've given is for a full-sized, rather than a half-sized, bottle, it's quite a steal. Also, because of the longevity of the Auslese style, it's possible to pick up ridiculously affordable older vintages from knowledgeable merchants if you live in a market that enjoys a healthy influx of German imports.

WHAT FOOD DOES IT GO WITH?

The beauty of Auslese is its ability to swing with savory or sweet. The stick-your-finger-in-a-light-switch acidity will cut right through the fatty richness of main courses (especially those with sweet-and-sour notes) like tea-smoked duck, *kung pao* chicken or pork with a balsamic reduction. Yet it's also gorgeous alongside desserts that build upon fruit, spice, cream or doughy flavors. Think mango rice pudding, sweet-bean *mochi*, broiled figs with honey and mascarpone, marzipan cookies, rhubarb pie and the like.

TOP FOOD MATCH: *Bratwurst* and chutney with butternut squash tart

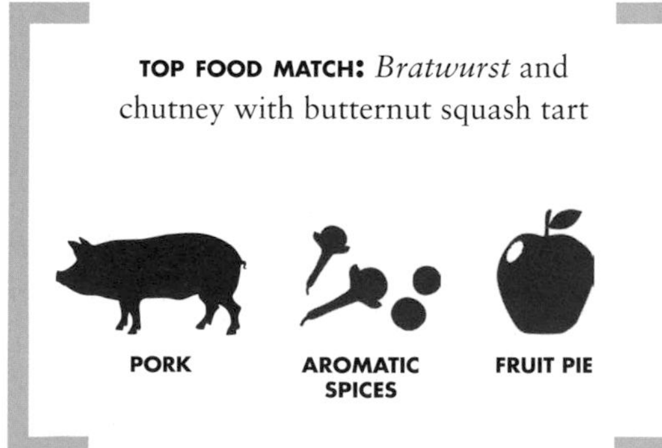

Left: The Mosel River and sloping vineyards allow the Riesling grapes to ripen even in this cool, northerly region.

10 OF THE BEST

GOLDEN GERMAN AUSLESE PRODUCERS

ANSGAR CLÜSSERATH	\$\$–\$\$\$
SCHLOSSGUT DIEL	\$\$–\$\$\$\$\$
WEINGUT DÖNNHOFF	\$\$\$\$–\$\$\$\$\$
GUNDERLOCH	\$\$\$\$
WEINGUT HANS LANG	\$\$\$_\$\$\$\$
LEITZ WEINGUT	\$\$–\$\$\$\$
MARKUS MOLITOR	\$\$–\$\$\$\$
EGON MÜLLER	\$\$\$\$\$
JOH. JOS. PRÜM	\$\$–\$\$\$\$\$
DOMDECHANT WERNER	\$\$–\$\$\$

AROUND THE WORLD

SIMILAR STYLE WINES FROM DIFFERENT COUNTRIES

Hermann J Wiemer,
Select Late Harvest, Riesling,
Finger Lakes, New York, U.S. \$\$\$–\$\$\$\$

Trimbach,
Cuvée Frédéric Emile
Sélection de Grains Nobles, Riesling,
Alsace, France \$\$\$\$–\$\$\$\$\$

Cave Spring,
Indian Summer Select Late Harvest,
Riesling, Niagara Peninsula, Canada \$\$

CHOICE MADE SIMPLE

EXPERT'S PERSONAL FAVORITES

Recommended by John Szabo MS, Beverage Director at Trump Tower Toronto, Canada & Partner and Principal Critic in WineAlign.com

ESTATE ARGYROS, VINSANTO 20 YEARS BARREL-AGED (ASSYRTIKO / AIDANI / ATHIRI) SANTORINI, GREECE $$$$$

DONNAFUGATA, BEN RYÉ PASSITO DI PANTELLERIA (MUSCAT) SICILY, ITALY $$–$$$

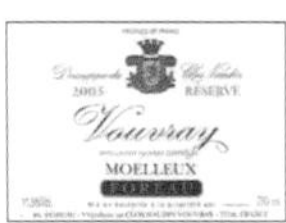

FOREAU, DOMAINE DU CLOS NAUDIN, VOUVRAY MOELLEUX (CHENIN BLANC) LOIRE VALLEY, FRANCE $$$

CHÂTEAU GILETTE, CRÈME DE TÊTE, SAUTERNES (SÉMILLON / SAUVIGNON BLANC) BORDEAUX, FRANCE $$$$$

INNISKILLIN, RIESLING ICEWINE, NIAGARA PENINSULA, ONTARIO, CANADA $$$

KIRÁLYUDVÁR, TOKAJI ASZÚ 6 PUTTONYOS (FURMINT / HÁRSLEVELŰ) TOKAJ, HUNGARY $$$

CHÂTEAU PIERRE-BISE, QUARTS DE CHAUME (CHENIN BLANC) LOIRE, FRANCE $$$

ΕΟΣΣ SAMOS, NECTAR (MUSCAT) SAMOS, GREECE $$

DOMAINE SCHOFFIT, RANGEN DE THANN CLOS SAINT-THÉOBALD, PINOT GRIS, SÉLECTIONS DE GRAINS NOBLES ALSACE, FRANCE $$$$$

WENZEL, SAZ RUSTER AUSBRUCH (MUSCAT / FURMINT) NEUSIEDLERSEE-HUEGELLAND, BURGENLAND, AUSTRIA $$$$

(Grape Varieties in Brackets)

WORLD OF FINE WINE RECOMMENDATIONS

MAXIMIN GRÜNHÄUSER ABTSBERG AUSLESE (RIESLING) MOSEL, GERMANY $$$

WEINGUT FRITZ HAAG, BRAUNEBERG JUFFER SONNENUHR AUSLESE LONG GOLD CAPSULE (RIESLING) MOSEL, GERMANY $$$$

TSCHIDA, SÄMLING TROCKENBEERENAUSLESE (SCHEUREBE) NEUSIEDLERSEE, AUSTRIA, $$$$

DOMAINE HUET, VOUVRAY CLOS DU BOURG MOELLEUX PREMIÈRE TRIE (CHENIN BLANC) LOIRE VALLEY, FRANCE $$$

CHÂTEAU CLIMENS, BARSAC (SÉMILLON / SAUVIGNON BLANC) BORDEAUX, FRANCE $$$$

CHÂTEAU SUDUIRAUT, SAUTERNES (SÉMILLON / SAUVIGNON BLANC) BORDEAUX, FRANCE $$$

ROYAL TOKAJI, MÉZES MÁLY TOKAJI ASZÚ 6 PUTTONYOS (FURMINT / HÁRSLEVELŰ / SÁRGA MUSKOTÁLY) TOKAJI, HUNGARY $$$$

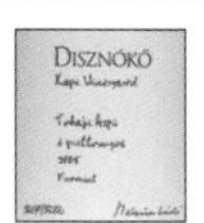

DISZNÓKÖ KAPI VINEYARD TOKAJI ASZÚ 6 PUTTONYOS, (FURMINT) TOKAJI, HUNGARY $$$$

AVIGNONESI, OCCHIO DI PERNICE VIN SANTO DI MONTEPULCIANO (SANGIOVESE) MONTEPULCIANO, TUSCANY, ITALY $$$$$

SAN GIUSTO A RENTENNANO, VIN SAN GIUSTO, VIN SANTO (MALVASIA / TREBBIANO) CHIANTI, TUSCANY, ITALY $$$$

VERSATILE FOOD WINES

DOMAINE DE BELLIVIÈRE, ELIXIR DU TUF (CHENIN BLANC)
JASNIÈRES, LOIRE, FRANCE $$$$

BROOKS, TETHYS LATE HARVEST RIESLING
WILLAMETTE VALLEY, OREGON, U.S.
$$–$$$

DE BORTOLI, NOBLE ONE, BOTRYTIS SÉMILLON
NEW SOUTH WALES, AUSTRALIA
$$–$$$

CAROLE BOUQUET, SANGUE D'ORO, MOSCATO PASSITO DI PANTELLERIA
(MUSCAT) SICILY, ITALY $$$

PHILLIPPE DELESVAUX, COTEAUX DU LAYON, SÉLECTION DE GRAINS NOBLES
(CHENIN BLANC) LOIRE, FRANCE
$$$–$$$$

CHÂTEAU DOISY-VÉDRINES, BARSAC
(SAUVIGNON BLANC / SÉMILLON)
BORDEAUX, FRANCE $$

FEILER-ARTINGER, RUSTER AUSBRUCH
(PINOT BLANC / NEUBURGER / PINOT GRIS / CHARDONNAY)
BURGENLAND, AUSTRIA $$$$

ISOLE E OLENA, VIN SANTO DEL CHIANTI CLASSICO
(MALVASIA / TREBBIANO)
TUSCANY, ITALY $$$–$$$$

KRACHER, GRANDE CUVÉE NOUVELLE VAGUE TROCKENBEERENAUSLESE NO. 6
(CHARDONNAY / WELSCHRIESLING)
BURGENLAND, AUSTRIA $$$–$$$$

CA' RUGATE, LA PERLARA RECIOTO DI SOAVE
(GARGANEGA)
VENETO, ITALY $$$

BEST ON A BUDGET

DOMAINE DES BERNARDINS, MUSCAT-DE-BEAUMES-DE-VENISE
RHÔNE, FRANCE $$

FALCHINI, PODERE CASALE 1°, VIN SANTO DEL CHIANTI
(MALVASIA / TREBBIANO)
TUSCANY, ITALY $$

FERRANDO, LA TORRAZZA, ERBALUCE DI CALUSO
(ERBALUCE)
PIEDMONT, ITALY $–$$

KEO, ST. JOHN XYNISTERI, COMMANDARIA
(MAVRO)
CYPRUS $–$$

OREMUS, LATE HARVEST TOKAJI
(FURMINT) TOKAJ, HUNGARY $$

ELIO PERRONE, SOURGAL, MOSCATO D'ASTI
(MUSCAT) PIEDMONT, ITALY $–$$

LA SPINETTA, BIANCOSPINO, MOSCATO D'ASTI
(MUSCAT) PIEDMONT, ITALY $–$$

ROBERT & BERNARD PLAGEOLES, DOMAINE DE TRES CANTOUS, MUSCADELLE
GAILLAC, FRANCE $$

CHARLES HOURS, UROULAT, JURANÇON
(PETIT MANSENG)
SOUTHWEST FRANCE $$

UVAGGIO, MOSCATO DOLCE,
(MUSCAT) LODI, CALIFORNIA, U.S.
$$

MASTERCLASS: SWEETNESS CLASSIFICATIONS

No more procrastinating; it's time to face the Kafka-esque classification systems of sweet wines. We'll start in France, where **doux** means sweet and **liquoreux** means extremely sweet. As we've learned in our previous discussion of the official terminology of the Loire Valley Chenin Blancs of Vouvray (in our section on Lively, Aromatic Whites), **Sec** means dry. Off-dry? **Demi-Sec.** And sweet, with more than 50 grams-per-liter of sugar, are **Moelleux.** Which is a wonderful word, by the way. It means soft, mellow, smooth or squishy. It's derived from the same Latin base as emollient, as in hand lotion, and mollifying, as in, the effect of consuming a nice glass of Domaine Huët "Le Haut-Lieu" Moelleux Vouvray. Mmmmmmmmm.

On to Alsace, which is a specialist in sweet Gewurztraminer and Pinot Gris, with a minor in after-dinner Riesling and Muscat. The Alsatians keep it simple, with the term **Vendanges Tardives,** meaning late harvest. Allowed to hang on the vine past ripeness, late-harvest grapes turn to raisins, sometimes contracting noble rot—which we'll get to in a minute. Alas, not all Vendanges Tardives in Alsace are sweet, confusingly. (But in New World regions, where we like to steal French wine terms because they sound fancy, they are.) But there's no mistaking the sweetness of a **Sélection de Grains Nobles,** pressed from the most dried-up, sugary and shriveled grapes of the harvest. I highly recommend this style of wine if you're dining on someone else's expense account. (Go for the Zind Humbrecht!)

And now, we must interrupt our regular programming to define the term noble rot, a.k.a. ***Botrytis cinerea.*** This gray fungus forms on ripe grapes, shriveling them and concentrating their sugars—provided said grapes are white, and you're in a region that tends toward foggy mornings and sun-soaked afternoons. Move to a cool location, where vignerons are attempting to make dry red wines in monsoon-like conditions (see: Burgundy and Oregon) and that rot turns ignoble, sucking the color out of the skins and turning the forlorn fruit moldy and mushy.

Properly botrytized white grapes look like shrunken heads in an archaeological museum: shriveled, *sui generis* approximations of their former selves. In Bordeaux, there's a noble rot sweet spot where the Ciron tributary branches off the Garonne River. Here, botrytis settles reliably on Sémillon, Sauvignon Blanc and Muscadelle, oozing a golden ambrosia, the most prestigious of which is bottled under the appellations of **Sauternes** or **Barsac** (the latter may also be labeled as Sauternes, but not vice versa). Other sweet-wine appellations in the region include Cadillac, Loupiac and Ste-Croix-du-Mont.

Ready to tackle Austria? Here we have the **Prädikat** system, which goes by the grams of sugar per milliliter of grape must (the juice of freshly crushed or pressed grapes). I won't bore you with the numbers. Suffice it to say that **Spätlese** is fully ripe; **Auslese,** which we met at the start of this chapter, is even riper; **Beerenauslese** is ultra-ripe and may include some noble rot; **Ausbruch** refers to raisins left hanging on the vine; and **Trockenbeerenauslese** (TBA for short) refers to the most shriveled of the noble rot lot. Germany's ratings are much the same, although they begin with the ethereally wispy Kabinett, (lighter than Spätlese), and they don't have Ausbruch. We can't all have Ausbruch, after all.

VARYING LEVELS OF RIPENESS AND ROT

HEALTHY GRAPES
Healthy, mature grapes are plump and juicy at harvest time.

ONSET OF BOTRYTIS
If purplish-pink spots begin to appear on the grapes, the vine tender knows that **noble rot (*Botrytis cinerea*)** is forming.

SPREAD OF BOTRYTIS
Vignerons watch the grape bunches carefully as noble rot spreads. The best producers go through the vineyard repeatedly during the fall and early winter, harvesting individual grapes for berry-select bottlings, which include **Sélection de Grains Nobles**, **Beerenauslese**,**Trockenbeerenauslese** and **Essencia**.

NOBLE ROT
When *Botrytis cinerea* settles on white grapes in ideal conditions, it turns the skins pink-to-brown and shrivels the flesh, concentrating the sugars and yielding a golden juice.

GRAY ROT
If the botrytized grapes don't get the chance to dry out in the afternoon sun, noble rot becomes **gray rot**. The grapes turn grayish and smell moldy; and a cobwebby film forms over the bunches.

RAISINED GRAPES
The French call grapes or bunches that simply dry out on the vine, without contracting botrytis, ***raisins dorés***.

MASTERCLASS: SIX WINES TO BUY

Grapes shrivel in many different ways, and each of these results in a different sort of wine. Here's a lineup of six of the best-known styles. You might be surprised to find that our first selection, Amarone, is actually a powerful dry red, and Vin Santo, also from Italy, has a nutty, Sherry-like note to it. We'll learn more about these wines, as well as Tokaji Aszú and Icewine, in the WHAT'S TRENDING section that follows this tasting. For now, just sip and compare. And if you can't find one of these suggested bottles, feel free to substitute a different style of dessert drink, such as Sauternes. Dessert wines are a relatively scarce commodity.

PIEROPAN AMARONE
(Corvina / Corvinone / Rondinella / Croatina) Amarone della Valpolicella, Italy $$$$

ALTERNATIVE CHOICES

MASI COSTASERA AMARONE
(Corvina / Rondinella / Molinara) Amarone della Valpolicella Classico, Italy $$$–$$$$

TEDESCHI AMARONE
(Trajadura / Loureiro) Vinho Verde, Minho, Portugal $$–$$$

ROYAL TOKAJI
TOKAJI ASZÚ 6 PUTTUNYOS
(Furmint / Hárslevelű / Sárga Muskotály) Tokaj, Hungary $$$–$$$$$

ALTERNATIVE CHOICES

SZEPSY TOKAJI ASZÚ 6 PUTTUNYOS
(Furmint / Hárslevelű) Tokaj, Hungary $$$$$

HÉTSZOLO TOKAJI ASZÚ 6 PUTTUNYOS
(Furmint / Hárslevelű Kövérszőlő / Sárga Muskotály) Tokaj, Hungary $$$–$$$$

AVIGNONESI
VIN SANTO
(Trebbiano / Malvasia) Vin Santo di Montepulciano, Tuscany, Italy $$$$$

ALTERNATIVE CHOICES

BADIA A COLTIBUONO VIN SANTO
(Trebbiano / Malvasia) Vin Santo del Chianti Classico, Tuscany, Italy $$$

VOLPAIA VIN SANTO
(Trebbiano / Malvasia) Vin Santo del Chianti Classico, Tuscany, Italy $$$

SELBACH-OSTER
ZELTINGER SONNENUHR TROCKENBEERENAUSLESE
(Riesling) Mosel, Germany $$$$$

ALTERNATIVE CHOICES

MEULENHOF ERDENER TREPPCHEN TROCKENBEERENAUSLESE
(Riesling) Mosel, Germany $$$$–$$$$$

WEINGUT ACKERMANN ZELTINGER SCHLOSSBERG TROCKENBEERENAUSLESE
(Riesling) Mosel, Germany $$

DOMAINE OSTERTAG
FRONHOLZ VENDANGES TARDIVES
(Gewurztraminer) Alsace, France $$$–$$$$

ALTERNATIVE CHOICES

ALBERT MANN
ALTENBOURG VENDANGES TARDIVES
(Gewurztraminer) Alsace, France $$$

AGATHE BURSIN
ZINNKOEPFLE VENDANGES TARDIVES
(Gewurztraminer) Alsace, France $$$

MISSION HILL
RESERVE ICEWINE
(Vidal) Okanagan Valley, British Columbia, Canada $$–$$$

ALTERNATIVE CHOICES

JACKSON-TRIGGS
PROPRIETORS' RESERVE ICEWINE
(Vidal) Niagara Peninsula, Ontario, Canada $$

PONDVIEW ESTATE
FOUR MILE CREEK ICEWINE
(Vidal) Niagara Peninsula, Ontario, Canada $$

HOW TO SERVE IT

You'll want to pour the Amarone in medium-to-large-bowled glasses; a smaller white-wine glass will work for the rest. So offer two stemware sizes to each taster. Although this is an ideal after-dinner tasting, be sure not to turn the lights down too low, since the gradations of color in sweet wines are beautiful to behold.

HOW TO TALK ABOUT IT

Here's a quick guide to pronunciation and enunciation. Amarone is AH-MAH-ROH-NAY. (Bonus points if you can roll your "R.")
Vendanges Tardives is VAHN-DAHNJ-TAHR-DEEV.
Tokaji Aszú is TOKE-AH-EE OSH-OO.
Trockenbeerenauslese is TROH-KUN-BEER-UN-OWS-LAY-SAY. (Again, try to roll those "Rs" a bit.)
As for Vin Santo and Icewine, I think you can figure those out for yourself.

AROMATIC AND SENSORY CLUES

As you smell and taste through these, try to find the commonality between them: the aroma of dried fruit. Then, revisit each wine to determine what sets it apart from the rest. Generally, dried-grape wines like Vin Santo have an oxidative, Sherry-like nose, while botrytis-affected TBA tends toward notes of honey, citrus and apricots. You might find a slight smoky or peppery character in Vendanges Tardives; and Icewines tend to be bright, juicy and fruity.

FOOD MATCHES

To best appreciate the nuances of sweet wines, don't pair them with sweet desserts, but rather, neutral foods such as oatmeal biscuits or *biscotti*. Or, create contrast with slices of savory, hard cheese such as Parmigiano, Asiago, Grana Padano, Manchego or Pecorino—drizzle of honey optional. Salted, toasted nuts and dried fruits also work very well.

MASTERCLASS: WHAT'S TRENDING?
RAISIN WINES

HOW TO SAY "SWEET" IN MAGYAR

The 1989 collapse of the Communist Bloc was momentous for torn-apart families, jailed political activists, spurned religious groups and…wine lovers. Because it gave us access to that Hungarian sweet spot where the Bodrog and Tisza Rivers meet, generating morning mists, followed by sunny afternoons, and—you guessed it—noble rot. From here we get Tokaji Aszú, noble wine from the Tokaj region. It's a blend of fragrant, juicy varieties boasting high natural acidity. The most prominent is Furmint, whose thin skin makes it particularly susceptible to rot. After that, there's the option to include Hárslevelű, Sárga Muskotály, Zéta or Kövérszőlő. Got that? Good.

To make traditional Tokaji Aszú, painstakingly sort out the shriveled berries at harvest, then gently smash them to make an *aszú* paste. Meanwhile, vinify your un-botrytized grapes into an ordinary white wine. Add the *aszú* paste to your white wine, and the wine will re-ferment, morphing into a sweet elixir that's low in alcohol, high in sugar and acidity and gloriously fragrant. The number of ***puttunyos***, or buckets, of *aszú* in the final blend, begins at three and goes up to six (noted on the label as numerals), followed by the ridiculously rich Aszú Essencia. Finally there's Essencia. This nectar of the gods is fermented *aszú*, nothing else. It's only around two percent alcohol, as thick as honey, and can age for hundreds of years. It's on my bucket—*puttunyo*, if you like—list.

MAKING RAISINS…OR SULTANAS

The problem with noble rot is that you've got to sit around and wait for it to happen, then hope that it goes the noble way, not the gray way. There is, however, a much simpler solution: Simply pick the grapes, and then dry them, either by hanging them from the winery rafters, spreading them out on straw mats or laying them into stacking racks, with plenty of air flow between the layers. In Italy, where it's most prevalent, this process is called ***passito***, and since it doesn't rely on morning fogs or fungus spores, it is employed wherever winemakers wish to give it a go.

ITALIAN EARTHLY DELIGHTS

In Tuscany, the syrupy pressed juice of dried Trebbiano and Malvasia (white grapes) is sealed in small barrels, along with some yeast left over from previous vintages, and left alone for at least three years, for an unmonitored orgy of fermentation and oxidative aging. The finished wine is tawny and sweet-and-savory, like roasted, salted, toffee-covered nuts, with an Amontillado Sherry-like oxidative tang thrown in as a bonus. The name for this sinful substance? Vin Santo. And in northeastern Italy, in and around the Veneto, the *passito* process is notably employed for red wines, not whites (apologies to Soave), and with a twist….

The sweet version, called **Recioto**, tastes quite like chocolate-dipped cherries when done properly. Then there's **Ripasso**, a *dry* red that has fermented a second time on the skins of the same dried grapes used to make Recioto—or, in higher-quality bottlings, fermented with a small proportion of dried grapes—to make a rich wine, redolent of cherries and licorice. Finally, at the top of the heap is **Amarone**, powerful and by no means sweet (*amaro* translates as "bitter"). Tasting of baked plums and coffee beans and weighing in at around 15 percent alcohol, it's like a Valpolicella on steroids.

JACK FROST'S ROLE IN SWEET WINES

To desiccate grapes, we've learned, you can let them hang on the vine past the usual harvest date; or you can cross your fingers and hope for that fabulous fungus, noble rot, to settle into your vineyard; or, just pick your fruit and lay it out to dry. But there's one more grape diuretic left to discuss: bone-chilling cold. In parts of Germany, Austria, Canada and the northern U.S., a deep frost occasionally settles on late-harvest grapes, turning them rock-hard. Winery workers quickly pluck these marbles, rush them to the chilly winery before they thaw, and press them. Out oozes an ethereally silky juice, leaving ice crystals behind. In Germany and Austria, this sweet wine is called **Eiswein.**

But some of the world's most interesting deep-freeze wines come out of Canada, where arctic temperatures are reliable as rain—or, in Canada's case, snow. Apart from Riesling, there are unusual options here, like a pink *vin de glace* made from Cabernet Franc, some sparkling versions, and the surprisingly successful Vidal. Sadly for the rest of the world, Canada hasn't exported much wine in the past, with the United States and Asia grabbing most of the **Icewine** share. (And yes, that's "Icewine," all one word.) And since frozen grapes only release about 15 percent of the juice that their thawed-out brethren do, this wine is, by its very nature, a highly prized rarity.

THE FACSIMILES

In viticultural destinations where tasting-room sales account for a large proportion of the revenue, winery owners know that sweet wines sell. Thanks to their lovely golden-to-amber hues and fetching small bottles, they're easy on the eyes. They fit in suitcases easily and make nice gifts. And tourists who have been out tasting dry wines all day are quickly beguiled by a single sip of something sweet. In short, if you can produce a solid dessert wine, you've guaranteed yourself an income stream of impulse buys. But in many New World wine regions, climatic conditions make ice wine, noble rot, late-harvest or even *passito*-style winemaking impossible. Here, keep an eye out for the *vin Frigidaire*.

Some winemakers freeze their grapes and then squeeze them; some squeeze 'n' freeze. Others use vacuum evaporators, and finally, there's the tried-and-true method of making wine, freezing it, slowly thawing it until it tastes just right, and throwing the remaining ice chunks out. However you slice it, it's an "ice-box wine," not a true ice wine. There's nothing wrong with *vin Frigidaire*, but purists insist on the real deal. Because the deeper we delve into wine appreciation, the more we come to believe that someone or something has to suffer before we'll consider this liquid to be an art form. Thus, the vignerons who froze their fingertips at the crack of dawn, picking frost-covered grapes in a subzero vineyard, deserve our utmost respect.

5 SPARKLING WHITES AND ROSÉS

5 SPARKLING WHITES AND ROSÉS

The Italian composer Ferruccio Busoni could distill the multifaceted, three-keyboard organ compositions of J.S. Bach down to piano pieces without losing one iota of nuance. This is not unlike the challenge of the sparkling winemaker: To synthesize a blend of grape varieties—often from dozens of vineyard sites, and multiple vintages—and to capture the ebullience emitted by a complicated process without losing the very soul of the wine. In short, sparkling winemaking calls for technical virtuosity and inspired brilliance.

Of course, I'm mostly referring to *méthode traditionnelle* sparkling wines here—Champagnes, Crémants, Cavas, Franciacortas and the like—made by the labor-intensive traditional method. These wines, at their very finest, smell like warm brioche and pirouette across your tongue with a fine, forceful *mousse* of foamy bubbles, like Busoni's outstretched right pinky finger gently caressing those high notes. But there are other, simpler styles that can be just as enjoyable: Italian Proseccos, many German or Austrian Sekts, Portuguese Espumantes and their brethren are frolicsome, accessible pleasures, along the lines of a George Gershwin piano tune.

Before we delve into these delights, a bit of exposition is necessary: Because many sparkling wines are made from a blend of vintage years, I'll make note throughout this section of which wines are **Vintage** (from a single year), and which are **Non-Vintage** (**NV**, blended from two or more years). An added twist to sparkling-wine production is the practice of pressing the clear juice off the skins of red grapes. If the label doesn't specify, the wine is often a blend of red and white grapes, even if it looks white. A ***blanc de noirs*** is a white made from black (red) grapes; a ***blanc de blancs*** is a white made from white grapes; and a ***rosé*** may be made from red grapes, or a blend of red and white.

It's all enough to make one's head spin. But don't worry: The winemaker has it under control. Just listen...to the pop of the cork, the hiss of the gas escaping from the bottle and the pleasant fizz as the wine hits the flute.

YOU'LL ENJOY THESE WINES IF...

- You thirst for the crisp bite of seltzer or soda water
- You aim for elegance in all things
- You'd rather dabble in small plates than tuck into something substantial

WHAT THE EXPERTS SAY

"My favorite food to match with sparkling wines is charcuterie—anything from salty cured lardo to spicy soppressata. There is something beautiful that happens in our mouths when the meaty fatness meets the high-acid cold bubbles. Bubbles are also great with fried food such as French fries or just potato chips."

Sandia Chang, co-owner and Sommelier, Bubbledogs and Kitchen Table, London, U.K.

GOOD TO DRINK WITH

BREAKFAST
POPCORN
SOUFFLÉ
FRIED CHICKEN
STUFFED MUSHROOMS
CRÈME BRÛLÉE

KEY

$	UNDER $15	$$$$	$50–100
$$	$15–30	$$$$$	$100+
$$$	$30–50		

THE NAMES TO LOOK FOR

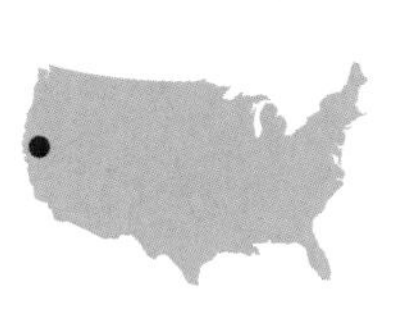

SPARKLING WINE WEST COAST, UNITED STATES

If you get all your information about the U.S. from hip-hop lyrics and footage of Super Bowl victory celebrations, you might think this New World nation is awash in sparkling wine. Not quite, but Americans do love their bubbly, so much that at least four French Champagne houses—and one Cava company—operate wineries in the US of A.

[**PRICE RANGE: $-$$$$**]

[**ABV: 11.5–13%**]

[**DRINK IT: 0–20 YEARS AFTER THE VINTAGE**]

CHOICE

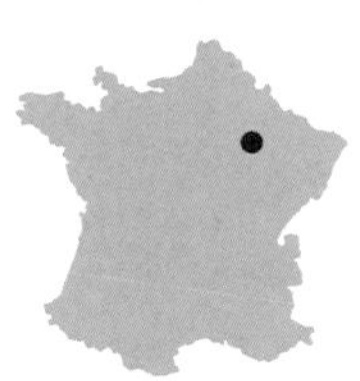

CHAMPAGNE CHAMPAGNE, FRANCE

While there are plenty of pretenders, no other winegrowing region boasts the blustery cool climate, the chalky soils and the courtly cultivation of Champagne. But is it overvalued? Look for vintage-dated bottles, small producers, single vineyards and sustainable farming practices to ensure that you're getting the *crème de la crème*.

[**PRICE RANGE: $$$-$$$$$**]

[**ABV: 11.5–12.5%**]

[**DRINK IT: 0–50 YEARS AFTER THE VINTAGE**]

CAVA CATALONIA, SPAIN

Salvador Dalí, Joan Miró, Antoni Gaudí, Ferran Adrià... Those Catalans know how to think outside the box. The Cordoníu bodega was the first to figure out how to make a dead ringer for Champagne for a fraction of the price; today, Cordoníu is the most prolific producer of *méthode traditionnelle* wines on the planet.

[**PRICE RANGE: $**]

[**ABV: 11–12.5%**]

[**DRINK IT: UPON RELEASE**]

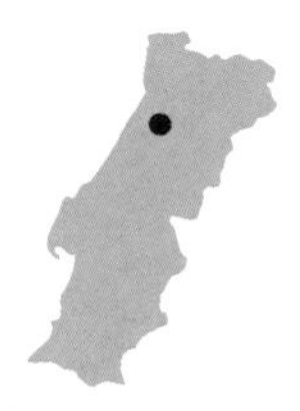

ESPUMANTE BAIRRADA, PORTUGAL

Sadly, there are selfish nations like Portugal that produce sensational sparkling wines...and keep them all to themselves. Word, however, has been leaking out, and lucky EU markets are beginning to gain access to Bairrada's deliciously affordable dry and sweet sparkling whites and—yes!—reds, for pairing with roast suckling pig.

[**PRICE RANGE: $**]

[**ABV: 12–13%**]

[**DRINK IT: UPON RELEASE**]

PROSECCO VENETO, ITALY

The featherweight Glera grape, vinified according to the stainless-steel Charmat method, makes the soda water of the wine world: Refreshing and neutral, Prosecco is a bartender's best friend. But just because it makes a beautiful Venetian-style Bellini doesn't mean you don't want to sip it solo. Sometimes, nothing tastes better.

[**PRICE RANGE: $-$$**]

[**ABV: 11–12%**]

[**DRINK IT: UPON RELEASE**]

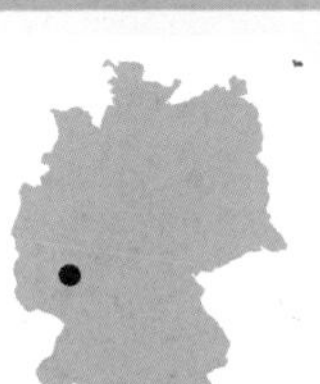

SEKT RHEINGAU, GERMANY

Sekt is a catch-all term, covering everything from light, Prosecco-like sparklers to luscious Champagne-style wines produced by small, quality-driven estates; they range from dry to sweet. The bottom line: Sekt quality has improved dramatically in recent years. Seek out the "Sekt b.A." or "Qualitätsschaumwein b.A." designations.

[**PRICE RANGE: $-$$$**]

[**ABV: 11–12.5%**]

[**DRINK IT: UPON RELEASE**]

TAKE ONE WINE: FRANCIS COPPOLA SOFIA BLANC DE BLANCS

THE BASICS

GRAPE VARIETIES: Pinot Blanc / Riesling / Muscat

REGION: Monterey County, California, U.S.

ALCOHOL LEVEL: 12%

PRICE: \$–\$\$

AVAILABILITY: Widely available

APPEARANCE: Pale straw, with *petite* bubbles and medium *pétillance*.

TASTING NOTE: Apples, white peaches, lemon chiffon, chalk, rose petals, grapefruit pith, honey.

FOOD MATCH: Spring rolls, shrimp cocktail, salad with pears or orange sections, risotto, Thai noodles, lemon curd tart, profiteroles, wedding cake.

DRINK OR KEEP: Drink now.

WHY DOES IT TASTE THAT WAY?

If you think that sparkling wine is all Champagne, think again. Simple, affordable, unfussy and effervescent wines are produced all over the planet, expressly for immediate enjoyment and consumption. Sofia falls into this category. It is made in a style that's crisp and light, lacking the toasty and caramel notes of fine Champagne, but far more affordable. The Sofia has an additional hit of fragrance and sweet fruitiness from its blend of aromatic grapes—Pinot Blanc accented by Riesling and Muscat—allowing this wine to transition from dinner to dessert. As an interesting side note, the inclusion of Pinot Blanc is a nod to Champagne. Today's Champagnes are mostly made from Pinot Noir, Chardonnay and Pinot Meunier, but historically, Pinot Blanc—a mutation of Pinot Noir—was prevalent, and it's still found in some Champagne blends today.

WHO MADE IT?

Much as we wine snobs would like to pretend it isn't happening, there is an unavoidable—and ever-growing—oenological trend rising from that oenological production zone known as Hollywood: the celebrity vintner. Antonio Banderas, Drew Barrymore, Gerard Depardieu, Greg Norman, Olivia Newton-John, Sting...these are the top echelon, but the list goes on, and on, and on... and on. Of these, filmmaker Francis Ford Coppola has shown perhaps the greatest commitment to quality winemaking, devoting 25 years to restoring the historic Inglenook winery in the Napa Valley to its former splendor. If Inglenook's \$250 Rubicon (a Cabernet Sauvignon-based blend) seems vainglorious, so be it. And if Sofia, Coppola's homage to his film-director daughter, isn't the wine of every oenophile's dreams, they don't have to drink it. The fact is, the majority of wine purchasers are women, and yet the consumer market is awash with off-the-mark, sub-par brands targeting female audiences with clumsy ad campaigns. Tasteful and restrained by contrast, Sofia makes many female consumers very, very happy.

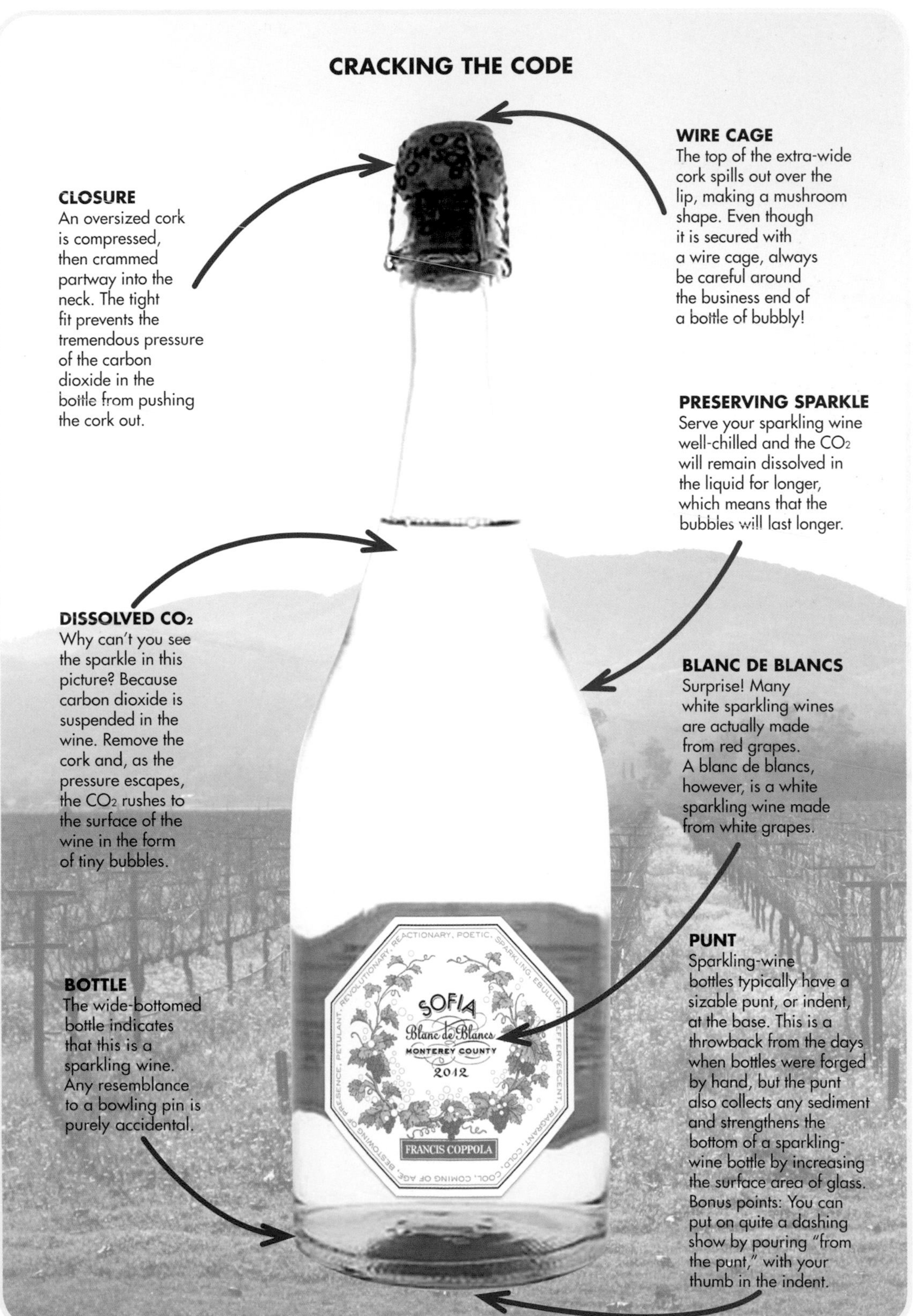
CRACKING THE CODE
CLOSURE
An oversized cork is compressed, then crammed partway into the neck. The tight fit prevents the tremendous pressure of the carbon dioxide in the bottle from pushing the cork out.
WIRE CAGE
The top of the extra-wide cork spills out over the lip, making a mushroom shape. Even though it is secured with a wire cage, always be careful around the business end of a bottle of bubbly!
PRESERVING SPARKLE
Serve your sparkling wine well-chilled and the CO_2 will remain dissolved in the liquid for longer, which means that the bubbles will last longer.
DISSOLVED CO_2
Why can't you see the sparkle in this picture? Because carbon dioxide is suspended in the wine. Remove the cork and, as the pressure escapes, the CO_2 rushes to the surface of the wine in the form of tiny bubbles.
BLANC DE BLANCS
Surprise! Many white sparkling wines are actually made from red grapes. A blanc de blancs, however, is a white sparkling wine made from white grapes.
BOTTLE
The wide-bottomed bottle indicates that this is a sparkling wine. Any resemblance to a bowling pin is purely accidental.
PUNT
Sparkling-wine bottles typically have a sizable punt, or indent, at the base. This is a throwback from the days when bottles were forged by hand, but the punt also collects any sediment and strengthens the bottom of a sparkling-wine bottle by increasing the surface area of glass. Bonus points: You can put on quite a dashing show by pouring "from the punt," with your thumb in the indent.
SOFIA
Blanc de Blancs
MONTEREY COUNTY
2012
FRANCIS COPPOLA

FRANCIS COPPOLA SOFIA BLANC DE BLANCS

WHY THAT PRICE?

Although sparkling winemaking is labor-intensive, the demand for this style of wine has made it affordable in almost every market—especially when it's produced by the Charmat method, which involves a secondary fermentation in large stainless-steel tanks rather than individual bottles. Sofia is made in this manner, in the style of an Italian Prosecco. The grapes are sourced from the cool and well-drained Arroyo Seco sub-appellation of coastal Monterey County, a vast winegrowing region where some of California's most cultish—as well as some of its most prolific—producers are based.

WHAT FOOD DOES IT GO WITH?

This class of wine is by nature quite acidic, so serve your sparkler as an aperitif or dinner companion. A Champagne, Cava or Franciacorta will have toasty, yeasty, nutty notes; these wines work well with caramelized onions, roasted red peppers, savory crêpes, *prosciutto* or *jamón Ibérico*, fried mushrooms, mac & cheese, pâté... the list goes on and on. Lighter styles, like Prosecco, complement tough-to-pair vegetables like asparagus, avocado or crisp salad with acidic vinaigrette. And I haven't yet met a sparkling wine that didn't work with raw oysters or caviar. All that said, Sofia is an exception to many of the rules: Its Muscat and Riesling add fruity and floral notes that work with Asian cuisine and shellfish, as well as with simple cookies, plain white cake or fresh fruit.

TOP FOOD MATCH: Lobster with Asparagus Mimosa

Left: The historic Inglenook winery, built in 1886 and restored to its former glory by Francis Ford Coppola.

10 OF THE BEST

AMERICAN BUBBLIES

ARGYLE	**$$-$$$$**
FRANK FAMILY VINEYARDS	**$$$**
GRUET	**$$-$$$**
IRON HORSE	**$$$-$$$$**
J VINEYARDS	**$$-$$$$**
MUMM NAPA VALLEY	**$$-$$$$$**
ROEDERER ESTATE	**$$-$$$$**
SCHARFFENBERGER	**$$**
SCHRAMSBERG	**$$$-$$$$$**
SOTER	**$$$-$$$$**

AROUND THE WORLD

SIMILAR STYLE WINES FROM DIFFERENT COUNTRIES

Graham Beck, Blanc de Blancs
Western Cape, South Africa $$

Huia, Blanc de Blancs
Marlborough, New Zealand $$

Jansz, Premium Cuvée
Tasmania, Australia $$

CHOICE MADE SIMPLE

EXPERT'S PERSONAL FAVORITES

Recommended by Clement Robert, Head Sommelier & Wine Buyer, Medlar, London, U.K.

AGRAPART & FILS, LES 7 CRUS, BLANC DE BLANCS BRUT NV
CHAMPAGNE, FRANCE $$$–$$$$

CAVALLERI, SATÈN (BLANC DE BLANCS) BRUT NV FRANCIACORTA, LOMBARDY, ITALY $$–$$$$

HENRI GIRAUD, FÛT DE CHÊNE BRUT VINTAGE
(PINOT NOIR / CHARDONNAY)
AŸ, CHAMPAGNE, FRANCE $$$$$

AUGUSTÍ TORELLÓ MATA, KRIPTA, VINTAGE (MACABEO / XAREL-LO / PARELLADA)
CAVA, CATALUNYA, SPAIN $$$$

NAUTILUS, CUVÉE MARLBOROUGH BRUT NV (PINOT NOIR / CHARDONNAY) MARLBOROUGH, NEW ZEALAND $$–$$$

NYETIMBER, CLASSIC CUVÉE BRUT VINTAGE (CHARDONNAY / PINOT NOIR / PINOT MEUNIER)
WEST SUSSEX, ENGLAND $$$

PELLER ESTATES, ICE CUVÉE MÉTHODE CLASSIQUE NV
(CHARDONNAY / PINOT NOIR)
NIAGARA PENINSULA, CANADA $$$

RENARDAT-FÂCHE, CERDON ROSÉ MÉTHODE ANCESTRALE NV
(GAMAY NOIR / POULSARD)
BUGEY, SAVOIE, FRANCE $–$$

JACQUES SELOSSE, INITIALE BLANC DE BLANCS BRUT NV
CHAMPAGNE, FRANCE, $$$$

LA TAILLE AUX LOUPS DE JACKY BLOT, TRIPLE ZÉRO NV
(CHENIN BLANC) MONTLOUIS-SUR-LOIRE, LOIRE, FRANCE $$

WORLD OF FINE WINE RECOMMENDATIONS

KRUG CLOS D'AMBONNAY BLANC DE NOIRS VINTAGE
(PINOT NOIR)
CHAMPAGNE, FRANCE $$$$$

BOLLINGER VIEILLES VIGNES FRANÇAISES VINTAGE
(PINOT NOIR)
CHAMPAGNE, FRANCE $$$$$

VEUVE CLICQUOT LA GRANDE DAME VINTAGE
(PINOT NOIR / CHARDONNAY)
CHAMPAGNE, FRANCE $$$$

HENRIOT CUVÉE DES ENCHANTELEURS VINTAGE
(CHARDONNAY / PINOT NOIR)
CHAMPAGNE, FRANCE $$$$

PHILIPPONNAT CLOS DES GOISSES VINTAGE
(PINOT NOIR / CHARDONNAY)
CHAMPAGNE, FRANCE $$$$

BILLECART-SALMON CLOS ST-HILAIRE VINTAGE
(PINOT NOIR)
CHAMPAGNE, FRANCE $$$$

DOM RUINART ROSÉ VINTAGE BRUT
(CHARDONNAY / PINOT NOIR)
CHAMPAGNE, FRANCE $$$$

POL ROGER VINTAGE
(PINOT NOIR / CHARDONNAY)
CHAMPAGNE, FRANCE $$$$

CHARLES HEIDSIECK BRUT RÉSERVE NV (PINOT NOIR / PINOT MEUNIER / CHARDONNAY)
CHAMPAGNE, FRANCE $$$$

CA' DEL BOSCO, ANNAMARIA CLEMENTE VINTAGE
(PINOT NOIR / PINOT BIANCO / CHARDONNAY) FRANCIACORTA, LOMBARDY, ITALY $$$$

(Grape Varieties in Brackets)

ORGANIC, BIODYNAMIC OR NATURAL

CHAMPALOU,
MÉTHODE TRADITIONELLE BRUT NV
(CHENIN BLANC)
VOUVRAY PÉTILLANT, LOIRE, FRANCE $-$$

DELMAS,
CUVÉE BERLÈNE BRUT VINTAGE
(MAUZAC) BLANQUETTE DE LIMOUX,
LANGUEDOC-ROUSSILLON, FRANCE $-$$

FLEURY PÈRE ET FILS,
ROSÉ SAIGNÉE NV
(PINOT NOIR)
CHAMPAGNE, FRANCE $$$-$$$$

PAUL GINGLINGER,
PRESTIGE BRUT NV
(PINOT BLANC)
ALSACE, FRANCE $-$$

CÉDRIC BOUCHARD, ROSES DE JEANNE
INFLORESCENCE, LA PARCELLE BLANC DE
NOIRS NV (PINOT NOIR)
AUBE, CHAMPAGNE, FRANCE $$$$

JAILLANCE,
CLAIRETTE BRUT & ELEGANT NV
(CLAIRETTE)
CLAIRETTE DE DIE, RHÔNE, FRANCE $-$$

PIZZOLATO NV
(GLERA)
PROSECCO, VENETO, ITALY $-$$

LOUIS ROEDERER CRISTAL VINTAGE
(PINOT NOIR / CHARDONNAY)
CHAMPAGNE, FRANCE $$$$$

TARANTAS BRUT NV
(MACABEO / PARALLEDA / XAREL-LO)
CAVA, CATALONIA, SPAIN $

VALENTIN ZUSSLIN,
BRUT ZERO SANS SOUFRE NV
(AUXERROIS / CHARDONNAY / PINOT GRIS)
CRÉMANT D'ALSACE, ALSACE, FRANCE $$

BEST ON A BUDGET

LE VIGNE DI ALICE,
EXTRA DRY VINTAGE
(GLERA)
PROSECCO, VENETO, ITALY $-$$

DE CHANCENY, ROSÉ BRUT
(CABERNET FRANC)
CRÉMANT DE LOIRE, LOIRE, FRANCE
$-$$

LOREDAN GASPARINI,
VENEGAZZU NV
(GLERA) ASOLO PROSECCO, VENETO,
ITALY $-$$

FREIXENET, MÉTODO TRADICIONAL
CORDON NEGRO BRUT NV
(PARELLADA / MACABEO / XAREL-LO)
CAVA, CATALONIA, SPAIN $

LUIS PATO,
MARIA GOMES BRUTO NV
(MARIA GOMES / BAGA)
BEIRAS, PORTUGAL $-$$

JAUME SERRA,
CRISTALINO BRUT ROSÉ NV
(PINOT NOIR)
CAVA, CATALONIA, SPAIN $

NINO FRANCO,
RUSTICO NV
(GLERA)
PROSECCO, VENETO, ITALY $-$$

SZIGETI,
MÉTHODE TRADITIONELLE BRUT NV
(GRÜNER VELTLINER)
BURGENLAND, AUSTRIA $-$$

TENUTA SANTOMÈ EXTRA DRY
(GLERA)
PROSECCO, VENETO, ITALY $-$$

VILARNAU
BRUT NV
(MACABEO / PARALLEDA / XAREL-LO)
CAVA, CATALONIA, SPAIN $

MASTERCLASS: PERLES ARE A GIRL'S BEST FRIEND

Dahhhrling, have you ever been to one of those soirées at which everyone appears to be richer, and skinnier, than you? I'd hate for you to feel tongue-tied at such affairs, so here are some conversation pointers. For example: A diamond isn't worth discussing if it's smaller than five carats. It's "fish roe" if it isn't beluga, sevruga or osetra. St Tropez and Ibiza are *over*. And the way it handles and hugs the road, the Lambo just *feels* faster than the Ferrari, you know?

And now for Champagne. Let us begin with the festive, familiar ***grandes marques***, those magnificent labels you can find on wine lists and shop shelves just about anywhere in the world: Billecart-Salmon, Krug, Laurent-Perrier, Moët et Chandon, Perrier-Jouët, Pommery, Veuve Clicquot and the like. These are the ***négociant-manipulants***. They purchase fruit from numerous vineyards throughout the Champagne region, then blend together as many as 60 wines from different vineyards and vintages to create a cuvée that upholds a consistent house style from year to year. Less ubiquitous is the ***cuvée de prestige***, or ***tête de cuvée***, a limited-release bottling of the finest grapes, with a proprietary name like Belle Epoque, Cristal or Dom Pérignon. These may or may not be vintage-dated but do get extended bottle age, and rich people are quite fond of them. Then there are **Vintage Champagnes**. As with Port, vintage-dated bottles are only released in the best years, and they can improve with age. After poor growing seasons, only **Non-Vintage** (NV) wines are released. So, as you can imagine, the Vintage bottlings are a big hit with collectors.

Some *grandes marques* release single-vineyard bottlings, but indie winos in search of something different go for **growers**. These are the small vignerons who produce their own boutique labels, often in addition to selling a portion of their fruit to the *négociant-manipulants*. These estate-produced wines show more vintage variation from year to year even in Non-Vintage bottlings. And they offer more quirky character for your money.

Speaking of money, if your Champagne wishes and caviar dreams conflict with a very different financial reality, never fear: There are affordable Champagne-style wines out there. Blanquette from the south of France, Crémant from almost any French region other than Champagne, and Cava from Spain—as well as many other sparkling wines—are all made by the same method as Champagne. If you're hosting a big party or simply sitting down to watch a movie with a bowl of popcorn, these wines can offer a slightly more rustic pleasure for a fraction of the price. You might also find this info useful, dahhhrling, if you want to bathe yourself in bubbles à la Marilyn Monroe.

HOW TO IDENTIFY THESE ELEMENTS

1: Because they go through a second bottle fermentation, in which the yeasty lees sit in the wine for more than a year—and often much longer—many Champagnes have a bready aroma. *Blanc de blancs* tends to be lighter and creamier on the palate; *blanc de noirs* more robust; rosé Champagnes fruitier. Oak-barrel-influenced Champagnes are fuller-bodied, with caramel notes.

2: In the glass, you can identify the best Champagnes by their tiny, numerous and endless bubbles, or ***perlage***. You might notice a pearl necklace-like ring of bubbles (*le collier de perles*) at the surface of the liquid. On your palate, the ***mousse***, or foam, of the best Champagnes should feel frothy rather than painfully prickly.

3: Outside Champagne, French wines made by the time-consuming and painstaking *méthode traditionnelle* are called Crémants. And in the foothills of the eastern Pyrenees, in southern France, the term ***Blanquette*** ("white" in Occitan, the local Provençal dialect) is comparable to *blanc de blancs*.

CRACKING THE CODE

GLASS
The glass walls of Champagne bottles are thick in order to stand up to the intense pressure created by the carbon dioxide trapped inside.

BUBBLES
Researchers have calculated that a single bottle of bubbly contains up to 250 million bubbles; the very finest bottles of Champagne have the tiniest bubbles, and more of them.

EMBOSSING
Special Club Champagnes are easy to identify because the bottles and the labels are nearly identical, no matter whom the producer is. They're also incredibly frustrating because...they look identical, no matter whom the producer is.

SPECIAL CLUB
This bottling is a **Special Club**, something like the grower Champagne version of the cuvée de prestige. The 26 artisan winery members of the **Club Trésors** evaluate one another's top wines each year and vote them into—or out of—Special Club status.

RM STATUS
If, on the front or back label of a bottle of bubbly, you find a tiny number that starts with the letters "RM," you know you've got a *récoltant-manipulant*, or grower, Champagne.

VINTAGE
The vintage year on the label is a hint that this is a wine made for cellar-aging.

BOTTLE
Champagne bottles look awfully self-important, don't they? Perhaps that's because the Cathedral at Reims was the traditional coronation site for the kings of France. For centuries—even before they were bubbly—Champagne wines were sipped by French royals on momentous occasions.

COLOR
Back in the day, wine bottles were green because glass-blowers didn't know how to remove the iron oxide that was causing the coloration. Today, Champagne bottles that are tinted green hint at history and tradition. Also, because light can damage wine, a dark-green bottle is better for aging.

DISGORGEMENT
If you are curious to know what the **disgorgement date** was (that is, the date when the wine was separated from the lees), look for six small numbers on the back label, which correspond to the year, month and day.

GRAPE VARIETY
This label says Chardonnay, but the more customary term used for a Champagne made from Chardonnay is **blanc de blancs**.

MASTERCLASS: SIX WINES TO BUY

This part is all about *schadenfreude*. Taste these wines with some pals, then sit around and gloat about all the bubbly you get to horde among yourselves for the remainder of the evening. (Of course, if you do open six bottles, please err on the side of more guests and less gloating.) Mix up the order of the wines and don't let your friends in on which is which. Can they tell which is the vintage-dated cuvée de prestige from a *grande marque* producer and which is the Special Club from a grower? How do the less-expensive alternatives stack up to the premier bottlings?

POL ROGER
SIR WINSTON CHURCHILL VINTAGE
(Pinot Noir / Chardonnay)
Champagne, France $$$$$

ALTERNATIVE CHOICES

MOËT & CHANDON DOM PÉRIGNON VINTAGE
(Pinot Noir / Chardonnay)
Champagne, France $$$$$

BOLLINGER
LA GRANDE ANNÉE VINTAGE
(Pinot Noir / Chardonnay)
Champagne, France $$$$–$$$$$

DOMAINE COLLIN
CUVÉE TRADITION BRUT NV
Crémant de Limoux,
Languedoc-Roussillon, France $

ALTERNATIVE CHOICES

DOMAINE DE MARTINOLLES BRUT VINTAGE
(Chardonnay / Chenin Blanc / Pinot Noir)
Crémant de Limoux, Languedoc-Roussillon, France $

SAINT-HILAIRE BRUT VINTAGE
(Mauzac) Blanquette de Limoux,
Languedoc-Roussillon, France $

J LASSALLE SPECIAL CLUB VINTAGE
(Chardonnay / Pinot Noir)
Chigny-lès-Roses, Champagne, France
$$$$

ALTERNATIVE CHOICES

GRONGNET SPECIAL CLUB VINTAGE
(Chardonnay / Pinot Noir)
Étoges, Champagne, France $$$$$

A MARGAINE SPECIAL CLUB VINTAGE
(Chardonnay)
Villers Marmery, Champagne, France $$$$

MONTE ROSSA SANSEVÉ SATÈN
(BLANC DE BLANCS) BRUT NV
(Chardonnay)
Franciacorta, Lombardy, Italy $$–$$$

ALTERNATIVE CHOICES

QUADRA BRUT NV
(Chardonnay / Pinot Blanc / Pinot Noir)
Franciacorta, Lombardy, Italy $$–$$$

QUATTRO MANI Q BRUT NV
(Chardonnay / Pinot Blanc / Pinot Noir)
Franciacorta, Lombardy, Italy $$

JACQUES LASSAIGNE
BLANC DE BLANCS BRUT NV
(Chardonnay)
Montgueux, Champagne, France $$$$

ALTERNATIVE CHOICES

CHARTOGNE-TAILLET
CUVÉE SAINTE-ANNE BRUT NV
(Chardonnay / Pinot Noir)
Merfy, Champagne, France $$$

CLAUDE GENET BLANC DE BLANCS BRUT
(Chardonnay)
Chouilly, Champagne, France $$$

AVINYÓ
BRUT RESERVA CAVA NV
(Macabeo / Parellada / Xarel-lo)
Cava, Catalonia, Spain $–$$

ALTERNATIVE CHOICES

ORIOL ROSSELL BRUT NATURE NV
(Xarel-lo / Macabeo / Parellada)
Cava, Catalonia, Spain $–$$

DIBON BRUT RESERVA NV
(Macabeo / Paralleda / Xarel-lo)
Cava, Catalonia, Spain $

HOW TO SERVE IT

Although some aficionados sip Champenois-style wines from oversized Burgundy glasses so as to enjoy the aromas, I'd suggest serving these wines in narrow flutes for optimal viewing and preservation of those delightful bubbles; fill them only half-way to best appreciate the spectacle. And since the bottles most likely will be sitting out and open while you taste, chill them down on ice before serving, as this will also preserve the *perlage*.

HOW TO TALK ABOUT IT

The best sparkling wines have a "fine *mousse*," with lots of tiny "beads" (bubbles) that create a foamy feeling in your mouth. "Persistent *perlage*" —a ceaseless cascade of bubbles—is also a good sign. On the palate, you might feel a texture of "chiffon" or "lace." A Vintage Champagne that needs more bottle-age might be "tart," "sharp" or "tight."

AROMATIC AND SENSORY CLUES

Provide comparison samples for guests in the form of lemons, apples and pear slices, brioche and even perhaps a hunk of bread dough. A particularly yeasty *méthode traditionnelle* wine might smell "bready," "doughy" or—bonus points!—"autolytic," with *goût de Champagne*.

FOOD MATCHES

Set out a stylish array of crackers, nuts, potato chips and mild cheeses for your guests. Warm puff-pastry *hors d'oeuvres* also work beautifully, as do teacups of *vichyssoise* or chestnut soup.

The *coup de grace*—if you can find them where you live—are *biscuits rosé de Reims*, the powdered-sugar-coated pink cookies that the Champenoise dip into their glasses of bubbly. Shortbread-style cookies, like Russian tea cakes (also called snowballs or *mantecados*) also work brilliantly.

MASTERCLASS: WHAT'S TRENDING?

ET TU, BRUT?

We're so used to seeing the word "Brut" on bottles of bubbly that we've ceased to question what it means. But increasingly, consumers are seeking out drier sparkling-wine styles. The very driest are Brut Nature or Brut Zero. These are made without *dosage*, or addition of sugar, after the second fermentation. They're rare, and considered by some connoisseurs to be the purest expression of Champagne. Up next is Extra Brut, made with a small *dosage*. Brut is not bone-dry, but not quite sweet, either. Then comes, confusingly, Extra Dry or Extra Sec, which is, in fact, slightly sweeter than Brut; and Dry, or Sec, which is even sweeter. Demi-Sec is sweeter still, and finally, Doux, or Sweet, actually delivers what it promises.

All Champagnes used to be Doux, in part to appeal to the tastes of Russian royals and nobles. It wasn't until the mid-19th century—when Louise Pommery introduced her Demi-Sec—that the British and American markets took serious notice of Champagne. Today, one of the world's great ironies (or tragedies?) is our insistence upon drinking bubblies with dessert. Grapes for sparkling-wine production are intentionally harvested early, to achieve the high acidity levels essential to this style. So it is totally irrational to drink this stuff with chocolate mousse. Serve most sparkling wines as aperitifs or dinner companions; then, when it's time to bring out the trifle, move to the absurdly named Dry or Demi-Sec styles, or—even better—bid adieu to your meal with a glass of Doux.

BUBBLY BEGINNINGS

According to legend, the monk Dom Pérignon "invented" bubbly in the 1660s, exclaiming, "I am drinking stars!" But historical documents show that the Abbey of St-Hilaire, in Limoux, produced sparkling wines much earlier, in 1531. And sparkling Champagne was actually created in the U.K. Frustrated by the fact that the delicate wines they imported from Champagne tended to spoil once the barrels had been tapped, 17th-century English merchants began bottling them prior to shipping in extra-strength British glass. The wines, which hadn't finished fermenting in the icy-cold cellars of Champagne, warmed up in their bottles, where they completed the process. The trapped carbon dioxide expressed itself as bubbles when the cork popped.

The Widow Clicquot: The Story of a Champagne Empire and the Woman Who Ruled It by Tilar J. Mazzeo

THE THROWBACKS: PET NATS

If you're curious as what the earliest Champagnes might have tasted like, look for labels with the words *méthode ancéstrale*, *méthode rurale* or *pétillant originel* (the latter is the only such designation officially recognized by the French governing body). This style of sparkling wine tends to be semisweet and mildly fizzy, and sometimes has a pleasing whiff of crabapples or cider vinegar to it; the alcohol is generally low, around 6–7%. What's the methodological—or, perhaps, philosophical—difference? *Méthode traditionnelle* wines are coaxed into their Champenois state by the addition of yeast and sugar to the bottle, which is then sealed, causing a second fermentation and, consequently, bubbles.

By contrast, proponents of *pétillants originels* claim that they are more natural, since they're made with no additions of yeast or sugar. They're simply wines in which fermentation has stopped midstream due to cold cellar temperatures (or refrigeration). They're bottled this way, with low alcohol and relatively high sugars; once the chill wears off, they continue fermenting in the bottle, in the same way that those 17th-century wines from Champagne suddenly sparkled once the British weather warmed up in spring. This style of winemaking is taking off in the French regions of Loire Valley, Limoux, the Jura and Bugey, neighboring Savoie. Their admirers refer to them as pétillant naturel, or, "pet nat." Ironically, one sometimes comes across an unintentional pet nat, from a small producer working in a particularly chilly cellar.

UNDER PRESSURE

We've all seen the scene: The sports team wins the championship, and someone shakes up a bottle of Champagne and pops the top over the coach's head. Why does sparkling wine erupt? Because the pressure of the carbon dioxide that's trapped inside that strong glass bottle is greater than the pressure of the air that's all around us. When it settles into the liquid, the CO_2 reaches a state of equilibrium; when you shake it up, you disrupt that equilibrium and get a great photo moment. If you're planning to pull this stunt on someone, be sure to purchase the sort of sparkling wine that will erupt with a bang, because not every style is as pressurized as Champagne.

A fully sparkling wine—such as Champagne, Crémant or Cava—is bottled at between 5 and 6 atmospheres of pressure. (Although it's not an apples-to-apples comparison, an automobile's tires are typically pressurized at approximately 2.5 atmospheres.) It's traditional to open a bottle of bubbly at a 45° angle, not only to tilt the cork away from overhead light fixtures, but also to increase the surface area available for those bubbles to escape through. At lower pressure levels, the fizz in the bottle is less aggressive, so you can hold your bottle upright to open it. These wines go by the names *pétillant*, *perlant*, *frizzante* or *spritzig*. At less than one atmosphere of pressure, you've reached the equivalent of the atmosphere around you, so your wine should be flat. Now, let's put all that we've learned to terrible use.

HOW TO SABER

1. Like many foolish and potentially fatal pursuits, the classic art of *sabrage*, or slicing off the top of a Champagne bottle with a lethal weapon, is inexplicably enjoyable to watch. Please, folks, don't try this at home. But if you must, at least follow these basic guidelines.

2. Are you sober? Don't saber unless you're sober.

3. To be honest, you can use a butter knife or just about any old thing, but a saber is the most impressive. If you happen to be, say, a pirate, and thus have a large saber lying around the house, this is the use for it.

4. Make sure you've got a fully pressurized bottle of bubbly, as per the discussion above. Prosecco, for example, won't work if it's done in the *frizzante* style.

5. Chill your bubbly as cold as you can get it. (It will explode spontaneously if it freezes; your goal is to get it as close to that point as possible without risking it.)

6. Only saber outside, well out of the way of anyone who might be hit by a flying shard of glass, or be walking around barefoot. Basically, only saber in a padded cell. An outdoor padded cell.

7. Remove the foil and wire cage. Locate one of the seams—the two thin lines, from base to neck—on the wine bottle. Position your seam so it is facing up.

8. Shake the bottle, keeping your thumb over the cork and your eye on the seam. Angle the bottle out in front of you, tilting it at 45 degrees.

9. Swiftly slide your saber along the bottle, making contact with the rim in the spot where the seam is.

10. Voilà! Fill those glasses, mop up the mess, and do not, under any circumstances, consider drinking straight from the shorn top. There. You've been warned.

FUN FACTS

The degree of pressure in the bottle determines the ferocity—not the size—of the bubbles. And large bubbles rise more slowly than small ones, due to drag.

6 ROSÉ

6 ROSÉ

According to Homer—that epic-producing epicure—the sea was, curiously, "wine-dark." Why? Because the early Greeks had no word for the color blue. But the dawn, oh, he knew how to describe that. It was "rosy-fingered." Thus, if any wine should stir the imaginations of poets, it must be rosé. One has the lacey delicacy of cherry blossoms; the next is the brilliant orange of a sliced mango. A Bandol might remind you of the Taj Mahal at sunset or the cliffs at Cassis while a Tavel recalls the firm, juicy flesh of a watermelon. Before you bring it to your lips, just hold that glass up, and look through it. It's impossible not to be cheered by the rose-colored spectacle.

Just a few years ago, I would have had to stop here, to make apologies and explanations, perforated by winks and witticisms: *No, proper rosé isn't sweet like Lancers.* But we live in an enlightened age. Dry rosé is now standard on the wine lists of stylish restaurants. And it's the one wine that solves the quandary of mixed company, because it occupies that liminal space between red and white.

Rosé both comforts and refreshes, offering a sneak preview of the vintage of red wines that's aging in barrels, along with the crisp acidity and quaffability of a white. We tend to associate it with balmy climates—most notably, Provence—but we ought to drink it in any weather, because it is so very flexible with food. It isn't just for beach-blanketed *flâneurs*. It's for everyone, everywhere.

So, yes, rosé can be fun. But it isn't frippery. The soldiers in *The Iliad* mixed their wine with water, steeling themselves for battle by drinking pink. As early wordsmiths put names to what they saw in the world around them, is it any surprise that the pink of sunrise and pale wine came before the blue of sky and water?

YOU'LL ENJOY THESE WINES IF...

- You have trouble deciding whether to order red or white
- You wish it were always summer
- You're an aesthete

WHAT THE EXPERTS SAY

"Lighter rosé is the prime choice to drink during searing-hot summers in the south of France, namely Provence. It's only logical, then, that it should go well with the seafood and herbs (rosemary, oregano, marjoram, thyme, mint) from that area. If the rosé is a little more full-bodied and complex, I don't hesitate to pair it with pork or veal, especially if the sides are nice summery vegetables, like peas, broad beans or tomatoes."

Laura Vidal, Wine Director, Frenchie, Paris, France

KEY

$	UNDER $15	**$$$$**	$50–100
$$	$15–30	**$$$$$**	$100+
$$$	$30–50		

THE NAMES TO LOOK FOR

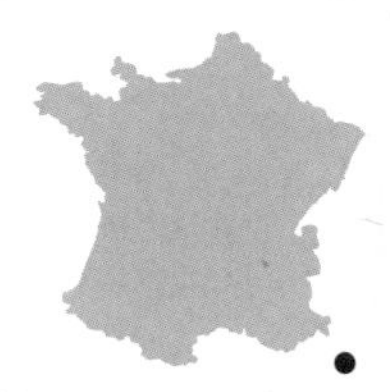

ROSÉ CORSICA, FRANCE

Tourists have been saying it for years: The pink wines in Corsica are to die for. But only recently have the vignerons of L'Île de Beauté made an effort to export their treasures. These wines are haunting and serious, ranging from seashell-pink to ruby-red grapefruit; they taste of rosewater, olive brine and citrus. Why did Napoleón ever leave?

PRICE RANGE: $-$$$

ABV: 12–14%

DRINK IT: 0–3 YEARS AFTER THE VINTAGE

CHOICE

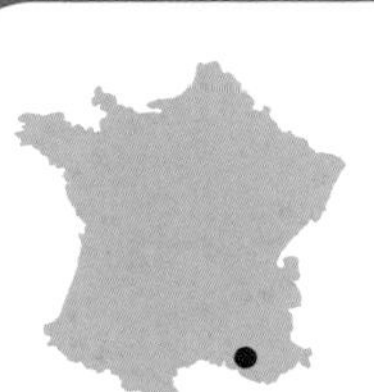

TAVEL & BANDOL PROVENCE, FRANCE

OK, so technically speaking, Tavel is from the southern Rhône. But it's near Avignon, and thus quite close to Bandol country (coastal Provence, between Toulon and Marseilles). These are the world's top two rosé regions, working in two different styles. Red currant-colored Tavel is fruity, while pale Bandol is minerally and crisp. Both are *magnifique*.

PRICE RANGE: $-$$$

ABV: 12–15%

DRINK IT: 0–3 YEARS AFTER THE VINTAGE

CERASUOLO ABRUZZO, ITALY

Abruzzo (and Puglia) vintners produce *bambini rossi* by steeping Montepulciano skins in their juice for a foreshortened timeframe. This cherry-colored beverage may bring about a craving for pasta with ricotta and *peperoncini*. And if it causes you to dust off the turntable and dance a polka around the living room, don't say I didn't warn you.

PRICE RANGE: $-$$

ABV: 12–13%

DRINK IT: 0–3 YEARS AFTER THE VINTAGE

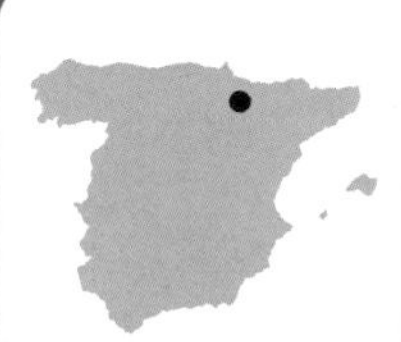

ROSADO DE GARNACHA NAVARRA, SPAIN

Spain is awash in *rosado*—made not just from Garnacha but also Tempranillo, Monastrell, et al. And in Rioja, there's the darker *clarete*, made by blending Garnacha with white Viura. But it's the strawberry-scented *rojillo* Garnacha from Navarra that has captured the attention of foreign markets with its unbeatable quality-price ratio.

PRICE RANGE: $

ABV: 12.5–14%

DRINK IT: 0–2 YEARS AFTER THE VINTAGE

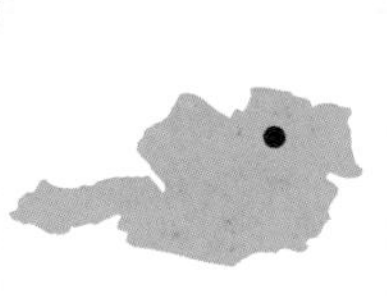

ROSÉ AUSTRIA

We knew about German rosés, but what are these Austrian pinks we've been seeing on store shelves lately, from thoughtful producers like Heidi Schröck and Tegernseerhof? Earnest wines, made from grapes like Zweigelt and Blaufränkisch and meant for contemplation at the table. *Ganz im ernst*!

PRICE RANGE: $-$$

ABV: 12–13%

DRINK IT: 0–3 YEARS AFTER THE VINTAGE

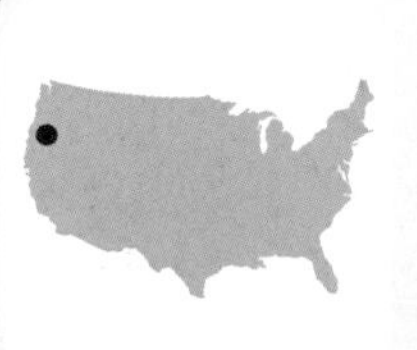

ROSÉ OF PINOT NOIR WEST COAST, UNITED STATES

Where there is red Pinot Noir, there is also pink Pinot Noir. In Burgundy, much of that becomes bubbly Crémant, but in the U.S., each summer season sees the release of pinks from a majority of Pinot producers. With an increasing demand for these wines in export markets and in the off-season, this is a growing category to keep your eye on.

PRICE RANGE: $-$$$

ABV: 12–15%

DRINK IT: 0–2 YEARS AFTER THE VINTAGE

TAKE ONE WINE:
DOMAINE COMTE ABBATUCCI CUVÉE FAUSTINE ROSÉ

THE BASICS

GRAPE VARIETY: Sciaccarellu

REGION: Corsica, France

ALCOHOL LEVEL: 13%

PRICE: $$–$$$

AVAILABILITY: Widely available

APPEARANCE: Translucent seashell pink

TASTING NOTE: Starfruit, kiwi, pineapple, lime; the sage-juniper-myrtle-olive notes of the Corsican *maquis*; strawberry-tree (*Artubus unedo*) fruit; fresh, with a mouthfeel of both chalk and silk.

FOOD MATCH: White fish or langoustines steamed with garlic, thyme and parsley. Corsican sheep's milk cheese, such as *brocciu*, or herb-crusted *brin d'amour*. Zucchini fritters (*beignets de courgette*).

DRINK OR KEEP: Drink it up before someone else does!

WHY DOES IT TASTE THAT WAY?

The word "cuvée" typically refers to a blend of grape varieties, but over the past couple of years this rosé has been made entirely from Sciaccarellu, a fragrant and peppery purple grape indigenous to Corsica. (In Italy, it's called Sciaccarello or Mammolo.) Despite its dark skins, it's not too tannic, and it has what the French call *sucrosité*—not sweetness, but a sort of ripe, juicy quality—making it a good candidate for rosé. Instead of crushing the grapes, the winemaker presses them gently into steel tanks, as though he were going to make a white wine. The fermentation is temperature-controlled to about 65°F (18°C) to capture the Sciaccarellu's natural notes of red berries and bright acidity. As with so many of the best Corsican wines, you really do get a sense of terroir, or place, from this wine—you can taste the wild herbs of the *maquis*, or the fragrant Corsican scrub brush, in every sip.

WHO MADE IT?

Corsican wines taste half French, half Italian... and all Corsican. This mountainous island was once governed by the Genoese—which explains the Italian sound of the name Abbatucci. French Revolutionary hero General Jean-Charles Abbatucci was a comrade-in-arms of Napoleón Bonaparte; his great grand-nephew is the present-day Count Jean-Charles Abbatucci, winemaker. In 1962, Abbatucci's father planted a vineyard with cuttings rescued from mountain villages, where he had seen that the old way of subsistence farming was coming to an end, imperiling the indigenous grape varieties of the island. Approximately 25 years later, Jean-Charles planted the vines that went into this rosé on an adjacent vineyard using the ***sélection massale*** method—selecting cuttings from the very best vines for the new vineyard block.

CRACKING THE CODE

DUAL HERITAGE
Corsica is a gorgeous French island just north of Sardinia, known as L'Île de Beauté. This winery's title is a glimpse into Corsica's fascinating history: the French "Comte" paired with the Italian-sounding name Abbatucci.

PRODUCER NAME
Sometimes it's difficult to locate the name of the producer. On this bottle, it's printed on the foil covering the neck.

FULL WINE NAME
Front labels can be maddeningly vague. The full name of this wine—Domaine Comte Abbatucci Cuvée Ajaccio Corsican Faustine Rosé—is printed on the back label. (At least, in the United States, it is!) Whenever you are looking for more information, just turn that bottle around.

WINE REGION
Ajaccio is the capital of Corsica and the name of the winegrowing region, or appellation d'origine contrôlée, on the west coast of Corsica. Once we become familiar with appellation names, they become a way to assess wines by sight alone. If you can't get enough of this bottle, the next time you see another wine labeled "Ajaccio," you'll know it's from Corsica, and probably made in a style that you'll enjoy.

IMPORTER
Also on the back label (of my American bottle) is the name of the importer. In this case, it's Kermit Lynch, the Berkeley, California-based shipper who famously turned American palates onto dry rosé in the late 1970s when he got his friend, the restaurateur Alice Waters, hooked on Domaine Tempier's pink wine from Bandol and she began serving it at her eatery, Chez Panisse. Today, Lynch is championing rosés from Corsica.

CUVÉE NAME
"Faustine" is the proprietary name for this cuvée, or blend, which should taste fairly consistent from year to year. It is named after the daughter of the vigneron.

DOMAINE COMTE ABBATUCCI CUVÉE FAUSTINE ROSÉ

WHY THAT PRICE?

While some rosés are quite inexpensive, Corsican pink wines are not, due to their scarcity. Over the past three decades or so, the industry has focused on quality rather than quantity, leaving very little, but very good, wine for tourists to drink on the island. As a long-time leader of the movement to establish Corsica as a stronghold of quality winemaking, Abbatucci is sought after in the world wine market. In addition, the estate is certified **biodynamic**. In keeping with this form of agriculture, Jean-Charles Abbatucci has set aside part of his estate as wild forest land, plows his soil behind horses instead of tractors and sends a herd of sheep down the vine rows to pull up weeds. He even plays music to his vines.

WHAT FOOD DOES IT GO WITH?

Mediterranean rosés go with Mediterranean foods, like grilled fish, *brandade* and Spanish spices like paprika and saffron. Their unique combination of acidity and depth, fruit and herbaceousness, makes them a formidable match for impossibly pungent vegetables, like roasted garlic or grilled artichokes and, of course, always safe with salad. The deeper-colored, fruitier rosés can match meats like pork or steak tartare; this one is on the lighter side, so better suited to lighter fare. Abbatucci recommends serving it as an aperitif, with scallop carpaccio, tuna tartare or Corsican veal brochette.

TOP FOOD MATCH:
Green Garlic Soup, Zucchini Beignets and White Beans with Fresh Herbs

GARLIC | FRESH HERBS | WHITE BEANS

Left: Corsica's wines reflect its ruggedly beautiful landscape.

10 OF THE BEST

PRETTY CORSICAN PINKS

DOMAINE ANTOINE ARENA	$$
CLOS ALIVU	$$
CLOS CANARELLI	$$–$$$
DOMAINE DE GIOIELLI	$$–$$$
DOMAINE SAPARALE	$–$$
DOMAINE LECCIA	$$
DOMAINE DE MARQUILIANI	$$
DOMAINE ORENGA DE GAFFORY	$–$$
CLOS SONNENTA	$–$$
CLOS TEDDI	$$

AROUND THE WORLD

WINES IN A SIMILAR STYLE FROM DIFFERENT COUNTRIES

Caves du Château d'Auvernier, Oeil de Perdrix
Auvernier, Neuchatel, Switzerland $–$$

Bermejo, Listán Rosado
Lanzarote, Canary Islands, Spain $–$$

Château Ksara, Gris de Gris
Bekaa Valley, Lebanon $–$$

CHOICE MADE SIMPLE

EXPERT'S PERSONAL FAVORITES

Recommended by Arnaud Goubet, Chef Sommelier, Le Manoir Aux Quat'Saisons, Oxford, U.K.

DOMAINE DANIEL CHOTARD ROSÉ
(PINOT NOIR)
SANCERRE, LOIRE, FRANCE $$

DOMAINE BRUNO CLAIR ROSÉ
(PINOT NOIR) MARSANNAY, BURGUNDY, FRANCE $$

DOMÄNE GOBELSBURG ROSÉ
(ZWEIGELT)
LANGENLOIS, AUSTRIA $–$$

CHÂTEAU LÉOUBE ROSÉ
(GRENACHE / CINSAULT / SYRAH / MOURVÈDRE)
PROVENCE, FRANCE $$

CLOS SAINTE MAGDELEINE ROSÉ
(GRENACHE / CINSAULT / MOURVÈDRE) CASSIS, PROVENCE, FRANCE $$–$$$

LA COURTADE, L'ALYCASTRE ROSÉ
(MOURVÈDRE / GRENACHE / TIBOUREN)
PROVENCE, FRANCE $–$$

CHÂTEAU SAINTE ROSELINE, LA CHAPELLE ROSÉ
(MOURVÈDRE / GRENACHE / ROLLE)
PROVENCE, FRANCE $$–$$$

DOMAINE TEMPIER ROSÉ
(MOURVÈDRE / GRENACHE / CINSAULT / CARIGNAN) BANDOL, PROVENCE, FRANCE $$–$$$

TURKEY FLAT VINEYARDS ROSÉ
(GRENACHE / SHIRAZ / CABERNET SAUVIGNON / DOLCETTO)
BAROSSA VALLEY, AUSTRALIA $$

UMATHUM ROSA
(BLAUFRÄNKISCH / ZWEIGELT / ST. LAURENT)
BURGENLAND, AUSTRIA $

WORLD OF FINE WINE RECOMMENDATIONS

DOMAINES OTT, CHÂTEAU DE SELLE
(SYRAH / CABERNET SAUVIGNON / GRENACHE / CINSAULT)
PROVENCE, FRANCE $$

CHÂTEAU D'ESCLANS
(GRENACHE / ROLLE)
PROVENCE, FRANCE $$$$

CHÂTEAU MIRAVAL ROSÉ
(CINSAULT / GRENACHE)
PROVENCE, FRANCE $$

SYLVAIN PATAILLE, MARSANNAY FLEUR DU PINOT
(PINOT NOIR)
BURGUNDY, FRANCE $$

CA' DEI FRATI, ROSATO DEI FRATI
(GROPPELLO / MARZEMINO / SANGIOVESE / BARBERA)
LOMBARDY, ITALY $$

COMM. GB BURLOTTO, ELATIS
(NEBBIOLO / PELAVERGA / BARBERA)
PIEDMONT, ITALY $$

ROSA DEL GOLFO
(NEGROAMARO)
PUGLIA, ITALY $$

ROCCA DI MONTEGROSSI, ROSATO
(SANGIOVESE / CANAIOLO / MERLOT) TUSCANY, ITALY $$

LÓPEZ DE HEREDIA, VIÑA TONDONIA ROSADO RESERVA
(GARNACHA / TEMPRANILLO / VIURA) RIOJA, SPAIN $$$$

NIEPOORT, REDOMA ROSÉ
(TINTA AMARELA / TOURIGA FRANCA / OTHERS)
DOURO, PORTUGAL $$

(Grape Varieties in Brackets)

LEFT-FIELD ALTERNATIVES

CAYUSE VINEYARDS,
EDITH ARMADA VINEYARD
(GRENACHE)
WALLA WALLA, WASHINGTON, U.S. $$$–$$$$

CHÂTEAU BELLEVUE LA FORÊT ROSÉ
(NÉGRETTE / GAMAY NOIR / SYRAH / CABERNET FRANC)
FRONTON, FRANCE $–$$

BRUMONT ROSÉ
(TANNAT / SYRAH / MERLOT)
VIN DE PAYS DE CÔTES DE GASCOGNE, FRANCE $

TSOMIN EXTANIZ ROSADO
(HONDARRABI ZURI / HONDARRABI BELTZA)
GETARIAKO TXAKOLINA, SPAIN $$

FUENTE DEL CONDE ROSADO
(TEMPRANILLO / VERDEJO / GRENACHE)
CIGALES, CASTILLA Y LEON, SPAIN $

LES CELLIERS DE MEKNÈS,
ZNIBER LES TROIS DOMAINES GRIS
(CINSAULT / GRENACHE)
GUERROUANE, MOROCCO $

DOMAINE DE L'OCTAVIN,
CUL ROND À LA CUISSE ROSÉ
(POULSARD)
ARBOIS, JURA, FRANCE $$

PROVENZA, CHIARETTO TENUTA MAIOLO
(BARBERA / SANGIOVESE / MARZEMINO / GROPPELLO)
GARDA, LOMBARDY, ITALY $

TURLEY WHITE ZINFANDEL
(ZINFANDEL)
CALIFORNIA, U.S. $$

WILD ROCK, VIN GRIS ROSÉ
(MERLOT / MALBEC / SYRAH / PINOT NOIR)
HAWKES BAY, NEW ZEALAND $–$$

BEST ON A BUDGET

COMMANDERIE DE LA BARGEMONE ROSÉ (SYRAH / GRENACHE / CINSAULT / CABERNET SAUVIGNON) COTEAUX D'AIX EN PROVENCE, FRANCE $–$$

BIELER PÈRE ET FILS ROSÉ
(SYRAH / GRENACHE / CABERNET SAUVIGNON / CINSAULT) COTEAUX D'AIX EN PROVENCE, FRANCE $

BORSAO ROSÉ
(GRENACHE)
CAMPO DE BORJA, ARAGON, SPAIN $

MARQUÉS DE CÁCERES ROSADO
(TEMPRANILLO / GRENACHE)
RIOJA, SPAIN $

GOATS DO ROAM ROSÉ
(SYRAH / MOURVÈDRE / GRENACHE / GAMAY NOIR)
SOUTH AFRICA $

RAFFAULT ROSÉ
(CABERNET FRANC)
CHINON, LOIRE, FRANCE $–$$

CHÂTEAU DE ROQUEFORT, CORAIL
(GRENACHE / SYRAH / CINSAULT / CARIGNAN / VERMENTINO / CLAIRETTE)
CÔTES DE PROVENCE, FRANCE $–$$

CHÂTEAU ROUTAS, ROUVIÈRE ROSÉ
(CINSAULT / GRENACHE / SYRAH)
COTEAUX VAROIS EN PROVENCE, PROVENCE, FRANCE $

TRIENNES ROSÉ
(CINSAULT)
VIN DE PAYS DU VAR, PROVENCE, FRANCE $$

TASCA D'ALMERITA REGALEALI LE ROSE
(NERELLO MASCALESE)
SICILY, ITALY $

MASTERCLASS: SKIN CONTACT

I know, I know: We shouldn't judge anyone or anything by looks alone. But I propose that you can deduce a great deal about a rosé in a single judgmental glance. The palest pinks tend to be dry and briney—excellent for cocktail hour. The more russet the hue, the better for matching heartier foods, like grilled meats or *bouillabaisse*. But what accounts for the extensive variegation of the rosé spectrum? Two words: skin contact.

Now, hold on a minute, there… I know where your mind is going…! Well, just cool off, because this sort of skin contact has nothing to do with the original, uncut, and unrated version of *9½ Weeks*. Rather, it's the amount of time the fruit's skins have spent soaking in the juice. As a general rule, the darker the wine, the more skin contact it's had. For example, in Abruzzo, central Italy, the rosé of the region is called Cerasuolo ("cherry colored" in the local dialect) because it's vinified as though it were destined to become a red. The black-skinned Montepulciano grapes are crushed and macerate for approximately 16 hours, as winemaker Stefano Illuminati explains it to me, before pressing. The result is a *vigne nuove*—a younger, fresher and lighter version of the robust red from the region (which typically gets 10 to 18 days of maceration time).

By contrast, the very palest rosés get their ghostly pallor from minimal skin contact. Some are made according to white wine protocol: The red grapes are pressed, rather than crushed, to get the juice off the skins as quickly as possible. Slightly pinker wines are often made by *saignée*, or the practice of siphoning juice off a tank of recently crushed red grapes. This bled-off liquid makes a wine that can be anywhere from pale pink to bold vermilion; the wine that's left behind to steep on the skins becomes a richer, more powerful red due to the increased skin contact by volume. In Bandol, winemaker Daniel Ravier of Domaine Tempier describes rosé as the hardest style of wine to make, because he's got to get a very pale pink wine out of the black, tannic Mourvèdre grape. His complex recipe: 10 percent *saignée*, and the rest split between direct pressing and approximately 18 hours of maceration prior to pressing.

The least-interesting and least-common way to make rosé is simply to blend together red and white wines. More intriguing is the method employed in Tavel in France's southern Rhône, where the fashion is for a hodgepodge of red and white fruit, all fermenting together in the same vat. (The white grape in question is typically Clairette or Bourboulenc.) The grapes soak on their motley array of skins for a couple of days, just long enough to extract the blazing color of red currants, without picking up those tongue-gripping tannins.

So there you have it: You can judge dry rosés just as easily as you can deduce what the fuss over *9½ Weeks* was all about just by taking a quick glance at the film posters. Go ahead: Google them. I'll wait. I'll just be sitting here passing judgment on the lineup of rosés in front of me.

HOW TO IDENTIFY THESE ELEMENTS

1: First, be sure to purchase that rosé at a proper wine shop or restaurant, not from the bottom shelf at the discount supermarket. The above discussion refers entirely to dry wines, not sweet pinks, like Lancers, Mateus or American White Zinfandel.

2: Go ahead: Make your selection by color. (I won't report you—remember, I do it, too.) The fact is, more color means more skin contact. And more skin contact generally means more red-fruited flavor.

SHADES OF PINK

The very palest rosés are made like white wines—the grapes are pressed almost immediately and the juice bleeds off the skins without soaking up much pigment. Another way to lighten a pink wine: Allow it to sit on the lees, which strip the color down.

There's a style of rosé, called gris de gris, that's most notably produced in the evocatively named Sables du Golfe du Lion—Sands of the Lion's Gulf—an appellation that dips into the azure Mediterranean around Montpellier. If ever a wine was made for sipping at the beach, this is it. It's all or mostly Grenache Gris, which ripens to a deep pink color and makes a prettily pale rosé.

Although Tavel and Bandol are close geographically, they make two very different wines. Bold Tavel is made like a red wine, with some white grapes mixed in; it macerates for a short time so as to extract less pigment from the skins. Bandol is made in a lighter vin gris style—the ideal match for coastal Provençal seafood dishes.

Deep-pink wines from Navarra are made by *saignée*, or the practice of spilling some juice out of a vat of crushed Garnacha (that's Spanish for Grenache Noir) grapes. The red wine that remains is richer and darker thanks to the reduced liquid; and the run-off makes a fruity and inexpensive rosado (that's Spanish for rosé).

Pinot Noir is a thin-skinned grape that thrives in regions where it's difficult to develop lots of concentration and flavor in cool, rainy seasons. So *saignée* rosés made from Pinot Noir are fairly common.

MASTERCLASS: 6 WINES TO BUY

First, indulge in the visual feast that is a lineup of rosés. Then taste through them. Do you hear the faintest whisper of Grenache in the inexpensive Gris de Gris, and a louder shout from the rosado of Navarra? Does the rosé of Pinot Noir remind you of a ghostly pale outline of its pigmented peer? How about the Cerasuolo—does it taste like a lighter version of an Italian red? And finally, reward yourself with the pale Bandol and bold Tavel. These two regions are the world's best for rosé, but—as you can see by looking at them—they follow very different winemaking procedures.

LISTEL ESTATE
PINK FLAMINGO TÊTE DE CUVÉE GRIS DE GRIS
(Grenache Gris)
Languedoc-Roussillon, France $

ALTERNATIVE CHOICES

DOMAINE DE FIGUEIRASSE GRIS DE GRIS
(Grenache Gris) Languedoc-Roussillon, France $

DOMAINE LE PIVE GRIS
(Grenache Gris / Grenache Noir / Merlot / Cabernet Franc) Languedoc-Roussillon, France $

LEZAUN
EGIARTE ROSADO
(Garnacha) Navarra, Spain $

ALTERNATIVE CHOICES

CHIVITE GRAN FEUDO ROSADO
(Garnacha) Navarra, Spain $

ARTAZURI ROSADO
(Garnacha) Navarra, Spain $

JK CARRIERE
GLASS WHITE PINOT NOIR
(Pinot Noir) Willamette Valley, Oregon, U.S. $$

ALTERNATIVE CHOICES

SOKOL BLOSSER ROSÉ OF PINOT NOIR
(Pinot Noir) Dundee Hills, Willamette Valley, Oregon, U.S. $$

ELK COVE VINEYARDS PINOT NOIR ROSÉ
(Pinot Noir) Willamette Valley, Oregon, U.S. $–$$

ILLUMINATI
CAMPIROSA CERASUOLO D'ABRUZZO
(Montepulciano) Montepulciano d'Abruzzo, Abruzzo, Italy $–$$

ALTERNATIVE CHOICES

VALLE REALE VIGNE NUOVE CERASUOLO D'ABRUZZO
(Montepulciano) Montepulciano d'Abruzzo, Abruzzo, Italy $–$$

TERRA D'ALIGI CERASUOLO
(Montepulciano) Montepulciano d'Abruzzo, Abruzzo, Italy $

DOMAINE DU GROS' NORÉ ROSÉ
(Mourvèdre / Cinsault / Grenache)
Bandol, Provence, France $$–$$$

ALTERNATIVE CHOICES

DOMAINES BUNAN
MAS DE LA ROUVIÈRE ROSÉ
(Mourvèdre / Cinsault / Grenache) Bandol, Provence, France $$

DOMAINE DE TERREBRUNE ROSÉ
(Mourvèdre / Grenache / Cinsault) Bandol, Provence, France $$–$$$

DOMAINE LAFOND
ROC EPINE ROSÉ
(Grenache / Cinsault / Syrah / Carignan)
Tavel, Rhône, France $–$$

ALTERNATIVE CHOICES

CHÂTEAU DES SÉGRIÈS ROSÉ
(Grenache / Cinsault / Clairette / Syrah) Tavel, Rhône, France $$

E GUIGAL ROSÉ
(Grenache / Cinsault / Clairette / Syrah) Tavel, Rhône, France $–$$

HOW TO SERVE IT

Chill these wines, but let them sit on the counter for 15 minutes or so before you get started. You'll best appreciate their fruity aromas if they're cool but not cold. And provide as many glasses to your guests as possible, so they can enjoy the visual spectrum.

HOW TO TALK ABOUT IT

Time to wax poetic. Half the fun of rosé is coming up with the proper metaphoric descriptor. Some are salmon, some are grapefruit, some watermelon, some as pink as a baby's bum. Just don't say the word "blush," OK? Just not cool.

AROMATIC AND SENSORY CLUES

Some of the aromatic notes I tend to find in rosé are lavender, rosemary, tarragon, white pepper, salt and even nutmeg in the lighter styles; and strawberries, cherry candy, raspberries, cranberries and red currants in the bolder styles. But this is such a broad category, since it can be made from any grape, that it's difficult to generalize.

FOOD MATCHES

Cold asparagus spears with vinaigrette. A basket of sliced baguette; a plate of large white beans, such as *gigante*, seasoned with fresh herbs (tarragon is nice) and olive oil. Thin slices of chorizo.

MASTERCLASS: WHAT'S TRENDING?
COLORS OTHER THAN RED, WHITE AND PINK

WHITE REDS

In the preceding MASTERCLASS, we touched upon the idea of vinifying red grapes according to white winemaking techniques: That is, pressing them gently to squeeze the juice out, instead of crushing them and allowing the skins to float around and color the liquid. When carried out carefully—as cellar masters in Champagne do when they're producing *blanc de noirs*—the pressed-out juice can be as pale as any white wine. But in Oregon, where I live, we've got more Pinot Noir vines planted than we know what to do with, and the last time I checked, at least a dozen producers were devoting part of their harvest to *blanc de noirs*-style still wine.

But Oregon and Champagne aren't the only places making white from red. The practice is followed in Germany, in Corsica, and in Italy, where this style of winemaking is called *nero bianco*—white black. There's no easy way to classify these wines, since, like rosé, they can be made from any red grape variety, and once the juice is pressed off the skins, there are any number of ways the wine can go in the cellar: a quick stay in a sealed steel vat, or a long rest in oak barrels. I've tasted fiercely acidic, enamel-stripping versions, candy-apple-like oddities and everything in between. One Willamette Valley winemaker calls his wine, simply, "Red Grape, White Juice." That about sums it up.

DON'T BELIEVE ME? HERE ARE SOME WHITE REDS

Ca'Montebello, Pinot Nero Bianco
(Pinot Noir) Oltrepo Pavese, Lombardy, Italy $–$$
Golden Delicious apples, peaches, almonds.

Domaine Comte Abbatucci, Cuvée Collection BR Blanc
(Barbarossa) Corsica, France $$$$
Minty and butter-creamy, with white pepper notes.

Domaine Serene, Coeur Blanc Barrel Fermented White
(Pinot Noir) Willamette Valley, Oregon, U.S. $$$$
Like an oaky Chardonnay, with notes of butterscotch and caramel.

YELLOW WINE

In Jerez, Spain, casks are partially filled with white wine to encourage the development of *flor*, a yeast that covers the liquid, rendering the pale, dry Sherries known as Fino and Manzanilla. If you've enjoyed these dry Sherries, check out a Vin Jaune from the Jura, the eastern French wine region bordering Switzerland, where the protective yeast layer is called the *voile*, or veil. Like Sherry, Vin Jaune is tangy and nutty; but unlike Sherry, it's not fortified, so it turns an unusual shade of mustard as it's exposed to oxygen over the many years it ages in barrel. It's naturally high in alcohol (13–15%) and can age almost indefinitely. And if geeking out on yellow wines sounds like your cup of tea, also seek out the *vins de voile* from Gaillac, France.

ORANGE WINE

To make a white or pink wine from red grapes, simply follow white-winemaking protocol: Press the juice out of the skins before they sully the liquid with their pigment. But what happens when you reverse this process, and vinify *white* grapes according to the *red* winemaking process? You get an **orange** wine. (That's right—orange wine is *not* made from fermented orange juice!) The fact is, if you look at a bunch of "white" wine grapes, you'll see an array of shades: green, gold, pink and gray. White wines look so pale, generally, because the juice is pressed off and separated from the skins. But allow the juice to macerate on those tinged skins and the resulting wine will be gold, or peachy or...yes, orange. Really—no joke.

The longer that liquid wallows with those astringent, flavorful skins, the more quirky character you'll get in the glass: notes of lemon curd, nutmeg, honey, dried apricot, chamomile, yellow plum, hay and also—let's be frank—sometimes, pleasantly funky hints of kefir or vinegar. (Those kookier flavors, and some of that yellow tint, get in there because the maceration generally takes place in an open-topped tank, allowing for plenty of oxygen contact.) The hotbed of orange wine production is the spot where Friuli, northeastern Italy, meets the Brda wine region of western Slovenia. Here, the favored orange-wine grape is pinkish-yellow Ribolla Gialla ("yellow"). But winemakers all over the world are experimenting with this style, and having success with Malvasia, Pinot Gris, Sauvignon Blanc and Trebbiano, among others.

SOME ORANGE WINES TO TRY

Paolo Bea, Arboreus
(Trebbiano) Umbria, Italy $$$$

La Biancara di Angiolino Maule, Pico
(Garganega) Veneto, Italy $$–$$$

Gravner, Anfora
(Ribolla Gialla) Friuli-Venezia-Giulia, Italy $$$–$$$$

Movia, Lunar
(Ribolla Gialla) Slovenia $$–$$$

La Stoppa, Ageno
(Malvasia Bianca) Emilia-Romagna, Italy $$–$$$

The Scholium Project, Prince in His Caves Farina Vineyards
(Sauvignon Blanc) California, U.S. $$$–$$$$

Edi Simčič, Rebula Rubikon
(Ribolla Gialla) Goriska Brda, Slovenia $$

Radikon, Ribolla Gialla
(Ribolla Gialla) Friuli-Venezia-Giulia, Italy $$–$$$$

A LEADING PRACTITIONER

Josko Gravner (*right*) is one of the most controversial and iconic producers of orange wine, produced in 45 large clay amphorae that he keeps in a specially built part of his cellar in Oslavia, Friuli, Italy. The amphorae, which are lined with beeswax to stop them leaking, come from the Caucasus, where wine producers have used similar vessels for thousands of years. Gravner ferments his white grapes in the amphorae and keeps them on their skins there for six months, then for another six months after pressing. The wines then spend another six years in large wooden casks of close-grained Slavonian oak. The finished product is a burnished amber-gold...or orange, if you will.

7 LIGHT, REFRESHING REDS

7 LIGHT, REFRESHING REDS

Continental Europeans are famously obsessed with the inner workings of the abdomen. Pasta must not be consumed at dinnertime: "It will sit in the gut all night!" Salad must follow the entrée, "To keep the digestive system flowing"; mineral water *con gas* is more essential than a daily multivitamin. An apéritif must be sipped before dinner, to stimulate the appetite, and a digestif after dinner, to soothe the stomach. And lunch without wine? It's positively not done. The problem is, so many red wines nowadays are so syrupy and alcoholic that you couldn't drink a glass at lunch without facing dire consequences back at the office (namely: falling asleep, face on keyboard).

Since most of us aren't allowed siestas at work, we gourmands must look to light-bodied reds. These wines come from cool-climate growing regions and are statements of acidity and minerality rather than fruit and force. They tend to be pale-to-ruby in color, low in mouth-coating tannins, and less than 13.5% ABV. Wine geeks love lighter red styles for their subtlety and purity; gastronomes are big fans because these wines tend to underscore, rather than overpower, food. You can drink a fresh, crisp, light red with almost anything; just avoid sweet desserts, which tend to clash with these wines' tart fruit flavors.

Believe it or not, just a few decades ago, almost any red wine, including Cabernet Sauvignon, could have been described as "light and refreshing." But the climate has changed considerably, and so have farming and winemaking styles. Fortunately, a new wave of interest in cool-climate viticulture has brought about a renaissance in light, refreshing reds in recent years. So don't be a bore and order a diet soda at that next lunch meeting; sip a subtle glass of *Schiava grigia* instead. You can explain that you have an Italian stomach.

YOU'LL ENJOY THESE WINES IF...

- You consider yourself a "white wine drinker"
- Red wines typically give you a headache
- You enjoy lighter fare, such as fish and vegetables

WHAT THE EXPERTS SAY

"It's always tricky to pair vegetables with reds: Asparagus or peas can be nightmares, for example, but they do go with Blaufränkisch from Austria or Gamay from Beaujolais. I love an earthy Pineau d'Aunis, from the Loire Valley, with our chef's pickled and roasted mushrooms drizzled with truffle oil. And the acidity in a light red wine will stand up to a vinaigrette or high-acid sauce."

Pascaline Lepeltier, Wine Director, Rouge Tomate, New York City, U.S.

KEY

$	UNDER $15	**$$$$**	$50–100
$$	$15–30	**$$$$$**	$100+
$$$	$30–50		

THE NAMES TO LOOK FOR

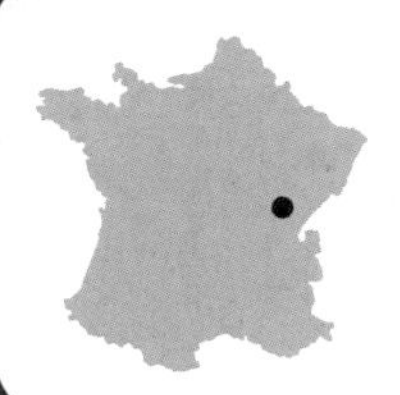

PINOT NOIR BURGUNDY, FRANCE

If you're accustomed to drinking Pinot Noir from New Zealand or California, you might wonder what this grape is doing in the "Light, Refreshing Reds" section. But in cool, damp Burgundy (also, in Canada and Oregon), Pinot declares its fragility and elegance. The best Burgundies are floral and haunting, with an intangible electricity about them.

PRICE RANGE: $-$$$$$

ABV: 12–14%

DRINK IT: 2–50 YEARS AFTER THE VINTAGE

CHOICE

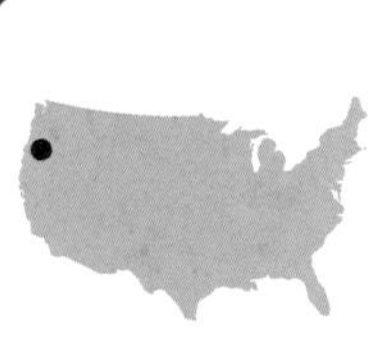

GAMAY NOIR WILLAMETTE VALLEY, OREGON, UNITED STATES

If you've only tasted cheap French Beaujolais, you might think of that region's grape, Gamay Noir, as the vinous equivalent of fruit punch. But look past Beaujolais Nouveau and you'll find Gamays that are earthy, gamey and spicy. You can also find tasty Gamays in France's Loire Valley, Canada's Niagara Peninsula and New York's Finger Lakes.

PRICE RANGE: $-$$

ABV: 12–13%

DRINK IT: 0–5 YEARS AFTER THE VINTAGE

CABERNET FRANC NIAGARA, ONTARIO, CANADA

Cab Franc is best-known as a blending grape in Bordeaux, the United States, Australia, Chile and many other parts of the world. But in cool-climate regions like Canada's Okanagan Valley and Niagara Peninsula, as well as New York's Finger Lakes and Long Island, this variety is surprisingly fleet-footed, brisk with acidity, and juicy, with notes of blackcurrant and snappy green pepper.

PRICE RANGE: $$

ABV: 12.5–13.5%

DRINK IT: 1–5 YEARS AFTER THE VINTAGE

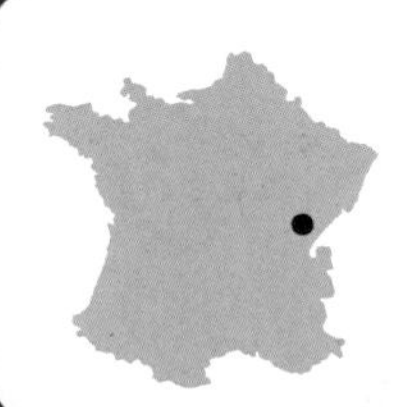

TROUSSEAU JURA, FRANCE

Famous for its Bresse chickens, the chilly Jura is rapidly gaining fame for its offbeat, surprisingly delicious varietal reds (in fact, they tend to be cloudy pink): Poulsard and Trousseau. Poulsard is the lighter of the two, tending toward watermelon and white pepper, while Trousseau displays more herbaceousness and depth. Both are delicious with—you guessed it—fowl.

PRICE RANGE: $-$$

ABV: 12.5–13.5%

DRINK IT: 3–5 YEARS AFTER THE VINTAGE

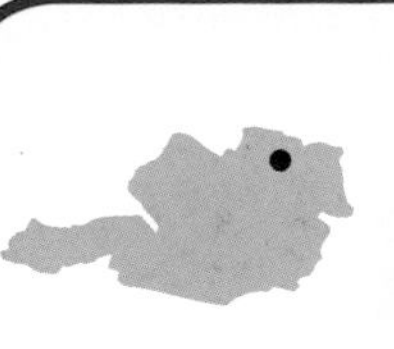

ZWEIGELT KAMPTAL, AUSTRIA

While Spätburgunder (Pinot Noir) gains ground in Germany, Blaufränkisch and Zweigelt from Austria are also having a moment. Blaufränkisch is spicier and silkier; Zweigelt is pleasingly drinkable, combining dark fruit with a light body. For a little cross-cultural experiment, serve these Austrians, slightly chilled, alongside corned beef and cabbage.

PRICE RANGE: $-$$

ABV: 12–13.5%

DRINK IT: 2–5 YEARS AFTER THE VINTAGE

LAMBRUSCO EMILIA-ROMAGNA, ITALY

Northern Italy's semi-sparkling reds are enjoying a *risorgimento* right now as wine lovers realize just how delicious these juicy, dry, effervescent, low-alcohol wines can be with food. Only recently have the very best small producers of Lambrusco in Emilia-Romagna and also Brachetto d'Acqui in Piedmont been available in fine-wine shops worldwide.

PRICE RANGE: $-$$

ABV: 10.5–11.5%

DRINK IT: NOW

TAKE ONE WINE:
JOSEPH DROUHIN LAFORÊT BOURGOGNE PINOT NOIR

THE BASICS

GRAPE VARIETY: Pinot Noir

REGION: Burgundy, France

ALCOHOL LEVEL: 12.5%

PRICE: \$–\$\$

AVAILABILITY: Widely available

APPEARANCE: Bright, translucent ruby

TASTING NOTE: Juicy tart raspberries; brambles; fresh-cut herbs; bracing acidity; white-pepper spice; forest-floor mushrooms; minerality; brisk energy.

FOOD MATCH: Salmon, subtly spiced vegetable dishes, poultry or pork.

DRINK OR KEEP: Drink this fresh, juicy Pinot Noir now; keep your higher-tier Burgundies for later.

WHY DOES IT TASTE THAT WAY?

If you've been raised on a vinous diet of plush, rich red wines, a sip of a brisk Pinot Noir can be like diving into ice-cold water: You might be tentative about making the plunge, but once you've done it, you realize it's sooooo good for you. Thin-skinned, high in acidity and grounded in minerality, Pinot Noir reaches its spine-tingling peak of deliciousness when grown in Burgundy, where methodical monks spent hundreds of years identifying the best microclimates and cultivars for this delicate, difficult-to-husband grape variety. The cool, moist climate here means that that the fruit barely ripens in time for harvest season—if it ripens at all. But when it does, there's a frisson to it that can't be duplicated anywhere else on the planet.

WHO MADE IT?

After 130 years in business, Domaine Joseph Drouhin remains in the family, with the thoughtful fourth generation—Philippe, Véronique, Laurent and Frédéric—running winemaking and viticulture under the watchful eye of *pater familias* Robert. Although it's a large company, with vineyards throughout Burgundy and a satellite winery (Domaine Drouhin Oregon) in the United States, the focus at Drouhin is on impeccable farming and wines of subtlety and finesse. Drouhin practices biodynamic agriculture (more on this subject later in this section) at its own estates; the fruit for this blend came from multiple growers, however.
The light body and fresh fruit style of this wine come in part from aging in stainless steel; the gentle spice and silkiness from partial aging in neutral, or previously used, oak barrels.

CRACKING THE CODE
CLOSURE
While rarer releases from Drouhin are closed with corks, this entry-level, drink-now bottling is topped with a screwcap, for ease and portability.
APPELLATION NAME
A wine labeled "Bourgogne" can be sourced from anywhere within the Burgundy appellation. A Bourgogne from a top-tier producer like Drouhin may be relatively simple, but it should still be delightful.
PRODUCER NAME
Joseph Drouhin is a family-owned winery and one of the best-known names in Burgundy, synonymous with quality at every price point.
ALCOHOL
At just 12.5% alcohol by volume, this light and refreshing Pinot Noir won't weigh you down during lunch, cocktail hour or a quick weeknight meal.
WINE NAME
"Laforêt" is the proprietary name for this cuvée, or blend, which should taste fairly consistent from year to year.
Joseph Drouhin
LAFORET
BOURGOGNE
Appellation Bourgogne Contrôlée
PINOT NOIR
www.drouhin.com
contains sulphites (SO 2)

JOSEPH DROUHIN LAFORÊT BOURGOGNE PINOT NOIR

WHY THAT PRICE?

OK, I'll come clean here: If I could buy any red from Joseph Drouhin, it might be the intoxicatingly fragrant "Amoureuses" ($$$$$), from a single vineyard in Chambolle-Musigny, Côte de Nuits. But how cool is it that Véronique Drouhin-Boss, the winemaker responsible for *that* dreamy collector's item, also makes *this* affordable light red for every-night enjoyment? Here's how: Drouhin isn't merely a *maison* managing precious single estates; it's also a *négociant*. That is, it's a winery that purchases grapes from small growers throughout Burgundy. Its large network of fruit sources allows Drouhin to deliver bargains—like this one—to consumers. Buying an inexpensive bottling from a top négociant like Drouhin is like purchasing pantry items from the bulk section of your gourmet grocery: You can be certain that the quality will be good and the price will be fair. And if you like a basic weeknight wine like "Lafôret," you can be quite sure that you'll enjoy exploring Drouhin's single-vineyard wines on the weekend, when you have the time to appreciate properly all that Burgundy has to offer.

WHAT FOOD DOES IT GO WITH?

You can't beat Pinot Noir for versatility. Poultry, pork and even a juicy steak respond with alacrity to the bright fruit and refreshing acidity in this elegant red wine. It's light enough to complement seafood or salad, but it has the earthy depth to go along for the ride with a mushroom lasagna. The only food that tastes truly terrible with Pinot Noir is a sweet, sticky dessert. (If you must finish a meal with Pinot, then serve fresh berries or dark bittersweet chocolate, please.)

Left: The roof of the Hospices de Beaune, the town where Drouhin and many other Burgundy négociants are based.

TOP FOOD MATCH:
Forest grouse with sautéed chanterelles

POULTRY

WILD MUSHROOMS

ROASTED VEGETABLES

10 OF THE BEST

GREAT BURGUNDIES, FROM SIMPLE TO SUBLIME

DOMAINE CHARLES AUDOIN	$$-$$$
DOMAINE FRANÇOIS GAY ET FILS	$$-$$$$$
MAISON LOUIS JADOT	$-$$$$$
DOMAINE MICHEL LAFARGE	$-$$$$$
DOMAINE J-F MUGNIER	$$$-$$$$$
DOMAINE P ET M RION	$$-$$$$$
DOMAINE MARC ROY	$$$-$$$$
DOMAINE DE LA ROMANÉE-CONTI	$$$$$
DOMAINE FANNY SABRE	$-$$$
DOMAINE COMTE GEORGES DE VOGÜÉ	$$$$$

AROUND THE WORLD

SIMILAR STYLE WINES FROM DIFFERENT COUNTRIES

Au Bon Climat Pinot Noir
Santa Barbara County, California, U.S. $$

Ata Rangi Pinot Noir
Martinborough, New Zealand $$$–$$$$

Le Clos Jordanne Village Reserve Pinot Noir
Niagara, Ontario, Canada $$$

CHOICE MADE SIMPLE

EXPERT'S PERSONAL FAVORITES

Recommended by Rajat Parr, Wine Director, Mina Group, and Partner/Sommelier, RN74, San Francisco, U.S.

DOMAINE DE BELLIVIÈRE, LE ROUGE-GORGE
(PINEAU D'AUNIS)
COTEAUX DU LOIR, FRANCE $$

CATHERINE & PIERRE BRETON, FRANC DE PIED
(CABERNET FRANC) BOURGUEIL, LOIRE, FRANCE $$–$$$

WEINGUT BRÜNDLMAYER
(ZWEIGELT)
KAMPTAL, AUSTRIA $

DOMAINE DUJAC, CHAMBOLLE-MUSIGNY PREMIER CRU LES GRUENCHERS (PINOT NOIR)
BURGUNDY, FRANCE $$$$$

JEAN FOILLARD, MORGON CÔTE DU PY
(GAMAY NOIR)
BEAUJOLAIS, FRANCE $$–$$$

THIERRY PUZELAT, LE ROUGE EST MIS
(PINOT MEUNIER)
LOIRE VALLEY, FRANCE $$

SOTTIMANO, MATÉ
(BRACHETTO)
PIEDMONT, ITALY $$

CANTINA TERLAN-KELLEREI GRAUVERNATSCH
(SCHIAVA GRIGIA)
ALTO ADIGE, ITALY $

BÉNÉDICT & STÉPHANE TISSOT SINGULIER
(TROUSSEAU)
ARBOIS, JURA, FRANCE $$

LE FILS DE CHARLES TROSSET, CUVÉE CONFIDENTIEL
(MONDEUSE)
ARBIN, SAVOIE, FRANCE $$

(Grape Varieties in Brackets)

WORLD OF FINE WINE RECOMMENDATIONS

VILLA PONCIAGO, FLEURIE
(GAMAY NOIR)
BEAUJOLAIS, FRANCE $$

GHISLAINE BARTHOD, BOURGOGNE ROUGE
(PINOT NOIR)
BURGUNDY, FRANCE $$

SYLVIE ESMONIN, GEVREY-CHAMBERTIN VIEILLES VIGNES (PINOT NOIR)
BURGUNDY, FRANCE $$$

J-F MUGNIER, CHAMBOLLE-MUSIGNY PREMIER CRU LES FUÉES
(PINOT NOIR)
BURGUNDY, FRANCE $$$$

ARMAND ROUSSEAU GEVREY-CHAMBERTIN PREMIER CRU CAZETIERS (PINOT NOIR)
BURGUNDY, FRANCE $$$$

CHARLES JOGUET, CHINON CLOS DE LA DIOTERIE
(CABERNET FRANC)
LOIRE, FRANCE $$$

JACKY BLOT, DOMAINE DE LA BUTTE, BOURGUEIL MI-PENTE
(CABERNET FRANC)
LOIRE, FRANCE $$$

FROMM WINERY, LA STRADA PINOT NOIR
MARLBOROUGH, NEW ZEALAND $$$

NIEPOORT, CHARME
(TOURIGA FRANCA / TINTA RORIZ)
DOURO, PORTUGAL $$$

FIORINO LAMBRUSCO
(LAMBRUSCO)
EMILIA-ROMAGNA, ITALY $$

ORGANIC, BIODYNAMIC OR NATURAL

BRICK HOUSE, GAMAY NOIR
(GAMAY NOIR) RIBBON RIDGE,
WILLAMETTE VALLEY, OREGON, U.S. $$

JEAN-PAUL DUBOST TRACOT,
MOULIN-À-VENT, EN BRENAY
(GAMAY NOIR)
BEAUJOLAIS, FRANCE $$

FELTON ROAD, BLOCK 5
(PINOT NOIR)
CENTRAL OTAGO,
NEW ZEALAND $$$$

DOMAINE HUBER-VERDEREAU, VOLNAY
(PINOT NOIR)
BURGUNDY, FRANCE $$$

JOHAN VINEYARDS, ESTATE
(PINOT NOIR)
WILLAMETTE VALLEY, OREGON, U.S. $$

FAMILLE PEILLOT, BUGEY MONDEUSE
(MONDEUSE)
BUGEY, SAVOIE, FRANCE $$

SOUTHBROOK VINEYARDS, TRIOMPHE
(CABERNET FRANC)
NIAGARA-ON-THE-LAKE, ONTARIO, CANADA $$

DOMAINE DE LA TOURNELLE,
L'UVA ARBOSIANA
(POULSARD)
ARBOIS, JURA, FRANCE $–$$

CHÂTEAU DE VAUX, LES HAUTES BASSIÈRES
(PINOT NOIR)
MOSELLE, FRANCE $$

DOMAINE DE VEILLOUX, ROUGE
(GAMAY NOIR / PINOT NOIR / MALBEC /
CABERNET FRANC)
CHEVERNY, LOIRE VALLEY, FRANCE $

BEST ON A BUDGET

AHA WINES, BEBAME RED
(CABERNET FRANC / GAMAY NOIR)
EL DORADO COUNTY, SIERRA
FOOTHILLS, CALIFORNIA, U.S. $$

EVENING LAND VINEYARDS,
CELEBRATION
(GAMAY NOIR) EOLA-AMITY HILLS,
WILLAMETTE VALLEY, OREGON, U.S. $$

TAMI'
FRAPPATO
(FRAPPATO) SICILY, ITALY $–$$

BOUCHARD AÎNÉ & FILS,
BOURGOGNE ROUGE
(PINOT NOIR) BURGUNDY, FRANCE $

CASTELFEDER, RIEDER
(LAGREIN)
ALTO ADIGE, ITALY $$

CLETO CHIARLI,
VIGNETO ENRICO CIALDINI
(LAMBRUSCO GRASPAROSSA)
CASTELVETRO, EMILIA-ROMAGNA, ITALY $

JACKY JANODET,
DOMAINE LES FINES GRAVES,
BEAUJOLAIS VILLAGES
(GAMAY NOIR) BEAUJOLAIS, FRANCE $

MONTINORE ESTATE
(PINOT NOIR)
WILLAMETTE VALLEY, OREGON, U.S.
$–$$

DOMAINE TAUPENOT-MERME,
PASSETOUTGRAIN
(PINOT NOIR / GAMAY NOIR)
BURGUNDY, FRANCE $$

VALLE DELL'ACATE,
IL FRAPPATO
(FRAPPATO)
VITTORIA, SICILY, ITALY $–$$

MASTERCLASS: NO-CRUSH WINEMAKING

In oeno-speak, the general term for the days and weeks of cellar work that surround harvest is "crush." Because all the time and labor spent picking, processing and overseeing fermentation can be crushing. And, of course, the grapes get crushed, too. Right? Well, not necessarily. Some winemakers, wishing to make a lighter, more traditional or spicier red wine, choose not to crush some or all of their red grapes. Instead, they leave the skins whole and the stems intact.

The most extreme example of no-crush winemaking is called **carbonic maceration**. The winemaker fills a vat with intact grape clusters, being careful not to break the skins (although the clusters at the bottom inevitably get squished and begin to ferment). He might then top off the tank with carbon dioxide gas before sealing it airtight. Over the next week or so, in this oxygen-free environment, each grape begins to ferment inside its own skin. The process results in a soft, juicy wine that's relatively light in color and low in tannins.

Famously, Beaujolais winemakers use this method to make Beaujolais Nouveau, the inexpensive and freakishly young rendition of the Gamay Noir grape that hits store shelves like clockwork every third Thursday in November —and often tastes like the alcoholic equivalent of tropical fruit punch. In parts of Spain's Rioja region, too, some winemakers use carbonic maceration to make juicy, inexpensive Tempranillos.

More commonly, vintners opt for **whole-cluster fermentation**, a process that—if managed correctly—captures fresh fruit flavors, increases spicy and savory aromas and smooths out tannins. The winemaker places some or all grape clusters into the fermentation tank whole, without crushing them or removing their stems. You'll find this technique used not only in more serious styles of Beaujolais, but also among Pinot Noir producers all over the world.

No-crush (or partial-crush) winemaking isn't solely the domain of the lighter red wine varieties, by the way. Rhône River Valley cult *vinificateur* Eric Texier tames his Syrahs with carbonic maceration. And according to the American sommelier Rajat Parr, a few old-school Piemontese *produttori* use this method on the brutally fierce Nebbiolo grape as well.

Parr is a big fan of whole-cluster fermentation; he favors on his restaurant wine lists wineries that do whole-cluster vinification, and he also utilizes this method at his own winery, Sandhi, in California's Santa Rita Hills. "A lot of my favorite producers use whole-cluster fermentation," Parr says. "I think whole-cluster wines age longer and better than destemmed wines."

HOW TO IDENTIFY THESE ELEMENTS

1: Put Gamay Noir grapes through carbonic maceration and you get the unmistakable aromas and flavors of Beaujolais: Think strawberry-cranberry-raspberry Kool-Aid (sometimes, even, a surreal scent of ripe bananas, although it is believed that this is actually caused by a certain yeast strain).

2: "Whole-cluster-fermented wines have this amazing texture," says Rajat Parr. "The process softens the mouthfeel so it's silkier, not as chewy. It's like the difference between sand and rocks: The tannins become more gritty; they aren't as chunky."

3: "On the nose, you'll find jasmine tea, rose petal, olive tapenade, bergamot, pomegranate, rhubarb and spices. You don't tend to get these aromas from a wine made with destemmed fruit," says Parr of whole-cluster-fermented wines.

WHOLE-BUNCH FERMENTATION

It's common to vinify a mix of whole-cluster and crushed fruit. The winemaker might fill the bottom of the tank with whole clusters, then layer destemmed and crushed fruit on top.

For carbonic maceration, the top of the tank is sealed and kept airtight. For whole-cluster fermentation, the top stays open.

If they want to be super-gentle, the winemakers can simply sit down and push the cap down carefully with their feet.

The cellar hands carefully "wet the cap," pushing down the layer of solids that floats to the top, to keep the skins macerating in the juice without disturbing the whole clusters and grapes at the bottom. This can be tiring work!

MASTERCLASS: 6 WINES TO BUY

If you look past "nouveau" bottlings, you'll find nuance and savory depth—without losing affordability—in Beaujolais. In Spain's Rioja, where the best grapes go into expensive barrels for the Crianza and Reserva bottlings, it's common to toss the rest into steel tanks for young or *joven* wines made by carbonic maceration. Yet another source for bargains is the Languedoc-Roussillon, where winemakers use partial carbonic or whole-cluster to tame the tannins of the Carignan grape. And if you've got a bit more to spend, explore Burgundy and beyond, where some vintners use whole-cluster fermentation to emphasize the fruit, spice and earth notes in Pinot Noir.

DOMAINE DE LA GRAND'COUR
CLOS DE LA GRAND'COUR
(Gamay Noir, carbonic maceration)
Fleurie, Beaujolais, France $$

ALTERNATIVE CHOICES

DOMAINE DE LA VOÛTE DES CROZES
(Gamay Noir, carbonic maceration)
Côte-de-Brouilly, Beaujolais, France $$

JEAN MAUPERTUIS LES PIERRES NOIRES
(Gamay Noir, carbonic maceration)
Vin de Table (Loire Valley), France $

LUBERRI ORLEGI
(Tempranillo, carbonic maceration)
Rioja Alavesa, Rioja, Spain $

ALTERNATIVE CHOICES

BODEGAS MEDRANO IRAZU JOVEN
(Tempranillo, carbonic maceration)
Rioja Alavesa, Rioja, Spain $

FERNANDO REMÍREZ DE GANUZA ERRE PUNTO
(Tempranillo / Graciano / Viura / Malvasia, carbonic maceration)
Rioja Alavesa, Rioja, Spain $

DOMAINE DES SCHISTES TRADITION
(Syrah / Carignan / Grenache, whole-cluster)
Côtes du Roussillon Villages,
Languedoc-Roussillon, France $

ALTERNATIVE CHOICES

DOMAINE DE FONTSAINTE CORBIÈRES ROUGE
(Carignan / Grenache / Syrah, whole-cluster)
Corbières, Languedoc-Roussillon, France $

PCHÂTEAU D'OUPIA LES HÉRÉTIQUES
(Carignan, partial carbonic maceration)
Vin de Pays de L'Hérault,
Languedoc-Roussillon, France $

DOMAINE DES LAMBRAYS
CLOS DES LAMBRAYS GRAND CRU
(Pinot Noir, whole-cluster)
Morey-St-Denis, Burgundy, France $$$$$

ALTERNATIVE CHOICES

CHÂTEAU DE LA TOUR
CLOS-VOUGEOT GRAND CRU
(Pinot Noir, whole-cluster)
Vougeot, Burgundy, France $$$$$

DOMAINE DE L'ARLOT NUITS-ST-GEORGES
PREMIER CRU CLOS DES FORETS ST-GEORGES
(Pinot Noir, whole-cluster) Burgundy, France $$$$

ESCARPMENT KUPE
(Pinot Noir, whole-cluster)
Martinborough, Wairarapa, New Zealand $$$

ALTERNATIVE CHOICES

RHYS VINEYARDS FAMILY FARM VINEYARD
(Pinot Noir, whole-cluster)
Santa Cruz Mountains, California, U.S. $$$$

DOMAINE CHANDON PINOT MEUNIER
(Pinot Meunier, whole-cluster)
Carneros, Napa Valley, California, U.S.

CRISTOM MT. JEFFERSON CUVÉE
(Pinot Noir, partial whole-cluster)
Willamette Valley, Oregon, U.S. $$–$$$

ALTERNATIVE CHOICES

BRICK HOUSE SELECT
(Pinot Noir, partial whole-cluster)
Willamette Valley, Oregon, U.S. $$–$$$

WILLAMETTE VALLEY VINEYARDS
WHOLE CLUSTER FERMENTED
(Pinot Meunier, whole-cluster)
Willamette Valley, Oregon, U.S. $$

HOW TO SERVE IT

A young carbonic maceration wine will taste best slightly chilled—to, say, 55°F (13°C)—so stick it in the fridge for 30 to 45 minutes before you pop the cork. A more complex, whole-cluster-fermented wine will also show better if it's cooler than room temperature. Try refrigerating Pinot Noir for 15 to 30 minutes before opening it, to best underscore its subtle spices and delicately fruity fragrance.

HOW TO TALK ABOUT IT

You're in fairly geeky territory once you start exploring carbonic maceration and whole-cluster fermentation, so it's worth being familiar with the lingo. Because few wines are made entirely by carbonic maceration or whole-cluster fermentation, you'll often hear terms such as "semi-carbonic," "partial carbonic" or "30-percent whole-cluster." Also, be aware that in New Zealand, Australia and the United Kingdom, oenophiles tend to say "whole bunch" instead of "whole cluster."

AROMATIC AND SENSORY CLUES

If you know Beaujolais Nouveau, you might assume that carbonic maceration always makes for simple, tutti-fruity aromas and flavors. But in higher-tier Beaujolais, Tempranillo from Rioja and Carignan in the Languedoc, it results in a wine of juicy succulence and subdued tannins. Clues that a wine has been through whole-cluster fermentation are fresh fruit, a silky texture and spicy notes of white pepper and cinnamon. Sometimes, alas, it can also result in an unpleasant green astringency.

FOOD MATCHES

The bright-red fruit notes of a carbonic-maceration wine play deliciously off salty, savory meats such as ham, while the classic Thanksgiving meal of roasted turkey, cranberry sauce, stuffing and yams absolutely begs to be washed down with a juicy Beaujolais. Whole-cluster-fermented wines are all about nuance, so try them with subtle dishes, like lightly spiced Moroccan couscous or herb-crusted pork.

MASTERCLASS: WHAT'S TRENDING?
ORGANIC, BIODYNAMIC AND NATURAL WINES

ORGANIC WINE

Back in the 1970s and '80s, "organic" wineries churned out the sort of funky hippie juice that only tasted swell if you'd recently smoked copious amounts of dope. But today, organic wines are among the best in the world. Why? First, consumer awareness of environmental and health issues has translated into an increased demand for high-quality organic foods and beverages. Second, in response to this demand, organic farming and production methods have improved. Finally, wine enthusiasm is at an all-time high, with more oenophiles than ever before exploring the notion of "terroir"—the idea that you can taste the vineyard in the wine. And if that vineyard had been sprayed with chemicals, would you want to taste them?

Vine tenders cite another reason: Unlike crops that are rotated from year to year, a grapevine can continue to produce fruit in the same spot for a century or longer. But as vines planted in past decades mature, some vignerons discover a slump in grape quality and vine health. Determined to save their old vines, they focus on restoring nutrients and microbial activity to the soil by growing cover crops and spreading organic compost. Consumers have embraced these changes, but buying organic can be confusing: There are countless sustainable and organic certifications, not to mention the language barrier: "organic" in the United States is *bio* in France. Also, many winegrowers don't bother with the certification paperwork and fees. Your best bet is to ask your sommelier or wine merchant to recommend organically or sustainably produced wines.

BIODYNAMIC WINE

"Biodynamic" might sound like a way-out exercise program, but it was the precursor to modern organic farming. An eccentric Austrian intellectual and spiritual leader named Rudolf Steiner codified this ultra-natural agriculture in a series of lectures delivered in 1924, in response to a growing sense of alarm among landowners. At that time, chemical munitions plants from World War I were staying in business by harnessing the new nitrogen-synthesizing technology to make chemical fertilizers rather than weapons. Steiner implored the public to consider the risks that these chemicals posed to human and environmental health. He suggested an alternative style of farming based on traditional farming methods and ancient religious beliefs.

Instead of using organic fertilizers and pesticides, Biodynamic farmers spray herbal "preparations"—something akin to homeopathic medicine for plants. Because they make some of these preparations using animal parts (such as cow horns), and tend to time their agricultural activities to the phases of the moon, practitioners are considered cultish and strange. But in fact, it's only in the past century that we have begun practicing "conventional" agriculture; for thousands of years prior to World War I, all farming was basically biodynamic. Because of their interest in terroir and tradition, winegrowers and wine lovers are among the most avid proponents of biodynamic farming. But critics advise caution, citing a lack of evidence that labor-intensive biodynamic farming is anything other than overpriced.

RECOMMENDED READING

Jamie Goode and Sam Harrop MW, *Authentic Wine: Toward Natural and Sustainable Winemaking* (University of California Press)

What's the difference between an "organic wine" and a wine "made with organic grapes"? Just what are those weird biodynamic preparations? What does "non-interventionist" mean? What must winemakers do (or not do) in the cellar to ensure that their wine will be organic or biodynamic? Eco-curious oenophiles can find answers to all these questions, and more, in this informative and refreshingly readable reference.

NATURAL WINE

All the cool kids on the gastronomic scene are talking about "natural" wines. But what in a wine constitutes natural-ness? In supermarkets, after all, this moniker is meaningless: The only products claiming to be "natural" seem to be hermetically sealed and pumped full of additives. In the sphere of wine, however, this word has more weight. The natural wine movement celebrates authenticity in an era when it's possible to mass-produce quaffable plonk using chemicals and machinery. And it's a consumer-driven revolution. Wineries seldom call themselves "natural"; it's more often sommeliers, merchants and oenophiles who apply this term, to producers who farm organically and refrain from using additives or modern techniques.

Although it's not short on gurus, the natural wine movement lacks a governing body or any specific directives. But here's a general description of what's expected of "natural" winemakers: After the ecologically sensitive farming is done, vineyard workers pick the grapes by hand—never machine harvesters. The grapes then go into a vessel, preferably a cement container or an oak cask rather than a stainless-steel tank, where the winemaker allows indigenous or "wild" yeast to promote primary and secondary fermentation instead of inoculating the macerating fruit with cultured yeast. Filters and fining agents (even "natural" substances, like egg whites) are frowned upon. Additives—enzymes, oak chips, water, sugar or acid—are a no-no. And the use of high-tech machinery, to smooth out tannins or increase concentration, is *verboten*.

THE TAKE-AWAY

Why are we discussing organic, biodynamic and natural wines in this section? Because if you created a Venn diagram of winemakers who aspire to more "natural" methods, and wineries producing light, refreshing red wines, you'd see a lot of crossover. Many top domaines in Burgundy, Oregon, New Zealand and California have bet on biodynamic agriculture as the best way to nurture delicate Pinot Noir; numerous Pinot and Cab Franc producers in the Loire Valley, too, believe in farming this way. Varieties like Mondeuse from Savoie or Poulsard and Trousseau from the Jura are practically synonymous with natural winemaking. And sustainable vine-tending and hands-off winemaking are practiced religiously by the better producers in Beaujolais. It's difficult to argue with the idea of lower-alcohol, handcrafted, naturally produced wines. But the movement has nevertheless sparked controversy. Consumers are confused by the lack of clarity in labeling, as well as by the absence of rigor in defining the term "natural." And then there are the quality issues: The *sans soufre* contingent of the natural wine movement, for example, believes in bottling wines without the addition of sulfur dioxide, an anti-oxidative and preservative. While it's never fun to open a bottle of over-sulfured wine and have to stand back while the scent of rotten eggs fills the room, it's also a huge disappointment to pop the cork on a *sans soufre* wine, only to discover it has spoiled. So, ask your sommelier or wine merchant for guidance in finding natural wines that you'll be sure to enjoy.

RECOMMENDED READING

Alice Feiring, *Naked Wine: Letting Grapes Do What Comes Naturally* (Da Capo Press)

An impassioned proponent of natural winemaking and biodynamic farming, Feiring takes her readers on a personal tour of Beaujolais, the Loire Valley and other hot spots, giving us a taste of how thrillingly subversive this movement feels for its followers and risk-taking practitioners. Steampunks might wear copper-rimmed goggles to affect a look, but Feiring's cast of characters—nuclear engineer-turned-natural winemaker Eric Texier, for example—are the real deal.

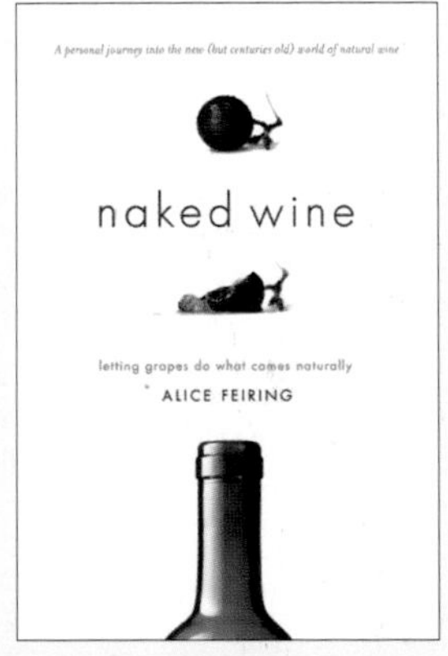

8 FIRM, MEDIUM-BODIED REDS

8 FIRM, MEDIUM-BODIED REDS

What is structure? Structure is the fifth-century Bolnisi Sioni in Georgia, still standing strong after more than 1,500 years. Structure is Florence's octagonal *duomo*, the Basilica di Santa Maria del Fiore. Structure is Frank Gehry's Hotel Marques de Riscal, a tangle of gleaming ribbons spilling over the vineyards of Rioja. Structure is stone and steel. It's clean lines and careful math. It's built on the trifecta foundation of history, bold statement and faith.

In wine, structure is the formation of a different trinity: tannin, acidity and fruit. These three must be balanced for the architecture of the wine to hold. But light reds tend toward high acidity; full-bodied reds often overdo the tannin and fruit. Structure lies at the center: those firm, midweight wines that don't tip the scales too low in any direction.

As is so often the case with the classics, the medium-bodied wines of structure—Tempranillo from Spain, Sangiovese from Chianti, Saperavi from Georgia, Xynomavro from Greece—might seem outmoded and old-fashioned to some of us today. But consider Agiorgitiko (also known as St. George): This grape has been grown and vinified since 500 BC. Surely there is some value in the sort of structure that can span 25 centuries and still taste fresh and alive to our contemporary palates.

Why such longevity? Because these varieties love food. They can go light or heavy, depending on the circumstances. They are built to hold up what you are eating for dinner tonight—not what you're dreaming of ordering at that *au courant* restaurant this weekend. Sure, they're divine alongside veal scaloppini or roasted venison loin. But they're also just right next to meat and potatoes, spaghetti and meatballs or a thick lentil soup.

The classical structures are crumbling temples and palaces, still graceful after all these years. Structured, classic wines are the pillars of our everyday lives: the Tintos and Tintas of Portugal, Garnachas from Spain or Dolcetto and Barbera from Piedmont. These wines may have spanned the centuries, but we tend to take them for granted. So let's stop a moment here and take in the view.

YOU'LL ENJOY THESE WINES IF...

- You just plain love to eat
- You appreciate the classics
- You lean toward savory midweight foods, like creamy pasta, hearty soups or roasted poultry

WHAT THE EXPERTS SAY

"I love matching medium-bodied reds with very tender meats. For example, a veal tenderloin filet from Limousin goes perfectly with a soft Saint Laurent from Austria. Sun-dried tomatoes balance out the tannins, or try it with a classic, savory sauce like a Choron or Boulangère. More unusually, last week, we served warm octopus, lightly poached in a spicy broth, with a velvety Grenache from Priorat—what a surprise! It was a gorgeous, sunny pairing."

Antoine Petrus, Restaurant Manager and Wine Director, Restaurant Lasserre, Paris, France

GOOD TO DRINK WITH

KEY

$	UNDER $15	$$$$	$50–100
$$	$15–30	$$$$$	$100+
$$$	$30–50		

THE NAMES TO LOOK FOR

SANGIOVESE CHIANTI, TUSCANY, ITALY

Half a century ago, your grandparents drank Chianti out of a straw *fiasco* at a neighborhood trattoria with red-checked tablecloths and big, drippy candles. But what is Chianti today? Underappreciated, and in the midst of an identity crisis. Yet it still has a Pavlovian effect on the salivary glands. Just one sip has you thinking, *Mangia*! (Let's eat!)

PRICE RANGE: $-$$$$

ABV: 12.5–14.5%

DRINK IT: 5–25 YEARS AFTER THE VINTAGE

CHOICE

TEMPRANILLO RIOJA, SPAIN

The cool crowd goes for the reds of Bierzo, Priorat or Ribera del Duero. But don't dismiss the Tempranillo-based reds of Rioja as trope. In the region that launched modern Spanish winemaking, a thought-provoking combination of new-wave *enólogos* and virtuosos of the classic style make this a region that remains relevant today.

PRICE RANGE: $-$$$$$

ABV: 12.5–15.5%

DRINK IT: 3–40 YEARS AFTER THE VINTAGE

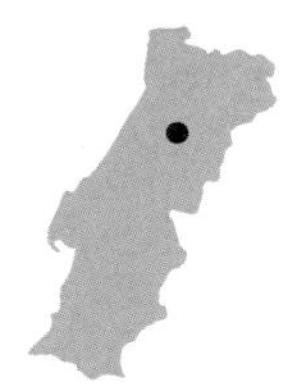

VINHO TINTO DÃO, PORTUGAL

Fine tannins, bright acidity and notes of leather, dark fruit and black pepper make the reds from Dão—or from the Douro—enchanting and collectible, just like those intricately hand-painted Portuguese ceramics I'm addicted to. Drinkers have discovered these spicy, layered Touriga Nacional-based blends and, darn it all, prices are on the rise.

PRICE RANGE: $-$$$$

ABV: 12.5–14%

DRINK IT: 2–15 YEARS AFTER THE VINTAGE

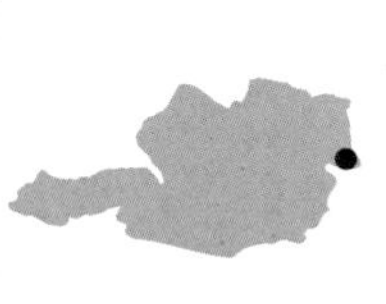

BLAUFRÄNKISCH BURGENLAND, AUSTRIA

So you know Grüner Veltliner. Congratulations. Now you're ready to move onto Austrian reds. Depending on the winemaker's whim, Blaufränkisch can be subtle or spicy, but it's always held up by a firm backbone of acidity. You'll find it under different names in central and east-central Europe, but Austria, at the moment, is where it's at.

PRICE RANGE: $-$$$

ABV: 12.5–13.5%

DRINK IT: 2–15 YEARS AFTER THE VINTAGE

AGIORGITIKO NEMÉA, GREECE

Not sure how to pronounce the original Greek? Don't despair: It also goes by "St. George." A smooth mouthfeel and juicy notes of plum, sour cherry, vinegar, herbs and spice make this a match not just for Greek cuisine, but Indian, African, Korean and Chinese, as well. Also, it's a comforting glass to relax with after you've slain a dragon.

PRICE RANGE: $-$$$

ABV: 12–13%

DRINK IT: 2–10 YEARS AFTER THE VINTAGE

SAPERAVI KAHKETI, GEORGIA

When archaeologists discovered an 8,000-year-old wine in Georgia, the public said, "8,000 years?" and oenophiles said, "Georgia?" Yes, Georgia—one of the few winemaking regions where it's truly legit to use amphorae, known there as *qvevri*. The cradle of viticulture is home to the red-fleshed Saperavi, a grape for the ages.

PRICE RANGE: $-$$$

ABV: 12–14.5%

DRINK IT: 5–50 YEARS AFTER THE VINTAGE

TAKE ONE WINE: CASTELLO D'ALBOLA CHIANTI CLASSICO RISERVA

THE BASICS

GRAPE VARIETY: Sangiovese (95%) / Canaiolo 5%

REGION: Tuscany, Italy

ALCOHOL LEVEL: 13%

PRICE: $$–$$$

AVAILABILITY: Widely available

APPEARANCE: Deep ruby

TASTING NOTE: Berry pie and incense on the nose; sour cherries, spice and subtle, cedar-y evidence of barrel age; food-friendly acidity balanced by soft tannins.

FOOD MATCH: A savory pasta like *spaghetti al pesto d'olive*; wild game such as rabbit; tomatoes and fresh herbs; oxtail stew.

DRINK OR KEEP: Since Chianti Classico Riservas get plenty of bottle age prior to release, this wine is ready to drink now. However, you could age it for an additional five to 10 years; the very best Chiantis will age for decades.

WHY DOES IT TASTE THAT WAY?

The formula for a wine that's ripe with fruit yet still brisk with acidity is simple: sun-soaked days and chilly nights. Albola's estate vineyards are in the heart of Chianti Classico, facing south for maximum sun exposure. The Sangiovese vines are planted on high hillsides at between 1,300 and 2,000 feet (400 and 600 m) of elevation; the clay-rich soil is studded by sun-reflecting calcareous stones, called *albarese*. The wine's rich character comes from 15 months of aging in wood—10 percent in modern French oak barriques and the rest in large Slavonian-oak casks. The wine then ages for an additional 12 months in stainless steel and three more months in bottle prior to release. The result is a wine that tastes both traditional and contemporary.

WHO MADE IT?

Winemaking has been happening in Chianti—and perhaps at Albola—since the Etruscan era. The oldest building on the Albola estate was built in the 12th century, and over the ages, the property has passed through numerous noble hands. In 1979, a dashing Prosecco magnate from the north, Gianni Zonin, zoomed up in a red Fiat, banged on the door of the magnificent 16th-century villa, and convinced its inhabitant, a certain Prince Ginolo Ginori Conti, to vacate the premises so that Zonin could realize his dream of growing Sangiovese and making Chianti. Conti sold; and Zonin added the estate to his portfolio of wineries. Casa Vinicola Zonin is today Italy's largest privately held wine company, with more than 4,500 acres (1,800 ha) under vine, and Albola is the jewel in the crown.

CRACKING THE CODE

CONSORZIO LOGO
The black rooster is the symbol of the Consorzio Vino Chianti Classico, a marketing and quality-control organization.

OFFICIAL STAMP
The pink label encircling the neck of the bottle acts as proof of authenticity, confirming that the grapes were grown within the Chianti Classico DOCG, or Denominazione di Origine Controllata e Garantita—that is, a top-quality winegrowing appellation in Italy.

WINE REGION
Chianti is the name of the place. The grape is called Sangiovese, but you don't typically see this on the front label of the wine. You're just supposed to know this. Or not—traditional winegrowers in classic regions such as Chianti believe that the terroir, or the place, is far more important than the grape variety.

BOTTLE
Chianti used to come in a fat-bottomed bottle, cutely swaddled in a straw basket, called a fiasco. Today, it tends to be packaged in a square-shouldered Bordeaux-style bottle.

RISERVA STATUS
In order to be labeled as a "Riserva," the wine must have aged in the winery's cellar for at least 27 months, but many wineries keep their riservas for longer. These wines tend to be richer and more concentrated than Chianti Classicos, with the added richness that comes from some aging in new oak barriques.

WINE SUBREGION
Chianti Classico was delimited—that is, designated as a special winegrowing zone—in 1716. It's a hilly, verdant subregion of the greater Chianti region.

CASTELLO D'ALBOLA CHIANTI CLASSICO RISERVA

WHY THAT PRICE?

The estate has been planted with the optimal Sangiovese clonal selections (cultivars) that recent research has shown to fare best in Chianti, and the vines are densely planted at 2,000 vines per acre (5,000 / ha), as is practice at the region's top estates. How, then, is this wine so affordable? By Chianti standards, Albola is a huge property, with 388 acres (157 ha) under vine and, it must be added, an additional 1,712 acres (693 ha) devoted to olive trees and overall Tuscan fabulousness. Volume of this sort makes for value. Also, collectors don't go for traditional Chianti Classico when buying the wines of Tuscany. Instead, they invest in Super-Tuscans (heavy Bordeaux-style blends), Brunello di Montalcino and Vino Nobile de Montepulciano. Which leaves the more affordable—and, I might argue, more enjoyable—Chianti Classico for you and me to enjoy.

WHAT FOOD DOES IT GO WITH?

If there is a God, he created Chianti for pasta—it's one of the few wines that doesn't lose its inherent character when paired with a savory-yet-acidic tomato sauce. Perhaps this is due to the fact that Sangiovese, as interpreted by the Tuscan countryside, has notes of balsamic vinegar and basil to it. Due to its greater depth and concentration, Chianti Riserva can stand up to roasted meats and game, especially in the slow-cooked ragù format of Tuscany. But I would serve it alongside any ethnic food with those slow-cooked or roasted flavors: mujaddara and shawarma from the Middle East, for example, or Korean bulgogi. Or, something with a savory gravy, like a good old English shepherd's pie.

Left: A typically idyllic Tuscan landscape, with Castello d'Albola surrounded by vineyards and cyprus and olive trees.

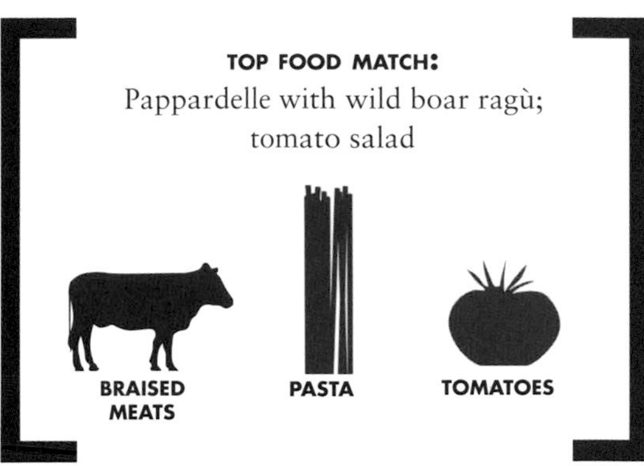

10 OF THE BEST

CHARISMATIC CHIANTI CLASSICOS

FÈLSINA BERARDENGA	\$\$–\$\$\$\$
FONTODI	\$\$–\$\$\$\$
MAZZEI CASTELLO DI FONTERUTOLI	\$\$–\$\$\$\$
TENUTA DI NOZZOLE RISERVA	\$\$–\$\$\$\$
POGGERINO	\$\$–\$\$\$\$
QUERCIABELLA	\$\$–\$\$\$\$
BARONE RICASOLI	\$\$–\$\$\$\$
SAN VINCENTI	\$\$–\$\$\$
SELVAPIANA (CHIANTI RUFINA)	\$–\$\$
CASA SOLA	\$\$

AROUND THE WORLD

SIMILAR STYLE WINES FROM DIFFERENT COUNTRIES

Castagna, La Chiave
Beechworth, Victoria, Australia \$\$\$\$

Elki, Sangiovese
Elqui Valley, Chile \$

Leonetti Cellar, Sangiovese
Walla Walla, Washington, U.S. \$\$\$\$

CHOICE MADE SIMPLE

EXPERT'S PERSONAL FAVORITES

Recommended by Angelo Sabbadin, Wine Director, Le Calandre and Quadri, Padua and Venice, Italy

FRATELLI ALESSANDRIA, SPEZIALE VERDUNO PELAVERGA
(PELAVERGA) PIEDMONT, ITALY $–$$

MARCHESI ANTINORI, BADIA A PASSIGNANO
(SANGIOVESE) CHIANTI CLASSICO RISERVA, TUSCANY, ITALY $$$

CASCINA BRUCIATA, VIGNETI IN RIO SORDO
(DOLCETTO) DOLCETTO D'ALBA, PIEDMONT, ITALY $$

PIETRO CACIORGNA, N'ANTICCHIA
(NERELLO MASCALESE) ETNA, SICILY, ITALY $$$$

ROMANO DOGLIOTTI, MONTEVENERE
(BARBERA) BARBERA D'ASTI SUPERIORE, PIEDMONT, ITALY $$

MASCIARELLI, MARINA CVETIC
(MONTEPULCIANO) MONTEPULCIANO D'ABRUZZO, ABRUZZO, ITALY $$–$$$

FATTORIA LA MASSA, LA MASSA
(SANGIOVESE / MERLOT / CABERNET SAUVIGNON) TUSCANY, ITALY $$–$$$$

PASETTI, TESTAROSSA
(MONTEPULCIANO) MONTEPULCIANO D'ABRUZZO, ABRUZZO, ITALY $$–$$$

TENUTA DELLE TERRE NERE, GUARDIOLA
(NERELLO MASCALESE) ETNA, SICILIA, ITALY $$$–$$$$

I VIGNERI 1435, VINUPETRA
(NERELLO MASCALESE / NERELLO CAPUCCIO / ALICANTE / FRANCISIS) ETNA, SICILY, ITALY $$$–$$$$

WORLD OF FINE WINE RECOMMENDATIONS

CHÂTEAU BRANE-CANTENAC
(CABERNET SAUVIGNON / MERLOT / CABERNET FRANC) MARGAUX, BORDEAUX, FRANCE $$$

CHÂTEAU RAUZAN-SÉGLA
(CABERNET SAUVIGNON / MERLOT / PETIT VERDOT) MARGAUX, BORDEAUX, FRANCE $$$

GIANFRANCO SOLDERA, CASE BASSE (SANGIOVESE)
BRUNELLO DI MONTALCINO, TUSCANY, ITALY $$$$$

FATTORIA LE TERRAZZE, ROSSO CONERO SASSI NERI
(MONTEPULCIANO) MARCHE, ITALY $$

CANTINA DEL NOTAIO, LA FIRMA
(AGLIANICO) BASILICATA, ITALY $$

BRICCO BATTISTA, BARBERA DEL MONFERATO
(BARBERA) PIEDMONT, ITALY $$

LÓPEZ DE HEREDIA, VIÑA TONDONIA RIOJA RESERVA
(TEMPRANILLO / GARNACHA / GRACIANO) RIOJA, SPAIN $$$$

LA RIOJA ALTA, RIOJA GRAN RESERVA 890
(TEMPRANILLO / GRACIANO / MAZUELO) RIOJA, SPAIN $$$$

MORIC, NECKENMARKT ALTE REBEN
(BLAUFRÄNKISCH) BURGENLAND, AUSTRIA $$$

BUSSACO WINES, BUÇACO RESERVA TINTO VINHO DE MESA
(BAGA / TOURIGA NACIONAL) BAIRRADA, PORTUGAL $$$

(*Grape Varieties in Brackets*)

LEFT-FIELD ALTERNATIVES

ARGIOLAS, PERDERA
(MONICA) ISOLA DEI NURAGHI,
SARDINIA, ITALY $–$$

COMM. GB BURLOTTO,
VERDUNO PELAVERGA
(PELAVERGA)
VERDUNO PELAVERGA, PIEDMONT, ITALY $–$$

DOMAINE DU CROS,
LO SANG DEL PAIS
(FER) MARCILLAC, FRANCE $–$$

JOSÉ MARIA DA FONSECA, PERIQUITA
(CASTELÃO) TERRAS DO SADO,
SETUBAL PENINSULA, PORTUGAL $

FORADORI, TEROLDEGO
(TEROLDEGO) VIGNETI DELLE DOLOMITI,
TRENTINO-ALTO ADIGE, ITALY $$

GAI'A, AGIORGITIKO
(AGIORGITIKO)
NEMEA, GREECE $$

TESTALONGA, ROSSESE DI DOLCE ACQUA
(ROSSESE) LIGURIA, ITALY $$$

THYMIOPOULOS, YOUNG VINES
(XYNOMAVRO) NAOUSSA, GREECE $–$$

D VENTURA, VIÑA DO BURATO
(MENCIA)
RIBEIRA SACRA, GALICIA, SPAIN $–$$

TAJINASTE, TINTO TRADITIONAL
(LISTÁN NEGRO) VALLE DE LA OROTAVA
TENERIFE, CANARY ISLANDS, SPAIN $$

BEST ON A BUDGET

ALLEGRINI, PALAZZO DELLA TORRE
(CORVINA / RONDINELLA /
SANGIOVESE)
VERONESE, VENETO, ITALY $$

ALTANO, DOURO RED
(TOURIGA FRANCA / TINTA RORIZ /
TINTA BARROCA)
DOURO, PORTUGAL $–$$

ARGENTO, BONARDA
(BONARDA)
MENDOZA, ARGENTINA $

BOLLA, VALPOLICELLA
(CORVINA / CORVINONE /
RONDINELLA)
VALPOLICELLA, VENETO, ITALY $

CUATRO PASOS
(MENCIA)
BIERZO, CASTILLA Y LEON, SPAIN $–$$

QUINTA DA GARRIDA, SINGLE ESTATE
(TINTA RORIZ / TOURIGA NACIONAL)
DÃO, PORTUGAL $

MORIC, BLAUFRÄNKISCH
(BLAUFRÄNKISCH)
BURGENLAND, AUSTRIA $–$$

PHEASANT'S TEARS, SAPERAVI
(SAPERAVI) KHAKETI, GEORGIA $$

MARCO PORELLO, MOMMIANO
(BARBERA) BARBERA D'ALBA,
PIEDMONT, ITALY $–$$

VIETTI, TRE VIGNE
(DOLCETTO)
ALBA, PIEMONTE, ITALY $$

MASTERCLASS: WHAT IS A "RESERVE"?

We often see the word **reserve** on wine labels and think that it must be a marker of quality. But is it? Confusingly, in New World wine regions, this term has little to no weight. Any winery can wield it, whether it's producing wine by the jug, the box or the bottle. However, it can be a useful marker once you get into the realm of higher end labels. Since my own tastes tend toward wines with a lighter body, higher acidity and less new-wood influence, I usually prefer a New World producer's run-of-the-mill everyday bottling to its "reserve." Which is convenient, because the reserve bottlings tend to cost more.

In the Old World—Italy and Spain, in particular—the good news is that the term is governed by regulations. The bad news is that the regulations differ by region. As we learned at the beginning of this unit, a Chianti Classico Riserva must be released a minimum of two years after the harvest. Basic Chianti Classico allows for more grapes in the blend, a slightly lower alcohol (12% as opposed to 12.5% for a Riserva), and less cellar-aging. And you can apply this basic principle—a little more alcohol, a lot more cellar age—to other styles of Italian wine as well. A Barolo Riserva, for example, must age five years prior to release.

In Spain, the Tempranillo hotbeds of Rioja and Ribera del Duero apply multiple reserve-style designations in stairsteps. A label that doesn't state anything other than the region is most likely a ***joven***, or a young wine, that's seen little to no oak, unless it mentions the word *barrica* (barrique), in which case some barrel-aging has happened. If the wine was in barrel for at least a year, with an additional year of bottle-age, it's labeled a ***Crianza***, meaning it's had some "breeding" or "education" (I love that). A ***Reserva*** has aged at least a year in oak and another two years in bottle. And a ***Gran Reserva*** has spent a minimum of two years in barrel and another three in bottle. That's something like a graduate-school degree.

However, don't assume that a Spanish Gran Reserva is going to be as powerful and concentrated as a "reserve" from a New World trophy producer. *Au contraire*: Spanish bodegas traditionally use older, mellower, American oak casks (as distinct from new French barriques), making for Reservas and Gran Reservas that are subtly spicy, brownish in color and taste more of dried leaves and earth than bold fruit. But that practice is changing as more Spanish producers begin to use new barriques as part or all of their oak regime, making contemporary Spanish Reservas more and more like New World "reserves."

HOW TO IDENTIFY THESE ELEMENTS

1: When you see the word "Riserva" or "Reserva" on an Italian or Spanish wine label, you can infer that the wine has aged in barrel and bottle prior to release. (When you think about it, the word "reserve" means "hold back," after all.) So don't be deterred by that older vintage date; if a winery can afford to hold a wine for years prior to release, it will normally be a sign of quality.

2: The term "Reserve" isn't regulated in New World winegrowing regions. As a rule of thumb, however, if you aren't a fan of concentrated fruit and heavy oak, you'll probably be wasting your money on a bottle labeled "Reserve."

A SPANISH WINE LABEL
WINE COLOR
Tinto simply means red, and while it also appears on other wine labels, it is not normally as prominent as it is here.
WINE NAME
Janus is a proprietary name, or a special name the winemaker has given to this particular bottling to differentiate it from others like it. Winemaker Alejandro Fernández planted the Ribera del Duero's first modern vineyard, the gravelly Viña Alta, in 1972. In exceptional vintages, Fernandez bottles the fruit from this property as Janus, named after the Roman god. The most recent Janus was released in 2003.
PRODUCER NAME
Elaborado y embotellado por means "produced and bottled by"; verbiage like this is quite helpful in Europe, where wineries and bodegas tend to predate their current owners, and thus bear different names. For example, Pesquera is named after the village of Pesquera del Duero rather than the vintner, Alejandro Fernández. But you might be surprised by how many wines (particularly inexpensive ones) are produced by contract, by a second winery. Look at the fine print to find out who really made the wine.
GRAN RESERVA STATUS
Since this is a Gran Reserva from Ribera del Duero, we can infer that the wine aged in barrel for at least two years (this wine actually barrel-aged for three years) and in bottle for an additional three years.
WINE REGION
Ribera del Duero is a winegrowing region in north-central Spain, slightly southwest of Rioja and Navarra. The Duero River is known as the Douro River in Portugal, where it also runs through an important wine region.
APPELLATION
The words Denomenación de Origen, or DO for short, indicate that Ribera del Duero is a quality winegrowing region, or controlled appellation. Most winegrowing nations regulate the use of geographic terms on wine labels to prevent fraud and ensure quality.
TINTO
PESQUERA
JANUS GRAN RESERVA
RIBERA DEL DUERO

MASTERCLASS: 5 WINES TO BUY

Here's a chance to try one grape—Tempranillo—at five different levels. We'll start with basic bottlings. I've sourced these suggestions from three different appellations, so if you're on a tight budget, you can just compare these three against one another. Then I've stuck with Rioja and Ribera del Duero for the rest. (Of course, you could ask your wine merchant to special-order the *joven*, Crianza, Reserva and Gran Reserva all from the same producer.) Finally, there are the cult wines that, like the Super-Tuscans in Chianti, fall outside any official category. How does a modern collector's wine compare with a Gran Reserva, in your opinion?

FAUSTINO VII
(Tempranillo / Garnacha) Rioja, Spain $

ALTERNATIVE CHOICES
RAMÓN ROQUETA
(Tempranillo) Catalonia, Spain $

CAMPOS REALES
(Tempranillo) La Mancha, Spain $

LA RIOJA ALTA
GRAN RESERVA 904
(Tempranillo / Graciano) Rioja, Spain $$$–$$$$

ALTERNATIVE CHOICES
MARQUÉS DE RISCAL GRAN RESERVA
(Tempranillo / Graciano / Mazuelo)
Rioja, Spain $$–$$$

BARÓN DE LEY GRAN RESERVA
(Tempranillo / Graciano / Mazuelo)
Rioja, Spain $$–$$$

IZADI CRIANZA
(Tempranillo) Rioja, Spain $–$$

ALTERNATIVE CHOICES
LAN CRIANZA
(Tempranillo) Rioja, Spain $

BODEGAS PALACIO GLORIOSO CRIANZA
(Tempranillo) Rioja, Spain $

DOMINIO DE PINGUS PINGUS
(Tempranillo) Ribera del Duero, Spain $$$$$

ALTERNATIVE CHOICES
BODEGAS RODA CIRSION
(Tempranillo) Rioja, Spain $$$$$

SIERRA CANTABRIA FINCA EL BOSQUE
(Tempranillo) Rioja, Spain $$$$–$$$$$

MUGA RESERVA
(Tempranillo / Garnacha / Mazuelo / Graciano)
Rioja, Spain $$–$$$

ALTERNATIVE CHOICES
BERONIA RESERVA
(Tempranillo / Mazuelo / Graciano)
Rioja, Spain $$

CVNE RESERVA
(Tempranillo / Garnacha / Mazuelo / Graciano)
Rioja, Spain $–$$

HOW TO SERVE IT

Here's a dilemma: These wines are best appreciated in order, from the simplest to the most complex. But you're going to be spending the big bucks on bottle number five, so insist that your guests taste and spit (you can provide paper cups for this) as they work through the lineup, so that their senses aren't clouded by the time they get to the last wine. Also, I'd recommend decanting this last bruiser. It's a big one and could use some air.

HOW TO TALK ABOUT IT

We've learned the differences between the basic *joven* bottling, the Crianza and the Reservas: oak aging. Now for the last category: These wines may have only aged as long as a Crianza, but in small new French oak barriques instead of older American oak barrels. So you'll find them to be opulent, with deep fruit and smoky wood notes, which you can describe as markers of "modern" or "international"-style winemaking.

AROMATIC AND SENSORY CLUES

The *jovens* have quaffable notes of fresh strawberry, blueberry and blackberry; added to this, Crianzas have an overlay of vanilla and sweet spice. The Reservas should show more depth, with cinnamon, nutmeg, red roses, dark chocolate and rhubarb rather than overt fruit. The Gran Reservas will show their age with notes of dried leaves, cigars, tea leaves and worn leather. Expect an inky-black color, high alcohol and mouth-coating richness from the cult labels.

FOOD MATCHES

Here's your chance to stock up on those fun Spanish crackers that you're always eyeing at the gourmet grocery. Specifically, *picos*, those pinky-finger-shaped olive-oil-infused breadsticks, and round, crisp *tortas de aceite*. Serve them with an olive dip. If you'd like to plan a dinner around these wines, I'd suggest roasted lamb or, for more of a casual, eat-on-your feet kind of party, Mexican tacos (do them right, with good *queso fresco* and fresh corn tortillas).

MASTERCLASS: WHAT'S TRENDING?
IN WITH THE OLD, OUT WITH THE NEW?

MODERNISTS VS. CLASSICISTS

As we deepen our appreciation of wine, we come to realize that—as is so often the case in life—wine lovers fall into three camps. There are the steadfast traditionalists, and there are the modernists. And then there are those of us who fall somewhere in between. (It all depends on what we're thirsty for, and who's paying.) In Rioja and Chianti, two regions we've looked at closely in this unit, this stylistic push-and-pull is in full evidence. There are those who follow the rules, producing Chianti Classico or Rioja Reserva as generations before them did. And then there are those who break the mold. This latter group doesn't have a name in Spain, but in Tuscany, their wines are called, rather heroically, Super-Tuscans.

The modernists eschew tradition—grape varieties and aging requirements codified by regional bureaucracies—in favor of bold statement. They prune their vines down so that each grape's juice will be thick with concentration. They put their wines into new French barriques, accessorizing them with the sheen of caramel and smoke. And some use equipment in the cellar to further **extract**, or condense, their wines. All of this is shocking to the traditionalists. But it depends on which side of the coin you're looking at. Like Marcel Duchamp's *Nude Descending a Staircase, No. 2*, a modernist expression is a recognizable, yet unrecognizable, reconfiguration of what you assumed to be true. The question for you as a consumer is: Do you love the modern style? Or hate it? And, perhaps more to the point, can you afford it?

THE POINTS PROBLEM

Why can't you afford the modern style? Well, in large part because over the past two to three decades, a few very powerful wine critics have taken a shining to it. And, although this is a sweeping generalization, the fact remains that powerful, concentrated wines, treated with plenty of new French oak, tend to score very well among reviewers who use the revered-and-feared **100-point scale**. You've seen it in wine shops, web sites and magazines: This wine gets a 95, while the one next to it only comes in at 88. For as long as I've been writing about wine, I've heard winemakers moan, complain, tear their hair out—and, occasionally, gloat—over these apparently arbitrary numbers.

As a budding wine aficionado, you should be aware of a few things. First, a wine that scores well with the critics is going to cost more, due to the simple rule of supply and demand. Second, each critic comes to the tasting table with his or her own sense of what makes the ideal wine, and your palate might not be in alignment. The numerical scores are still useful to you, however, even if you're not looking to be sucker-punched in the solar plexus with a plank of berry-slathered oak. Read all the wine criticism you can, and follow the writer whose palate is in closest alignment with your own.

TALKING TANNINS

A key concept to wrap your mind around is **tannins**. I mentioned this term at the beginning of this unit in my explanation of structure. Remember? Structure is built from fruit, acidity and tannin. But what is tannin, exactly? If fruit is the meat of the wine, and acidity is the skeleton, tannins are the muscle and gristle—the chewy, mouth-coating stuff that makes big, burly reds so unapproachable in their youth, and so needy of decanting. And they're something that wine critics have a lot of experience with. For those of us sipping casually, excessive tannins can feel like a Spanish Inquisition torture. But a seasoned reviewer can get that same gravel-and-cotton ball sensation and declare, "This wine will be delicious after 30 years of cellar age!"

Semi-porous oak barrels can soften tannins, but smoky new barriques also can add further woody tannins to a wine. So oak and tannin often work hand-in-hand. The bottom line: If tannins turn you off, get your hands on some older wines. Many wine shops and restaurants hold special tastings of **verticals**—that is, a series of ascending vintages from a single producer. That famous Barolo or Barbaresco may be difficult to tolerate upon release, but once you've tried the same bottling after a couple of decades of cellar age, you'll begin to understand what structure is all about. The tannins that were so unapproachable in youth hold the wine up with age, when it will release its perfume of dried roses and make you want to weep silently while listening to Kiri te Kanawa's rendition of *O mio babbino caro*.

WHAT IS TERROIR?

You may have noticed the term **terroir** in discussions of wine, and in this book. But what is terroir, exactly? It's a concept that gets to the heart of the question, "What is winemaking?" Here's why: The best winemakers claim not to have created what's in the bottle. "The terroir was always there, in the soil, in the vineyard," they say. "The wine is simply a conductor of the terroir." OK. So terroir is a statement made by a site. And wine is the mouthpiece for that statement. Of course, the winemaker who avers simply to be translating terroir is like the artist who describes painting as an act of channeling, rather than creating; or the novelist who claims that "the characters simply speak to me." And yet they happily take credit for their work, don't they?

But I do believe in terroir. When I taste a Pinot Noir from Oregon's Willamette Valley, I think of that Philip Larkin line, "Earth's immeasurable surprise": chanterelles! loganberries! marionberries! nettles! red soil! and Douglas fir! How did those distinctly Oregonian aromas get into that bottle? In the previous WHAT'S TRENDING, we discussed the idea that the more naturally the vineyard is farmed, the more terroir is translated into the wine. The traditionalists—or terroiristes—feel the same way about winemaking. The more natural the vinification process, they argue, the more evident the terroir in the wine. They claim that modern winemaking calls for so much manipulation (new oak barrels and equipment that concentrates flavor) that the terroir is lost.

RECOMMENDED READING

Elin McCoy, *The Emperor of Wine: The Rise of Robert M. Parker, Jr. and the Reign of American Taste* (Harper Perennial)

In discussions of points scores, traditional versus modern winemaking and the "international style," one name tends to crop up again and again: that of Robert Parker, founder of the American newsletter *The Wine Advocate*. While Parker's era is nearly over (he's sold control of his business to investors), an understanding of the contemporary wine market is incomplete without McCoy's thoughtful biography of Parker. Criticism is dead. Long live the critics.

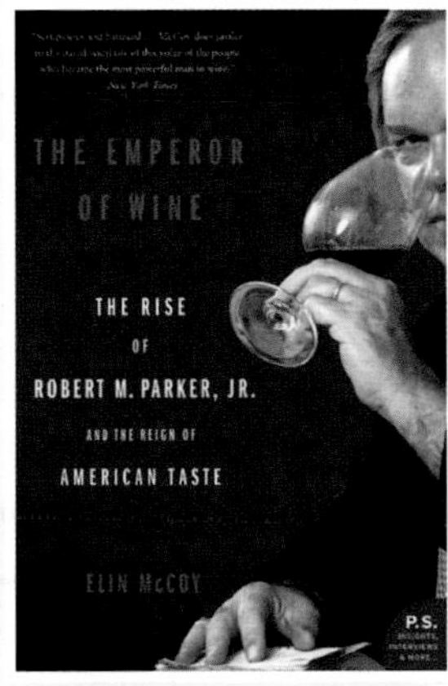

YOUR ROLE

As you begin to get hooked on wine appreciation, you'll start spending more and more time reading wine publications, participating in newsgroups, following blogs and catching the vinous conversations that happen over twitter and facebook. With time, you'll see that the oenophilic world is a democracy, percolating with contrasting philosophies and competing interests. And you'll see where the lines are drawn. On newsgroups and in magazines' comment sections, you'll find the everyday enthusiasts lined up against the collectors ("They're driving prices up!").

You'll also find the traditionalists railing against the modernists ("That isn't wine! It's blackberry-flavored lighter fluid!"). And the promoters of family wineries complaining about the power of the corporate conglomerates ("They're creating monopolies! It's unfair!"). And the small importers aligned against the large distributors. In this democracy, you have a vote. And no, you don't have to start a wine blog or to tweet outrageous statements in order to participate. Just take the time to try every style of wine in this book. Then, revisit your favorites. Use your pocketbook and your palate to support the sort of winegrowing you believe in.

9 RICH, FULL-BODIED REDS

9 RICH, FULL-BODIED REDS

Are you tough enough to handle the biggest, baddest wines on the planet? Because the rich, full-bodied reds require bravado. They are the vinous equivalents to riding an old horse across the desert, with a hunk of beef jerky in one cheek and a plug of tobacco in the other. They smell like cigars, worn leather and blood, and taste like a face full of gravel. (See: Aglianico, Cabernet Sauvignon, Malbec, Nebbiolo, Petite Sirah, Syrah and Tannat.)

But wait! We're also in the realm of the preposterously plush and the sinfully syrupy. The chocolate truffle with the Chambord center, and a triple mochaccino on the side. In satin skirts and beribboned bustiers, these reds are the harlots on the cowboy's arm. (See: Caménère, Merlot, Pinotage, Zinfandel. And Shiraz, which is the same thing as Syrah, but isn't, somehow.)

Flamboyant flavors call for equally robust food matches. Cowboy dishes like Texas chili, a charred buffalo burger or pan-fried venison all stand up to the strength of these wines. Also, dishes that incorporate layers of smoke and spice, like lamb *tagine* or New Orleans *jambalaya*, underscore the fruit and nuance. And if you want to keep sipping them all the way through the dessert course, skip the cheese tray and go for sweets flavored with maple, coffee or bitter dark chocolate.

Three factors unify the powerhouse reds: Alcohol, concentration of fruit and, increasingly, maturation in new-oak barrels. And where those three factors exist, so, too, do the collectors, critics and futures markets. If you're the competitive type, you'll thrive among the chest-beating big spenders and the fiercely focused number crunchers.

But if you aren't, don't sweat it. There are bargains burrowed among the simple, unadorned Malbecs, the rustic Primitivos and the curious Carignans. And, depending on the climate of the wine region and the whim of the winemaker, the biggest and baddest red varietals can come out smelling and tasting surprisingly restrained and nuanced. Even the roughest, toughest Syrah can be subdued into something a lovesick cowboy poet could croon about.

So, don't just sit there. Saddle up.

YOU'LL ENJOY THESE WINES IF...

- You go for the intense flavors of dark chocolate, red meat and black coffee
- You enjoy a juicy, charred steak
- You're a points person who's into fantasy football

WHAT THE EXPERTS SAY

"Full-bodied reds always conjure up images of gatherings and mouthwateringly rich dishes for me. There is something nurturing about powerful, deep red wines that give a sense of fulfillment. I enjoy pairing these wines with braised meats, roast goose, lamb or aged hard cheeses. Whether it's an aromatically dense Syrah-driven wine from the Rhône Valley, or an intellectually challenging Sagrantino, these bold wines beg for equally flavorful foods to bring balance to weight."

Yvonne Cheung, Chef Sommelier, the Upper House and Café Gray Deluxe, Hong Kong

GOOD TO DRINK WITH

KEY

$	UNDER $15	**$$$$**	$50–100
$$	$15–30	**$$$$$**	$100+
$$$	$30–50		

THE NAMES TO LOOK FOR

MALBEC MENDOZA, ARGENTINA

Every bottle of Cahors, the Malbec of South West France, must be followed by a thorough tongue-scraping and an appointment with one's therapist. ("Why do I torture myself?") And then along comes Argentine Malbec: plush, velvety, coffee-tinged in all the right places. It's like licorice-scented, plum-flavored Zoloft, with fewer side effects.

[**PRICE RANGE: $-$$$$$**]

[**ABV: 12.5–15%**]

[**DRINK IT: 3–20 YEARS AFTER THE VINTAGE**]

CHOICE

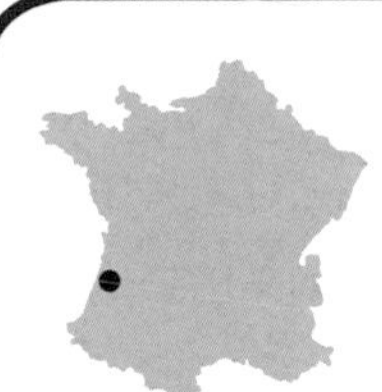

MERLOT BORDEAUX, FRANCE

To know rapture is to know the three Ps: Pomerol (the AOC), and Pétrus and Le Pin (the châteaux). Black cherries, red rose petals and a dusting of dark chocolate make these the sorts of wines grown men cry over—either because they cost thousands, or because they're that good. Oh, and Ornellaia's Masseto, made in Tuscany, ain't bad, either.

[**PRICE RANGE: $$$-$$$$$**]

[**ABV: 12.5–15%**]

[**DRINK IT: 10–60 YEARS AFTER THE VINTAGE**]

NEBBIOLO BAROLO AND BARBARESCO, PIEDMONT, ITALY

Nebbiolo is not for the impatient. Open Barolo too soon, and you'll face a wall of tannin so impenetrable that you'll never get to the wine inside. So put it in your cellar and sit on your hands for a decade. Or more. Until the door opens, and you can enter this mysterious place of dried rose petals, violets, figs, old leather, black tea and tobacco.

[**PRICE RANGE: $$-$$$$$**]

[**ABV: 13.5–14.5%**]

[**DRINK IT: 8–30 YEARS AFTER THE VINTAGE**]

SHIRAZ SOUTH AUSTRALIA, AUSTRALIA

In South Australia, the center of the action is the Barossa Valley, whence cometh the renowned Penfold's Grange, apex of the genre. In place of the gritty, spit-roasted pork notes of Syrah from France's Rhône Valley, Aussie Shiraz gushes purply-black gobs of blackberries and licorice, cracked pepper and mocha. Qué shiraz, shiraz.

[**PRICE RANGE: $-$$$$$**]

[**ABV: 13.5–15.5%**]

[**DRINK IT: 2–20 YEARS AFTER THE VINTAGE**]

CABERNET SAUVIGNON CENTRAL VALLEY, CHILE

Chile's winemaking tradition spans more than 450 years, but only over the past three decades has this Andean and antipodean nation emerged as the Second Coming of Bordeaux. Merlot thrives; Malbec is on the rise; long-lost Carménère has been born again; and Cabernet Sauvignon reigns supreme, with Old-World-funded status labels rocking the market.

[**PRICE RANGE: $-$$$$$**]

[**ABV: 12.5–14.5%**]

[**DRINK IT: 3–20 YEARS AFTER THE VINTAGE**]

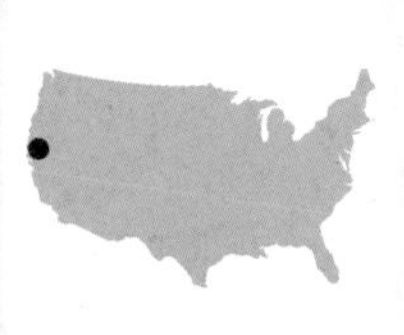

ZINFANDEL DRY CREEK VALLEY, SONOMA, CALIFORNIA, U.S.

The Gold Rush brought fortune-seekers to California in the mid-1800s, and with them, the cuttings (related to Italy's Primativo) that remain today as gnarled old vines. End result: Jammy, spicy wines that don't bat an eyelash at alcohol levels unthinkable in other varietals. Serve them with turkey, pork or goose. Golden egg optional.

[**PRICE RANGE: $-$$$$**]

[**ABV: 14–16%**]

[**DRINK IT: 8–30 YEARS AFTER THE VINTAGE**]

TAKE ONE WINE: ZUCCARDI Q MENDOZA MALBEC

THE BASICS

GRAPE VARIETY: Malbec

REGION: Mendoza, Argentina

ALCOHOL LEVEL: 14.5%

PRICE: $$

AVAILABILITY: Widely available

APPEARANCE: Inky, black-tinted red with purple undertones.

TASTING NOTE: Gravel, coffee, dark chocolate, leather, cayenne pepper and black olive, with vibrant acidity at the finish.

FOOD MATCH: Mole sauce, sweetbreads, braised red cabbage, rosemary-crusted lamb.

DRINK OR KEEP: Aerate this big wine in a decanter and drink now, or, keep 5 to 10 years after the vintage date.

WHY DOES IT TASTE THAT WAY?

Back in 1853, when it was one of Bordeaux's most prominent grapes, a French soil scientist planted Malbec in Mendoza, Argentina. A few years later, a pernicious root louse called phylloxera wiped out most of France's vineyards. The only way to hold off this menace was to graft the noble grape varieties onto phylloxera-resistant American rootstock; Malbec, sadly, didn't fare well on the rootstock. The Malbec story could have ended there, except that Argentina's sandy soils and dry climate have kept phylloxera at bay. Here, the variety thrives on its own roots, making wines of heady alcohol levels, invigorating acidity, forceful fruit and crackling spice. In its native France, Malbec is today the fifth wheel in Bordeaux—after Cabernet Sauvignon, Merlot, Cabernet Franc and Petit Verdot—and the inky-black, rather one-dimensional grape of Cahors. But in Argentina, it gives us a taste of the past while exemplifying modernity in winemaking.

WHO MADE IT?

Like the famous tango composer Ástor Piazzolla—and nearly half the population of Argentina—the Zuccardi family is of Italian descent. Engineer Alberto Zuccardi got into winegrowing in the early 1960s, developing his own irrigation system and designing a trellising method that creates a canopy of leaves, protecting the grapes from the unrelenting sunlight that the high-altitude desert of Mendoza gets an astounding 330 days per year. Over the years, the winery has built a reputation for inexpensive brands like Santa Julia and Fuzion, and experimenting with unusual grape varieties. Today, third-generation vineyard manager Sebastián Zuccardi oversees the Zuccardi label, sourcing fruit from ultra-high-elevation vineyards at 3,215 to 3,550 feet (or 980 to 1,080 m) above sea level. Winemaker Rubén Ruffo allows the Q Malbec to ferment spontaneously, from indigenous yeasts, making for a complex and relatively restrained style.

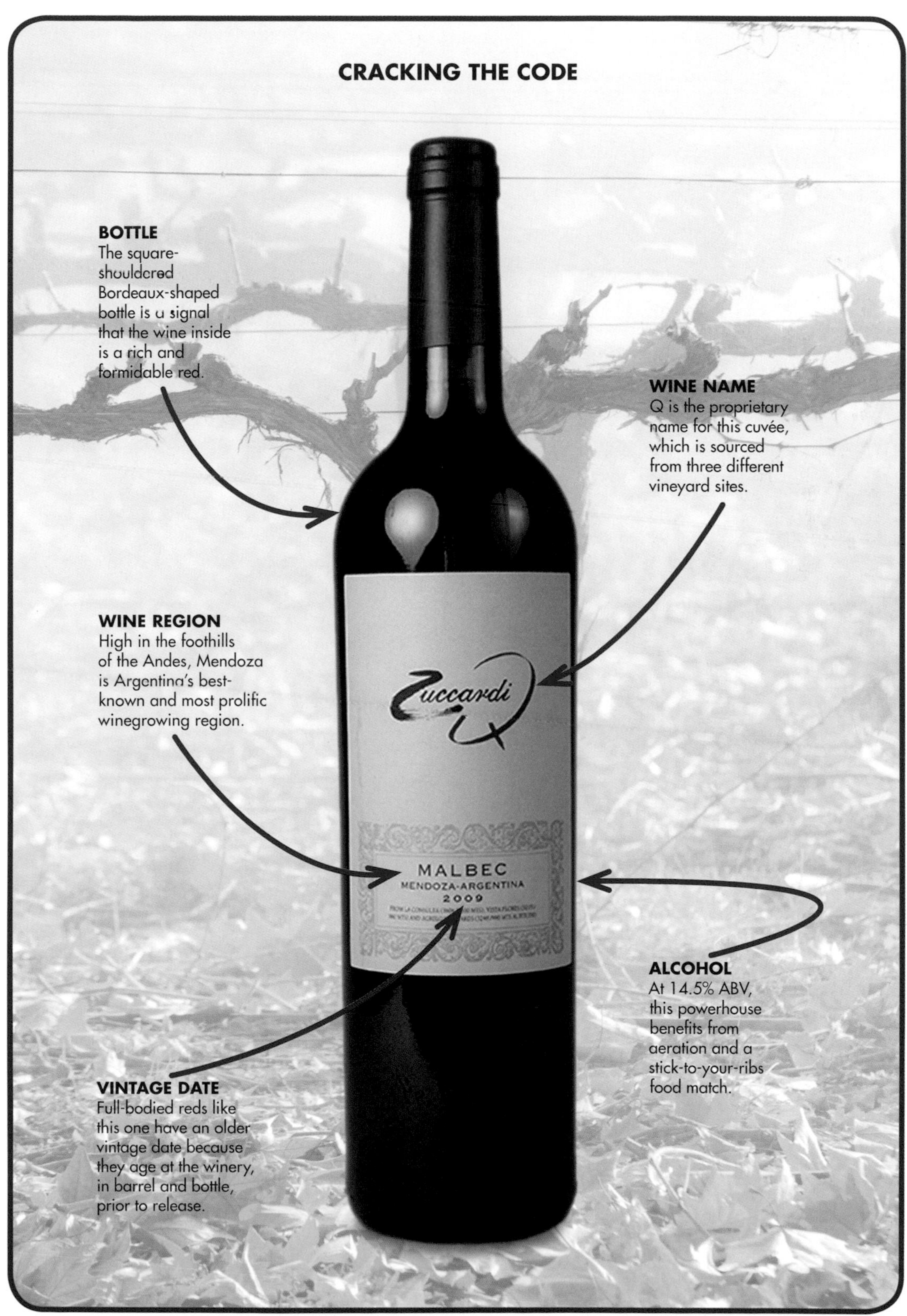
CRACKING THE CODE
BOTTLE
The square-shouldered Bordeaux-shaped bottle is a signal that the wine inside is a rich and formidable red.
WINE NAME
Q is the proprietary name for this cuvée, which is sourced from three different vineyard sites.
WINE REGION
High in the foothills of the Andes, Mendoza is Argentina's best-known and most prolific winegrowing region.
Zuccardi
Q
MALBEC
MENDOZA-ARGENTINA
2009
ALCOHOL
At 14.5% ABV, this powerhouse benefits from aeration and a stick-to-your-ribs food match.
VINTAGE DATE
Full-bodied reds like this one have an older vintage date because they age at the winery, in barrel and bottle, prior to release.

ZUCCARDI Q MENDOZA MALBEC

WHY THAT PRICE?

Like a fashionista who wears a Gap T-shirt with Stella McCartney trousers, Argentine Malbec manages to occupy both the high and the low with equal ease and panache. On the one hand, it's an extraordinary everyday value, which can satisfy the most discerning palate for less than $15. (Some lower end labels, like Alamos, Caro or Terrazas de los Andes, are so good that you can fool dinner guests by decanting them and pretending you paid three times as much as you did.) On the other hand are the collectors' wines, many funded by foreign investors from Old-World winegrowing regions, and costing as much as premium releases from Bordeaux or the Napa Valley. The third-largest exporter of wines from Argentina, the Zuccardi family, keeps the Q label in the middle ground, offering refinement and power at an every-night affordable price.

WHAT FOOD DOES IT GO WITH?

The natural match for Argentine Malbec is *churrascuria* cuisine: Meat (and, in some cases, vegetables) on skewers, charred over an open fire and served with fried potatoes. Apart from the obvious cultural connection, this works for two reasons: First, big, bold, red wines work best with hearty foods that can stand up to them. Second, the smoky aromas imparted by oak barrel aging match well with foods that have been grilled or charred. Just don't forget to spice up your meat-and-potatoes plan: Cracked black pepper, chile peppers and aromatic spices all agree with the velvety mouthfeel of rich reds like this one.

TOP FOOD MATCH: Grilled *chimichurri* skirt steak with fried sweet potatoes and charred bell peppers

BARBECUE | **GRILLED EGGPLANT** | **CHOCOLATE MOCHA CAKE**

Left: A Mendoza vineyard against the backdrop of Aconcagua, the highest mountain in the Americas.

10 OF THE BEST

BANG-FOR-THE-BUCK ARGENTINE MALBECS

ALAMOS	$
BODEGA COLOMÉ	$$
CAMPO NEGRO	$
DURIGUTTI	$
GOUGUENHEIM	$
IQUE	$
LUCA	$$
NÓMADE	$–$$
SEPTIMA	$
TRUMPETER	$

AROUND THE WORLD

SIMILAR STYLE WINES FROM DIFFERENT COUNTRIES

Bleasdale, Second Innings, Malbec
Langhorne Creek,
South Australia, Australia $$

Montes, Classic Series Malbec
Colchagua Valley, Chile $

Château Lagrézette
(Malbec) Cahors, France $–$$

CHOICE MADE SIMPLE

EXPERT'S PERSONAL FAVORITES

Recommended by Luca Gardini, Wine Director, Antica Osteria del Ponte, Milan, Italy & Acquarello, Mexico City, Mexico

ARNALDO CAPRAI, 25 ANNI
(SAGRANTINO)
MONTEFALCO, UMBRIA, ITALY
$$$$

ACHÁVAL FERRER,
FINCA ALTAMIRA LA CONSULTA
(MALBEC)
MENDOZA, ARGENTINA $$$$

FERRUCCIO CARLOTTO,
DI ORA IN ORA
(LAGREIN)
ALTO ADIGE, ITALY $$

GIANFRANCO FINO, ES
(PRIMITIVO)
MANDURIA, PUGLIA, ITALY
$$$–$$$$

KANONKOP
(PINOTAGE)
STELLENBOSCH,
SOUTH AFRICA $$–$$$

MASCARELLO, MONPRIVATO
CÀ D'MORISSIO RISERVA
(NEBBIOLO)
BAROLO, PIEDMONT, ITALY $$$$$

MASTROBERARDINO,
RADICI RISERVA
(AGLIANICO)
TAURASI, CAMPANIA, ITALY $$$

TENUTA DELL'ORNELLAIA,
MASSETO
(MERLOT)
TUSCANY, ITALY $$$$$

SCREAMING EAGLE
(CABERNET SAUVIGNON)
NAPA VALLEY, CALIFORNIA, U.S.
$$$$$

CONCHA Y TORRO, TERRUNYO
BLOCK 27 PEUMO VINEYARD
(CARMENÈRE)
CACHAPOAL VALLEY, CHILE $$–$$$

WORLD OF FINE WINE RECOMMENDATIONS

CHÂTEAU L'EGLISE-CLINET,
(MERLOT / CABERNET FRANC)
POMEROL, BORDEAUX, FRANCE
$$$$

CHÂTEAU RAYAS,
CHÂTEAUNEUF-DU-PAPE
(GRENACHE)
RHÔNE, FRANCE $$$$

DOMAINE DE TRÉVALLON
(CABERNET SAUVIGNON / SYRAH)
PROVENCE, FRANCE $$$$

GIACOMO CONTERNO,
BAROLO MONFORTINO
(NEBBIOLO)
PIEDMONT, ITALY $$$$$

TENUTA SAN LEONARDO,
TERRE DI SAN LEONARDO
(CABERNET SAUVIGNON / MERLOT)
TRENTINO, ITALY $$$

ROMANO DAL FORNO, AMARONE
DELLA VALPOLICELLA (CORVINA /
RONDINELLA / CROATINA /
OSELETA) VENETO, ITALY $$$$$

ÁLVARO PALACIOS,
L'ERMITA
(GARNACHA)
PRIORAT, SPAIN $$$$$

NIEPOORT, BATUTA
(TINTA AMARELA / TOURIGA FRANCA /
TINTA RORIZ / RUFETE / MALVAZIA
PRETA) DOURO, PORTUGAL $$$$

SADIE FAMILY WINES,
COLUMELLA
(SHIRAZ / MOURVÈDRE)
SWARTLAND, SOUTH AFRICA $$$$

PENFOLDS GRANGE
(SHIRAZ / CABERNET SAUVIGNON)
SOUTH AUSTRALIA, AUSTRALIA
$$$$$

(Grape Varieties in Brackets)

VERSATILE FOOD WINES

THIERRY ALLEMAND, CORNAS REYNARD
(SYRAH) RHÔNE, FRANCE $$$$–$$$$$

D'ARENBURG, THE DEAD ARM SHIRAZ
MCLAREN VALE, AUSTRALIA $$$

BOUZA, TANNAT
MONTEVIDEO, URUGUAY $$

CLOS LA COUTALE
(MALBEC) CAHORS, FRANCE $–$$

FATALONE, TERES
(PRIMITIVO) PUGLIA, ITALY $$

DOMAINE FAURY, VIN DE PAYS
(SYRAH) COLLINES RHODANIENNES, FRANCE $$

MAS DE GOURGONNIER
(CABERNET SAUVIGNON / GRENACHE / SYRAH / CARIGNAN) LES BAUX DE PROVENCE, PROVENCE, FRANCE $–$$

TENUTA CITA ASINARI DEI MARCHESI DI GRÉSY, MARTINENGA
(NEBBIOLO) BARBARESCO, PIEDMONT, ITALY $$$–$$$$

CHÂTEAU MONTUS, CUVÉE PRESTIGE
(TANNAT) MADIRAN, FRANCE $$$–$$$$

CHÂTEAU LE PUY, BARTHÉLEMY
(MERLOT / CABERNET SAUVIGNON) BORDEAUX, FRANCE $$$$–$$$$$

BEST ON A BUDGET

BODEGAS CARCHELO, C
(MONASTRELL / TEMPRANILLO / CABERNET SAUVIGNON)
JUMILLA, MURCIA, SPAIN $

CYCLES, GLADIATOR
(CABERNET SAUVIGNON)
CENTRAL COAST, CALIFORNIA, U.S. $

DRY CREEK VINEYARD, HERITAGE ZINFANDEL
SONOMA COUNTY, CALIFORNIA, U.S. $–$$

EMILIANA
(CARMÉNÈRE)
CENTRAL VALLEY, CHILE $

PETER LEHMANN, ART'N'SOUL
(SHIRAZ / CABERNET SAUVIGNON)
BAROSSA VALLEY, AUSTRALIA $

BODEGAS OLIVARES, ALTOS DE LA HOYA FINCA HOYA DE SANTA ANA
(MONASTRELL / GARNACHA)
JUMILLA, MURCIA, SPAIN $

CHÂTEAU ROUSTAING RÉSERVE VIEILLES VIGNES (CABERNET FRANC / CABERNET SAUVIGNON / MERLOT) BORDEAUX, FRANCE $

VALDIBELLA, KERASOS
(NERO D'AVOLA)
SICILY, ITALY $

VINUM CELLARS PETITE SIRAH
CLARKSBURG, CALIFORNIA, U.S. $

CHÂTEAU PINERAIE
(MALBEC / MERLOT)
CAHORS, FRANCE $

MASTERCLASS: ON OAK AND MODERNITY

Depending on whom you're speaking with, oak barrels are as traditional as church on Sunday, or as shocking and new as, well, *The Shock of the New.* Was. In 1980... For centuries, oak barrels were used to transport almost any product traveling more than a few miles. Waterproof and easy to roll, barrels carried everything from dried grains to gunpowder. The original wine barrel—called **puncheon, pipe** (Portugal), **butt, tun** or ***botti*** (Italy)—held anywhere from 84 to more than 250 gallons. That's enough wine to house the whale from *Free Willy*, so the oak didn't have much effect on the fluid inside.

But then came globalism. Winemakers from all over the world traveled to France and saw that small barrels, called **barriques**, were good for more than storage. Gently toasted by expert ***tonneliers***, or barrel-makers, over a flame, they could impart caramel aromas and spicy notes to wine.

Today's vintner thinks of oak as an ingredient, trying out **cooperage** (barrels) from France, the U.S., Russia, Hungary, Chile and elsewhere, to find the ideal match for his or her winemaking style. Then there's the matter of identifying which particular forest is the best source of wood, and which **toast level**, from light to heavy, is optimal.

Nowhere is oak more evident, or controversial, than in the richest red wines. A toasty oak barrel can take a Syrah, Merlot or Cabernet Sauvignon over the edge into a state of chocolate, vanilla and caramel-coated decadence. But if these flavors don't float your boat, don't swear off barriques altogether, because they perform other functions, as well: The transpiration of oxygen through the microscopic pores in the wood softens the aromatics and tannins, allowing the wine to evolve gently.

Over the years, I've found that I love the smooth mouthfeel and nutmeg notes that barriques can impart, but I'm not a fan of smoky s'more aromas and flavors. (I apologize here to any readers who may not have experienced a s'more. It's a marshmallow that has been blackened over a campfire and smashed with a square of chocolate between two graham crackers.) And so I've learned to look for wines aged in **air-dried** and/or **neutral oak**, and for ***tonneaux*** barrels, which are twice the size of barriques.

Air-dried barrels are made from staves that have sat outside to weather before being shaped; neutral barrels have already been used for three or four years, and no longer impart overtly smoky or woody aromas. I also like **light toast**—that is, barrels made from staves that have been warmed gently, as you might brown pine nuts in a frying pan, rather than charred. Ask your sommelier or wine merchant to help you to taste wines made using a variety of cooperage techniques. You might find that you're a fan of toasty new oak, lightly toasted oak, neutral oak or no oak at all.

HOW TO IDENTIFY THESE ELEMENTS

1: Oak barrels are expensive. If the wine was cheap, and it smells offensively of oak, you're probably dealing with a case of **oak chips** or **staves**, which have been dunked unceremoniously into a tank of wine, solely for aroma and flavor.

2: Pricier bottlings are generally those that see more **new French oak**. If you aren't a fan of woody aromas and flavors, you might actually prefer a less expensive wine that has aged in older, less toasty barrels. Tell your sommelier or wine merchant that you prefer wines that have been aged in **neutral oak**.

3: French oak brings savory and brambly notes to wine, while **American oak** imparts vanilla and spice. Slow warming over low heat produces cedar, clove and cinnamon notes, while rapid roasting over high heat produces sappy, butterscotch-slathered campfire flavors. Which do you prefer?

OLD AND NEW IN THE CELLAR

Tenute Cisa Asinari dei Marchesi di Grésy is a historic winery in Piedmont, Italy, owned by Alberto di Grésy, the descendent of a Marquis. While he honors the traditions of the Barbaresco region, di Grésy also uses modern winemaking techniques in his cellar. For some of his wines, the crushed red grapes sit in stainless-steel fermentation tanks for up to 35 days, their juice soaking up character and color from their skins.

Long-term aging generally happens in large underground cellars, where it's cool, dark and damp. The naturally low temperature stabilizes the wine and prevents it from aging prematurely, while a bit of moisture in the air keeps the liquid in the barrels from evaporating rapidly. Smaller French barrels, also called barriques, impart smoky aromas, soften tannins and bring sweet notes to the wine. They also stabilize color.

In Piedmont, large Slovenian oak casks are called *botti*. These last for 25 to 30 years, while expensive barriques must be replaced every three or four years. After aging a year in barriques, the higher-end reds are transferred to *botti* for additional aging. The increased air space in the *botti* softens and mellows the wines.

A wine that has bottle-aged in the winery's cellar is a better deal for consumers, because it has been stored in the ideal environment—cool, dark and humid—where the cork won't dry out and where the wine will gradually ease into its new glass-walled home. Fine wines, when opened too young, can sometimes exhibit "bottle shock," tasting clunky or lacking their usual aromatics.

MASTERCLASS: BIG WINES, WITH AND WITHOUT OAK

Budding wine enthusiasts tend to associate rich, full-bodied reds with toasty new-oak barrels. But barriques have only come into use quite recently in many top regions. In Piedmont, Italy, Nebbiolo is traditionally aged in massive oak casks that don't impart sweet or smoky notes to the wine. In France's Rhône Valley, most winemakers claim that Grenache can't handle the strong flavors imparted by new, small, toasted-oak barrels, preferring to age this variety in large casks or cement tanks. Meanwhile, their counterparts in the New World command big bucks for putting the same variety into barriques. And in southern Italy, leathery Aglianico is finding plusher personality when aged in barriques.

GIACOMO CONTERNO
CASCINA FRANCIA
(Nebbiolo [*Botti* / oak casks])
Barolo, Piedmont, Italy $$$$$

ALTERNATIVE CHOICES

BRUNO GIACOSA ALBESANI SANTO STEFANO
(Nebbiolo [*Botti* / oak casks])
Barbaresco, Piedmont, Italy $$$$$

PRODUTTORI DEL BARBARESCO
(Nebbiolo [*Botti* / oak casks])
Barbaresco, Piedmont, Italy $$$$$

GAJA BARBARESCO
(Nebbiolo [Barriques and casks])
Barbaresco, Piedmont, Italy $$$$$

ALTERNATIVE CHOICES

BOROLI, BAROLO VILLERO
(Nebbiolo [Barrels and barriques])
Barolo, Piedmont, Italy $$$$$

CA'ROME', ROMANO MARENGO CHIARAMANTI BARBARESCO
(Nebbiolo [Barriques])
Barbaresco, Piedmont, Italy $$$$$

DOMAINE DE LA BISCARELLE
LES ANGLAISES
(Grenache / Mourvèdre [Concrete vats])
Châteauneuf-du-Pape, Rhône, France $$

ALTERNATIVE CHOICES

DOMAINE RABASSE CHARAVIN RASTEAU
(Grenache / Mourvèdre [Enamel-lined concrete vats]) Rhône, France $$

PIERRE-HENRI MOREL SIGNARGUES
(Grenache / Syrah / Mourvèdre [Concrete vats])
Rhône, France $

TORBRECK LES AMIS
(Grenache [Barriques])
Barossa Valley, Australia $$$$$

ALTERNATIVE CHOICES

SINE QUA NON ATLANTIS FE203
(Grenache [Barriques])
Santa Rita Hills, California, USA $$$$$

ALBAN VINEYARDS ALBAN ESTATE VINEYARDS
(Grenache [Barriques])
Edna Valley, California, USA $$$$$

LUIGI TECCE POLIPHEMO
(Aglianico [Chestnut and oak *botti*])
Taurasi, Campania, Italy $$$

ALTERNATIVE CHOICES

CANTINE ANTONIO CAGGIANO
MACCHIA DEI GOTTI
(Aglianico [*Botti*])
Taurasi, Campania, Italy $$$

VILLA MATILDE TENUTE DI ALTAVILLA
(Aglianico [*Botti*])
Taurasi, Campania, Italy $$–$$$

TORMARESCA BOCCA DI LUPO
(Aglianico [Barriques])
Castel del Monte, Puglia, Italy $$$

ALTERNATIVE CHOICES

SALVATORE MOLETTIERI CINQUE QUERCE
(Aglianico [Barriques])
Irpinia, Campania, Italy $$

TERREDORA FATICA CONTADINA
(Aglianico [Barriques])
Taurasi, Campania, Italy $$–$$$

HOW TO SERVE IT

Set out the bottles in a row and invite your guests to taste through them, without revealing which wines have aged in small, new oak barrels and which haven't. Provide two glasses to each taster and let each person compare the wines in pairs. Which is the wine that aged in barriques? Which style of aging do you prefer for each grape variety?

HOW TO TALK ABOUT IT

If you think you may have just licked the inside of a barrel, your wine is **oaky** or **planky** or tastes of **new wood**. If it has charred vanilla or caramel notes, it's **toasty**. A rich, full red wine that has nicely integrated new oak might be **voluptuous** or **opulent**. Wines aged in large casks, on the other hand, are often described as **herbaceous**, with notes of **tobacco** and **dried leaves**, **flowers** or **fruit**.

AROMATIC AND SENSORY CLUES

Aromatics of smoke, toasted wood, charred marshmallows, caramel, vanilla or mocha, accompanied by flavors of ripe, concentrated fruit, are all clues that the wine has aged in new-oak barriques. A wine aged in a large puncheon or *botti* typically has more pronounced acidity, fiercer tannins and more herbal, leathery aromatics.

FOOD MATCHES

When tasting big red wines, it's best to snack on something that will cleanse those mouth-coating tannins off your overworked tongue. Slices of cold beef or cheddar cheese do the trick (the tannins bind with the proteins). And since truffles are a classic match for Nebbiolo, serve bread with truffle-infused olive oil.

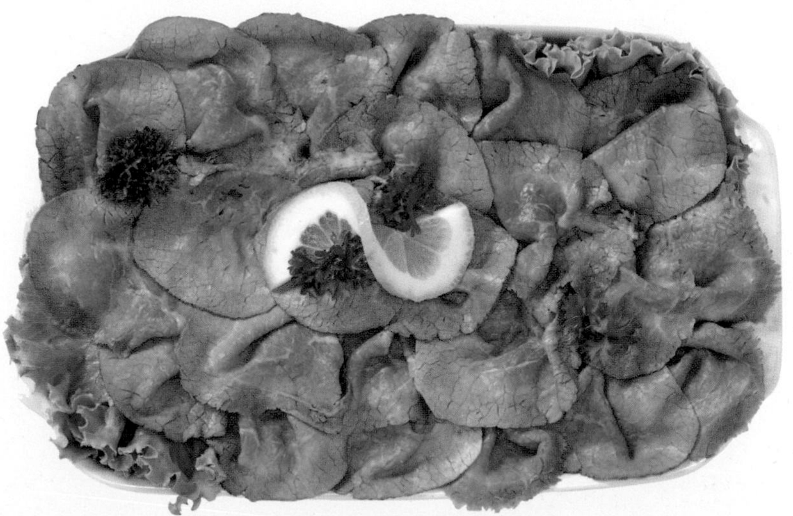

MASTERCLASS: WHAT'S TRENDING?

WHAT'S TRENDING: WHAT'S OLD IS NEW IN ÉLEVAGE

WHERE ANGELS DON'T FEAR TO TREAD

Barrels may be water-tight, but they aren't air-tight (trees, after all, respire oxygen). That's why barrel-aged wines taste richer and more concentrated. Winemakers call evaporated wine "the angel's share," and keep their aging cuvées from oxidizing by periodically **topping them off** with more wine, as well as injecting a bit of sulfur dioxide, nitrogen gas or carbon dioxide, to displace the air in the **head space**. In past centuries, according to wine writer Paul Lukacs, vintners would add ash, dye or (unwisely) lead as a preservative, light stinky sulfur candles over their wine, or burn powdered sulfur and dried herbs in their barrels before filling them. Still, wine was referred to as "the sour," writes Lukacs, because it often tasted like vinegar.

RECOMMENDED READING

Paul Lukacs, *Inventing Wine: A New History of One of the World's Most Ancient Pleasures* (Norton)

The field of wine study is largely devoted to the memorization of grape names, official winegrowing appellations, vintages and villages. But by focusing on the minutiae, we often forget to absorb the big picture. Lukacs has taken the time to look at the grand tapestry of wine through the ages, providing much-needed historical context to our connoisseurship.

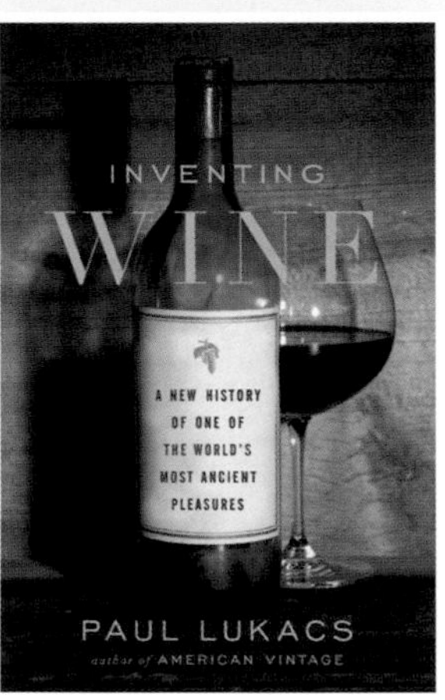

SITUATION, CULTIVATION, ETC.

Wine was once thought to be nothing short of a miracle, twice over. First, grape juice began bubbling, then somehow picked up an alcoholic kick. Then, over time, this heady beverage built character. Today, we can explain **fermentation** and **maturation**, but we're still experimenting with the best ways to instigate them. What's certain is that the container makes a difference. Modern wineries fine-tune their fermentations in temperature-controlled stainless-steel tanks, while traditionalists prefer the softening effect of handsome wooden *foudres* (large upright casks). And then there's the camp that believes in concrete (more on them soon).

But wine typically only sits in a fermenter for a few weeks, until it's done doing you-know-what. The next step—especially important for rich reds—is maturation, or what the French call *élevage*. As many oeno-pundits have pointed out, this term translates as "bringing up," as though the young wine were a baby in need of some life lessons before it could be introduced to the world. As we've just learned in the preceding Master Class, *élevage* doesn't always happen in the rows of small barrels we see in magazine advertisements. If you want your red to be bright-eyed and bushy-tailed, keep the maturation time to a minimum, in steel tanks. Or, if you're raising up a wine to be rather cryptic and sibylline, perhaps *botti* are better.

THE CONCRETE CAMP LAYS AN EGG

If you want to get a group of wine geeks buzzing, just say the word "concrete." Whether raw or lined with glass, enamel tiles, wax or steel, masonry has long been the material of choice for fermentation in places like Portugal. But it has recently gained converts in exclusive bastions of high-end red-wine production. In Bordeaux, Pétrus is committed to concrete; and when Château Cheval Blanc rolled out its new winery in 2011, the *pièce de résistance* was a stunning display of 52 concrete fermenters that could pass as decorative sculptures (*below*). Today, many big-red producers are praising these monolithic structures—some are shaped like pyramids, others like dinosaur eggs, others just simple cubes—for their natural temperature stability.

And that's not all. Unlined concrete is just porous enough to offer the tannin-smoothing benefit of micro-oxygenation, or **micro-ox**, as the trade calls it. (The unnatural alternative: Hooking your excessively tannic red up to an oxygen tank-like device, as though it were a hospital patient.) The Rhône River Valley, where superstar vintner Michel Chapoutier commissioned the first egg-shaped fermenter in 2001, is particularly pro-concrete: Despite the fact that unlined concrete is notoriously difficult to clean, many Rhône producers are moving their fermented wines back into concrete to mature, because it smooths out the sharp edges of grapes like Grenache without adding unwanted woody notes. Could the concrete egg soon be as ubiquitous as the barrique is now?

FROM CONCRETE TO CLAY

If a concrete egg isn't outlandish enough, allow me to introduce the very latest in cutting-edge winemaking technology: the amphora. As in, the kind of thing that archaeologists dig up. For the same reasons that Rhône winemakers love concrete, Italian vintners are embracing amphorae: they're porous, don't impart woody barrel notes to wine, and are made from a natural material, terra-cotta. Azienda Agricola COS, in Sicily, has more than 150 giant Spanish-made amphorae buried dramatically in its white-pebbled winery floor. Both white and red grapes macerate on their skins in these naturally cool containers for an astonishing eight to nine months, according to the owners.

10 FORTIFIED WINES

10 FORTIFIED

"Waiter, bring me your brownest wine, one with no vintage date, and preferably one that doesn't smell or taste the least bit like fruit. Be sure it's dry, or sweet, been exposed to lots of oxygen, and maybe heated up, as well." These are the words of a lunatic...a lunatic for the wine-liquor half-breeds that break every rule in the oenological textbook. Which must mean that we've arrived at the really fun part: fortified wines.

It would horrify an oenologist just about anywhere other than Jerez to see a partially full barrel in which a layer of white foamy yeast flowers. But this is how bone-dry Fino and Manzanilla Sherries come to look like coconut water and smell like something that could coax a seaweed-draped mermaid from the depths of the Strait of Gibraltar. Or, consider a winemaker blending together multiple vintages, and incessantly rearranging barrels as though he were stacking wood? Wines of uncertain age and amber-to-mahogany hues—Amontillado, Palo Cortado and Oloroso Sherries, as well as many Madeiras and Tawny Ports, are raised in this unconventional manner. But they taste of toasted hazelnuts and toffee. So who gives a damn about their outré upbringing?

Portugal is home to kingly Port, as well as mother to mad Madeira, the wildest wine of all. Born on a steeply cliffed island off Africa, it's everything from rangy Rainwater, to citrusy Sercial, to caramelly Verdelho. It's root-beer-hued Bual, rich with brown sugar and spices, and molasses-y Malmsey. Open a bottle of any of these, pour a small glass, pop the cork back in, then walk away and leave it a few months. That's right: Act like a lunatic. This wine will come along for the ride.

Wine connoisseurship can be so dogmatic. But we can forget most of those admonitions about vintage dates and proper storage as we enter the land of fortified wines, where the rules are meant to be broken. Like centenarians who swig whiskey and smoke cigarettes, these wines live longest of all.

YOU'LL ENJOY THESE WINES IF...

- You love sweet-and-savory flavor combinations
- You don't have the proper cellar conditions to age fragile wines
- A nightly apéritif or digestif fits your lifestyle

WHAT THE EXPERTS SAY

"Young, pale, dry fortified wines work perfectly with deep-fried fish, and all kinds of salty appetizers. Deeper-colored dry fortified wines work best with game meat, as well as almonds, hazelnuts, cocoa and coffee because they share so many aromas. Sweet fortified wines tend to be full-bodied and aromatic; I think that desserts and pastry are the best matches, especially those with bittersweet chocolate and dried fruit. But I get the most pleasure from them when I drink them alone, as a digestif."

Ferran Centelles, sommelier (1999–2011), elBulli, Spain; co-founder, wineissocial.com and Barcelona Wine School

KEY

$	UNDER $15	$$$$	$50–100
$$	$15–30	$$$$$	$100+
$$$	$30–50		

THE NAMES TO LOOK FOR

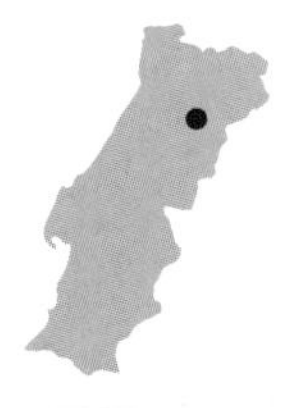

PORT DOURO, PORTUGAL

Vintage Ports are purple, smoky, spicy and blackberry cordial–like when young, growing plummy, leathery, even citrus-tinged with age. How long do they live? Well, expert Michael Broadbent praises the "Waterloo Vintage" of 1815. But you can enjoy any number of Non-Vintage Tawny, Ruby, White, Pink or Reserve Ports right now.

[**PRICE RANGE: $-$$$$$**]

[**ABV: 16–20%**]

[**DRINK IT: 1–250 YEARS AFTER THE VINTAGE**]

★ **CHOICE**

SHERRY ANDALUCIA, SPAIN

¡*Atención*! Get to know Jerez de la Frontera, Sanlúcar de Barrameda and El Puerto de Santa María in southwest Spain. Because the vinerati and the bright young things are all tippling the tangy-to-sweet array of barrel-aged beverages from these seaside towns at this very moment. Bonus: For now, they're ridiculously affordable. ¡*Olé*!

[**PRICE RANGE: $-$$$$$**]

[**ABV: 15–22%**]

[**DRINK IT: IMMEDIATELY**]

MADEIRA MADEIRA, PORTUGAL

When the founding fathers of the United States signed their Declaration of Independence, guess what they toasted with? A wine that comes from a subtropical island off the coast of Africa. Because it didn't spoil during long sea voyages, it was all the rage more than two centuries ago; and still tastes delicious today.

[**PRICE RANGE: $-$$$$$**]

[**ABV: 15–22%**]

[**DRINK IT: 1–300 YEARS AFTER THE VINTAGE**]

MARSALA SICILY, ITALY

In most oenological reference books, you'll see Marsala wine written off as ancient history. But the post-mafia era has introduced a new wave of vintners in Sicily—and renewed interest in Marsala, under quality designations such as Superiore, Riserva, Vergine, Soleras and Stravecchio. Watch this space.

[**PRICE RANGE: $-$$$$$**]

[**ABV: 15–20%**]

[**DRINK IT: 1–20 YEARS AFTER THE VINTAGE**]

BANYULS LANGUEDOC-ROUSSILLON, FRANCE

The finest of the *vins doux naturels* (see also: Rivesaltes, Maury), Banyuls is, at its best, the product of old-vine Grenache, grown on steep, windblown schist terraces overlooking the Mediterranean Sea, and aged like Sherry in barrels—or else in glass jars called, deliciously, *bonbonnes*—where flavors of nuts, licorice and red fruit unfold.

[**PRICE RANGE: $-$$$$**]

[**ABV: 16–17%**]

[**DRINK IT: 0–60 YEARS AFTER THE VINTAGE**]

LIQUEUR MUSCAT RUTHERGLEN, VICTORIA, AUSTRALIA

The Brits love fortified wines, so it would make sense that this former British colony would have a strong tradition in techniques similar to those used for Sherry, Port and Madeira. But the Aussies also have a way of allowing the grapes to raisin on the vine before vinifying and fortifying. This "brown Muscat," mate, is heavy stuff.

[**PRICE RANGE: $-$$$$$**]

[**ABV: 18%**]

[**DRINK IT: IMMEDIATELY**]

TAKE ONE WINE: QUINTA DO VESUVIO VINTAGE PORT

THE BASICS

GRAPE VARIETIES: Touriga Nacional-based blend of indigenous Douro Valley grape varieties.

REGION: Douro Valley, Portugal

ALCOHOL LEVEL: 20%

PRICE: $$$$

AVAILABILITY: Widely available

APPEARANCE: Inky purple in its youth, taking on copper tones with age.

TASTING NOTE: Upon release, blackberry cordial, blueberry preserves, fennel pollen, granite, licorice, lip-stinging black pepper, fragrant fresh herbs, dark chocolate and cinnamon.

FOOD MATCH: Dark chocolate; Camembert; venison with juniper berries.

DRINK OR KEEP: This wine is released late to allow for immediate enjoyment; however, you may prefer to keep a Single-Quinta Port for 10 to 25 years after the vintage date.

WHY DOES IT TASTE THAT WAY?

In Portugal's Douro River Valley, steep **patamares**, or terraces, rise from the wide, winding Douro River like stairsteps for the gods. In these vineyards, hodgepodges of indigenous grapes are typically planted together as insurance against harvest-season weather conditions that might favor one variety over another. (In the past, these were **field blends**, or random potpourris of varieties, but today's vineyard managers are more strategic, taking elevation and microclimate into account when deciding what to plant where.) These grape blends make rich and spicy dry red table wines. But for Port production, the *enólogo* adds **aguardente**, or grape brandy, to the percolating grape must when it has reached only 6% to 8% alcohol, stopping fermentation. The resulting wine combines juicy dark fruit with the heady alcoholic kick of the brandy; the blend of grapes makes for aromatics of complexity and depth.

WHO MADE IT?

Vesuvio is arguably the most breathtaking estate on the Douro, with a history that spans centuries and north-facing slopes that provide protection from the punishing heat of this sun-soaked region. In the latter half of the 19th century, it belonged to the legendary businesswoman Dona Antonia Ferreira, who built its reputation for quality while simultaneously running 30 quintas. However, after 1870, the practice of bottling the fruit of a single vineyard fell away, as larger Port houses or **shippers** began buying wines from estates like Vesuvio and adding them to larger blends. Then, in the late 1980s, as oenophiles began to take an interest in single-vineyard wines, the Port trade responded; when the Symington family purchased Vesuvio in 1989, they went about restoring it to its historic roots. Today, winemaking goes on much the same way it did in the early- to mid-19th century, with harvest workers treading the grapes by foot in granite ***lagares*** (which look like small swimming pools), often singing and dancing to pass the time. Yes, they do wash their feet before jumping in.

CRACKING THE CODE
CLOSURE
The driven cork, like that in a bottle of dry wine, must be removed with a corkscrew and is an indicator that the wine inside is high in quality, relatively fragile, and should be consumed within a day or two of opening the bottle. By contrast, Ports produced for everyday drinking are topped with T-shaped, plastic-topped corks. These can be enjoyed for up to a month if recorked and refrigerated between servings.
OFFICIAL STAMP
The seal on the neck of the bottle says "Vinho do Porto Garantia," proof that the IVDP, or Instituto do Vinho do Porto, has tested the wine for quality.
PRODUCER NAME
Symington is the name of the family that owns this quinta, as well as many other prominent quintas in the Douro Valley and famous Port brands such as Dow's, Graham's and Warre's.
WINE NAME
Quinta means "Estate." Vesuvio is a single-quinta Port, one of a new breed of single-vineyard wines that are slightly more affordable and individual alternatives to Vintage Port.
VINTAGE DATE
The single vintage year indicates that this is one of the highest-quality Ports, intended for aging. Ports marked with decades (as in "20-year-old"), terms such as Reserve or special proprietary names, like Warrior or Six Grapes, can be opened and enjoyed immediately.
ALCOHOL
The alcohol level is 20% because the wine has been fortified with brandy.
794873
04
GARANTIA
SYMINGTON'S
2009
Quinta do Vesuvio
VINTAGE PORT
BOTTLED 2011
PRODUCT of PORTUGAL
20% vol.
e75cl

QUINTA DO VESUVIO VINTAGE PORT

WHY THAT PRICE?

While most wine lovers are familiar with affordable higher-quality Ruby Ports (called Premium Ruby, or Reserve), amber-hued Tawnies, and expensive, cellar-worthy Vintage Ports, in-the-know oenophiles are increasingly seeking out Single-Quinta Ports like the Quinta do Vesuvio. These bottlings offer quality, with the added appeal of terroir, or the notion that we might be able to taste the characteristics of a specific place in the finished wine; Vintage Ports, by contrast, are typically blends sourced from multiple sites. While priced like the collectors' items that they are—only 600 cases of Vesuvio are produced annually—the Single-Quinta Ports are slightly more affordable than Vintage Ports because they tend to be released even in **undeclared vintages**, or those years when harvest conditions weren't ideal.

WHAT FOOD DOES IT GO WITH?

Blue cheese, such as Stilton, is often cited as a classic pairing with Port, but I find the combination of two such strong flavors to be overwhelming. For a more subtle combination, try the Vesuvio with baked brie topped with toasted pecans and dried fruits or preserves. Also, dark chocolate and Port are a match made in heaven. But don't feel that you must pair Port with cheese or dessert. With gamey meats like duck, Single-Quinta Port acts like a blackberry sauce; you could even try braised short ribs.

TOP FOOD MATCH: Venison loin with oaxacan-style mole sauce

Left: The magnificent Quinta do Vesuvio, lovingly restored by the Symington family, on the upper reaches of the Douro.

10 OF THE BEST

SINGLE-QUINTA PORTS FOR ADVENTUROUS PALATES

GRAHAM'S MALVEDOS	$$$-$$$$
NIEPOORT PISCA	$$$$
QUINTA DE LA ROSA	$$$-$$$$
QUINTA DE ROMANEIRA	$$$-$$$$
QUINTA DO CRASTO	$$$-$$$$
QUINTA DO INFANTADO	$$$-$$$$
QUINTA DO NOVAL	$$$$-$$$$$
QUINTA DO PASSADOURO	$$$-$$$$
TAYLOR'S VARGELLAS	$$$$$
VALLADO ADELAIDE	$$$$

AROUND THE WORLD

SIMILAR STYLE WINES FROM DIFFERENT COUNTRIES

Boplaas, Cape Vintage Reserve Port
Western Cape, South Africa $$

Ficklin Vineyards, Vintage Port
Madera, California, U.S. $$$

Seppeltsfield, VP Shiraz / Touriga
Barossa Valley, Australia $$

CHOICE MADE SIMPLE

EXPERT'S PERSONAL FAVORITES

Recommended by Carla Rzeszewski, Wine Director, The Breslin Bar & Dining Room, The John Dory Oyster Bar, and The Spotted Pig, New York City, U.S.

CHÂTEAU D'ARLAY,
MACVIN DU JURA BLANC
(CHARDONNAY / SAVAGNIN)
JURA, FRANCE $$–$$$

COUME DEL MAS,
GALATEO BANYULS
(GRENACHE) LANGEUDOC-ROUSSILLON, FRANCE $$–$$$

EQUIPO NAVAZOS, LA BOTA DE MANZANILLA PASADA 10
(PALOMINO) SANLÚCAR DE BARRAMEDA, SPAIN $$$$

FERNANDO DE CASTILLA,
ANTIQUE FINO
(PALOMINO)
JEREZ, SPAIN $$–$$$

GONZÁLEZ BYASS,
FINO TRES PALMAS
(PALOMINO)
JEREZ, SPAIN $$–$$$$

HIDALGO,
LA PANESA ESPECIAL FINO
(PALOMINO)
JEREZ, SPAIN $$–$$$

CHÂTEAU DE MONTIFAUD,
VIEUX PINEAU DES CHARENTES
(COLOMBARD) PINEAU DES CHARENTES, COGNAC, FRANCE $$

BARBEITO,
1978 SERCIAL FRASQUEIRA
(SERCIAL)
MADEIRA, PORTUGAL $$$$$

ROAGNA,
BAROLO CHINATO
(NEBBIOLO)
PIEDMONT, ITALY $$$$–$$$$$

AR VALDESPINO,
MOSCATEL TONELES VIEJISIMO
(MUSCAT)
JEREZ, SPAIN $$$$$

WORLD OF FINE WINE RECOMMENDATIONS

AR VALDESPINO,
FINO INOCENTE
(PALOMINO)
JEREZ, SPAIN $$$

OSBORNE,
PALO CORTADO SOLERA PΔP
(PALOMINO)
JEREZ, SPAIN $$$$

BODEGAS TRADICION,
OLOROSO
(PALOMINO)
JEREZ, SPAIN $$$$

EMILIO HIDALGO, SANTA ANNA PEDRO XIMÉNEZ 1860
(PEDRO XIMÉNEZ)
JEREZ, SPAIN $$$$$

BARBEITO,
10 YEAR OLD MALVASIA
(MALVASIA)
MADEIRA, PORTUGAL $$$

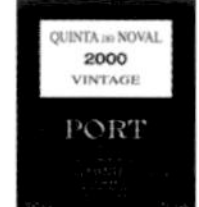

QUINTA DO NOVAL,
VINTAGE PORT
(DOURO BLEND)
DOURO, PORTUGAL $$$

TAYLOR'S,
VINHA VELHA VINTAGE PORT
(DOURO BLEND)
DOURO, PORTUGAL $$$$

DOW'S,QUINTA SENHORA DA RIBERA PORT
(DOURO BLEND)
DOURO, PORTUGAL $$$

NIEPOORT,
30 YEAR OLD TAWNY PORT
(DOURO BLEND)
DOURO, PORTUGAL $$$$

CHAMBERS, ROSEWOOD RUTHERGLEN GRAND MUSCAT
(MUSCAT) RUTHERGLEN, VICTORIA, AUSTRALIA $$$$

(*Grape Varieties in Brackets*)

LEFT-FIELD ALTERNATIVES

ANTOINE ARENA,
MUSCAT DU CAP CORSE
(MUSCAT) CORSICA, FRANCE $$–$$$

BARBADILLO, SOLEAR MANZANILLA
EN RAMA SACA DE INVIERNO
(PALOMINO) SANLÚCAR DE BARRAMEDA,
JEREZ, SPAIN $–$$

CAMPBELLS,
MERCHANT PRINCE RARE MUSCAT
(MUSCAT) RUTHERGLEN, VICTORIA,
AUSTRALIA $$$$–$$$$$

COCCHI, APERITIVO AMERICANO
(MUSCAT)
PIEDMONT, ITALY $–$$

KOPKE, WHITE PORTO 10 YEARS OLD
(ARINTO / MALVASIA BLANCA /
MARIA GOMEZ)
DOURO, PORTUGAL $$$

D'OLIVEIRA,
1988 HARVEST TERRANTEZ MADEIRA
(TERRANTEZ)
MADEIRA, PORTUGAL $$$$–$$$$$

QUADY, PALOMINO FINO
(PALOMINO)
CALIFORNIA, U.S. $$

THE RARE WINE CO., HISTORIC SERIES
NEW ORLEANS SPECIAL RESERVE MADEIRA
(TERRANTEZ / MALVASIA)
MADEIRA, PORTUGAL $$$$

BODEGAS TORO ALBALÁ,
GRAN RESERVA PX 1985 (UNFORTIFIED)
(PEDRO XIMENEZ) MONTILLA-MORILES,
ANDALUCIA, SPAIN $$–$$$

VEVI, DORADO 1954
(VERDEJO / VIURA)
RUEDA, SPAIN $$

BEST ON A BUDGET

CARPANO, PUNT E MES
(VERMOUTH)
VERMOUTH DI TORINO, ITALY $–$$

DOMAINE CAZES, RIVESALTES AMBRÉ
(GRENACHE BLANC)
RIVESALTES, LANGUEDOC-ROUSSILLON,
FRANCE $–$$

CHAMBERS ROSEWOOD VINEYARDS,
MUSCADELLE
(MUSCADELLE) RUTHERGLEN, VICTORIA,
AUSTRALIA $–$$

DOLIN,
BLANC VERMOUTH DE CHAMBÉRY
(WHITE VERMOUTH)
CHAMBÉRY, SAVOIE, FRANCE $

BODEGAS CÉSAR FLORIDO,
MOSCATEL ESPECIAL
(MUSCAT)
ANDALUSIA, SPAIN $–$$

DOMAINE FONTANEL,
RIVESALTES AMBRÉ
(GRENACHE BLANC) RIVESALTES,
LANGUEDOC-ROUSSILLON, FRANCE $$

W & J GRAHAM'S,
SIX GRAPES RESERVE PORT
(BLEND)
DOURO, PORTUGAL $–$$

KOURTAKI, SWEET RED WINE
(MAVRODAPHNE / BLACK KORINTHIAKI)
MAVRODAPHNE, PATRAS, GREECE $

MILES, RAINWATER MADEIRA
(TINTA NEGRA MOLE)
MADEIRA, PORTUGAL $–$$

DOMAINE LA TOUR VIEILLE,
BANYULS (GRENACHE)
LANGUEDOC-ROUSSILLON,
FRANCE $–$$

MASTERCLASS: ON SADNESS AND THE SOLERA

The Portuguese speak of a sadness that does not translate into other languages. *Saudade* is a melancholic longing for someone or something from long ago and far away. It can even be applied to the present, a way of expressing a yearning that may be fulfilled now, but will inevitably be lost later. It's fitting, then, that the Portuguese specialize in fortified wines that can be cellared almost *ad infinitum*. Buy a Vintage Madeira now for that child you love with such *saudade*, and his great-grandchildren's great-grandchildren can open and enjoy it.

But there's a segment of fortified wine that combines past and present in an immediately accessible manner, thanks to the fine art of **fractional blending**. These fortified wines are stored in rows of barrels, by year. Each year, a fraction of the wine from each of the older barrels is sold; and the remaining headspace is filled with wine from a more recent row of barrels, and so on. The wines are anywhere from amber to cola in color, from aging in wood for so long.

In Portugal, fractionally blended wines are composed of a medley of vintages at least as old as the number of years stated on the label; they range from a five-year-old Madeira to a 40-year-old Tawny Port. In Spanish, the term for this system is solera, and it's applied to Sherries. A crisp, young **Fino** that ages in solera for more than around 15 years becomes an **Amontillado**; if it hasn't enjoyed the protective coating of yeast (*flor*) that's particular to Finos, it's a **Palo Cortado** or **Oloroso**. But the Iberians don't have a lock on this method. You can find fractionally blended fortified wines from Australia, Greece, Cyprus, France and elsewhere. In Sicily, the profoundly Latin-inflected term for this traditional method is ***invecchiamento in perpetuum***—aging for all time.

Whatever you do, don't think too hard about how the solera system works, because you'll begin to have school math nightmares. In college calculus textbooks, the solera model is a fairly standard tear-your-hair-out problem: "for the amount of n-year-old wine removed from a solera with k *tiers* each year...." Instead, just think of the solera as a framework that allows us to enjoy a taste of incredibly old wine at any given moment.

Or, just imagine the Portuguese diva, who warbles about *saudade* in her mournful *fado* song while her audience silently weeps over their glasses of Port and Madeira. The framework for the *fadista*'s song is strummed on a steel-string guitar. And the word for a guitar's wooden frame, in the language of music everywhere, is solera.

HOW TO IDENTIFY THESE ELEMENTS

1: Fortified wines that don't bear the date of a single vintage year are often the product of a fractional aging system. These include Tawny Ports and Madeiras labeled by decade ("10-year," etc.); Amontillado, Palo Cortado, Oloroso and Cream Sherries; and Marsalas.

2: These are just about the only wines in the world that are prized for being brown in color and bearing no vintage date! They get their tawny color from the exposure to oxygen they get as they age in wooden casks.

3: If you aren't in Spain or Portugal, you'll find solera-aged fortified wines at the very end of restaurant wine lists, among the dessert drinks. But that doesn't mean you should save them for the last act of the meal. The nutty, saline and molasses notes that result from solera age can be dynamite with salty, savory foods.

THE SHERRY BODEGA

The *capataz*, or cellar master, is constantly evaluating the wines to determine what type of Sherry they will become. He marks the end of each barrel with a chalk symbol to designate its destiny.

In a traditional solera system, the barrels containing the oldest wines, at the bottom of the stack, are called soleras, as well. The word solera comes from *suelo*, meaning ground or earth. The upper rows are called *criaderas*.

In Spain, the wine thief, or tool used to remove a sample of wine from the cask, is traditionally long and metal, and called *la venencia*.

Sherry bodegas tend to be ground-floor warehouses rather than underground cellars. To keep the conditions cool and moist in the summer, water is sprinkled on the sandy floor.

In the bodega, 500-to-600-liter barrels, called butts, are stacked atop one another. The butts are made from American white oak, *Quercus alba*, which is less porous than European oaks—an important factor in a bodega that plans to barrel-age its wines for decades.

In the fractional blending of vintages, the winemaker can draw off as much as one third of the contents of each barrel each year; this wine is replaced with wines from newer vintages. The current vintage's wines are added to the top row, called the *añada*.

MASTERCLASS: STRONG SOLERA-STYLE WINES

I've designed this tasting to expose you to the breadth of solera-style winemaking as well as a spread in aging times. But feel free to improvise: For example, you could taste through a progression of 10-, 20-, 30- and 40-year-old Tawny Ports from the same producer to see how the wine changes with increased time in the solera. This lineup mixes things up, with a 10-year-old Bual Madeira, an Amontillado with at least 15 years of age (if not more), a 20-year-old Tawny, a 15-to-20-year-old Marsala; a VORS (Very Old Rare Sherry), which is a 30-year Oloroso; and finally, a 40-year Tawny.

BARBEITO
OLD RESERVE, 10 YEAR OLD BUAL
(Bual) Madeira, Portugal $$$

ALTERNATIVE CHOICES

COSSART GORDON
10 YEARS, MEDIUM RICH BUAL
(Bual) Madeira, Portugal $$$

BLANDY'S AGED 10 YEARS BUAL
(Bual) Madeira, Portugal $$–$$$

MARCO DE BARTOLI
VECCHIO SAMPERI VENTENNALE
(Grillo) Marsala Superiore, Sicily, Italy $$$$–$$$$$

ALTERNATIVE CHOICES

RALLO SOLERAS VERGINE RISERVA 20 ANNI
(Grillo) Marsala, Sicily, Italy $$–$$$

FLORIO
DONNA FRANCA RISERVA OLTRE 15 ANNI
(Grillo) Marsala, Sicily, Italy $$$

ALVEAR
CARLOS VII AMONTILLADO
(Pedro Ximénez) Montilla-Morilles, Andalucia, Spain $$–$$$

ALTERNATIVE CHOICES

BODEGAS TRADICIÓN 30 AÑOS AMONTILLADO
(Palomino) Jerez, Spain $$$–$$$$

LUSTAU LOS ARCOS SOLERA RESERVA DRY AMONTILLADO
(Palomino) Jerez, Spain $–$$

BODEGAS DIOS BACO
BACO IMPERIAL VORS OLOROSO
(Palomino) Jerez, Spain $$$$–$$$$$

ALTERNATIVE CHOICES

OSBORNE SOLERA INDIA VORS OLOROSO
(Palomino) Jerez, Spain $$$$–$$$$$

HARVEYS RICH OLD VORS OLOROSO
(Palomino) Jerez, Spain $$–$$$

RAMOS PINTO RP 20 QUINTA DO BOM RETIRO TAWNY 20 AÑOS
(Blend) Douro, Portugal $$$–$$$$

ALTERNATIVE CHOICES

FERREIRA
DUQUE DE BRAGANÇA TAWNY 20 AÑOS
(Blend) Douro, Portugal $$$–$$$$

FONSECA 20-YEAR-OLD AGED TAWNY
(Blend) Douro, Portugal $$–$$$

DOW'S 40 YEARS TAWNY
(Blend) Douro, Portugal $$$$$

ALTERNATIVE CHOICES

PRESIDENTIAL PORTO 40 YEARS TAWNY
(Blend) Douro, Portugal $$$$–$$$$$

CASA DE STA. EUFEMIA
40 YEARS OLD TAWNY
(Blend) Douro, Portugal $$$$$

HOW TO SERVE IT

The tiny glass used in Spain for sipping Sherry is called a *copita*, but any small wine glass will do. In fact, fortified wines are so aromatic that you can have fun with the presentation and pour them into Granny's antique cut-crystal *coupes*. And even though you could get away with storing Madeira in a sauna without damaging it, serve these wines slightly cool for optimal aromatics. Finally, remember that you needn't feel compelled to drink Non-Vintage fortified wines in one sitting. Everyone can recork a bottle, take it home, keep it in the refrigerator, and continue to enjoy it over the course of a few weeks.

HOW TO TALK ABOUT IT

Bual is BOO-AHL;
Amontillado is AH-MAHNT-EE-YA-DOH;
Oloroso is OH-LOH-ROH-SOH; and I'll
let you work out Tawny and Marsala for yourself. You might notice the term **VORS** used in conjunction with the Olorosos—this stands for "very old rare Sherry" and indicates that the solera was a minimum of 30 years old.

AROMATIC AND SENSORY CLUES

Solera-aged wines tend to show notes of roasted nuts, leather and molasses on the nose, and spiced dried dates and raisins on the palate. As you progress through the lineup, take note of the intensity of these aromatics. Do they smell and taste more developed in the older wines?

FOOD MATCHES

Toasted, salted nuts—almonds, walnuts, even spiced pecans—will complement the wines and help you to identify what you're smelling and tasting. If you prefer something sweeter, neutral (not chocolate-dipped!) *biscotti* work well; or, even better, bake up that classic pairing for Madeira, gingerbread. And while I don't condone smoking, if you were to light up a cigar after tasting through these wines, I wouldn't blame you.

MASTERCLASS: WHAT'S TRENDING?
SPIRITS + AROMATICS

VINIFERA BRANDIES

In almost any wine region, you'll find someone distilling fermented grapes. The best-known of the wine brandies is **Cognac**, produced on the west coast of France just north of Bordeaux, where the chalky soils, sea breezes and mild maritime climate make for fragrant, acidic Ugni Blanc grapes. Just like winemakers, producers aim to capture the terroir of the vineyard in the brandy, so Cognac has designated superior crus, where the best estates are located (these are named, confusingly, Grande Champagne and Petite Champagne). As with many fortified wines, Cognacs get their tawny color from extended barrel age; the length of time is indicated on the label by the letters **VS**, **VSOP** and **XO**.

Cognac's cousin in Gascony, in the southwest, is **Armagnac**. It's made from a blend of grapes, including Ugni Blanc, and due in part to a slightly different distillation process, tends to taste a bit more rustic and earthy than Cognac. And in South America (bet you didn't see *that* coming!) the Spanish introduced the technique of distilling spirits from wine back in the early 1600s. Today that tradition lives on in the **Pisco** of Peru, Chile and Bolivia. Until recently, this spirit was known as the key ingredient in a Pisco Sour cocktail, but a new movement toward quality production, most notably in Peru, has rendered this a sipping beverage worth seeking out; the best bottles are designated **Gran Pisco.**

SYMBIOTIC WINES AND SPIRITS

It should come as no surprise that most top Jerez bodegas also produce brandy, because a quality spirit is an essential ingredient in a good fortified wine. In Spanish Sherry country, distillation has been a tradition for more than a millennium. The aging process is nearly identical to that of Sherry: It takes place in used Sherry barrels, arranged in a solera system. Sherry enjoys worldwide acclaim while the equally fine Brandy de Jerez is more of a local specialty; ironically, the reverse is true in France, where Cognac gets all the glitz and glamour and charming **Pineau des Charentes**—a red, white or rosé ***mistelle*** of unfermented grape juice with young brandy—is little more than a footnote.

On to Italy, and **Grappa** (or **Marc** in French), the brandy that's made from the stuff that would normally be headed for the compost bin. That is, it's distilled from **pomace**—***vinaccia***—or the crushed skins, seeds and stems that are leftover from winemaking. But there's nothing trashy about this heady beverage, which is literally the pure essence of whichever grape variety it's made from. The most famous of the *grappaoili* is Poli, in the heart of Grappa country in northern Italy's Veneto. Poli produces clear and tawny (barrique-aged) grappas, sourced from Italian white and red grapes as well as from Port and Sherry, and even a special bottling culled from the cultish Bordeaux-style blend, Sassicaia.

AND THE REST IS HISTORY

The story behind Port, Madeira, Marsala and Sherry is much the same: The English and the Dutch wanted wine, but didn't have the climate to produce it. They did have ships, however, so they traveled to places like Spain, Portugal and Italy to get it. And then a funny thing happened during the long return voyage: The wines spoiled. In the mid-16th century, someone discovered that the addition of spirits to the barrels rendered wine stable for travel. And more alcoholic. And tastier, too. (Winemaking wasn't what it is today.) So, the next time you're feeling critical of globalism, just remember: Without it, you wouldn't have that nice little glass of Madeira.

VA-VA VERMOUTH

What other category of beverage must a wine lover know? **Vermouth**, wine's bastard cousin, aperitif, digestif, cocktail ingredient and standalone sipper. In Classical times, healers cooked up **wormwood** infusions to treat all sorts of maladies, adding sugar and spices to this bitter tonic to make it more palatable. By the late-18th century, Italians had begun blending it with wine, and about 100 years later, Giuseppe Cappellano, a Piedmontese pharmacist, mixed quinine and other curatives with the fine local wine, Barolo, to create the noble **Chinato** (from the Italian word for quinine). At the same time, the Swiss were distilling wormwood with anise and fennel to make that addictive muse, **Absinthe.** But thanks to the marketing of Cinzano and Noilly Prat, Vermouth has been far more successful; this blend of wine and spirits, macerated with herbs and spices, is in the "bistro umbrella" section of every thinking person's brain even today. There are two basic styles: The **dry**, white variety, redolent of citrus, chamomile, lavender and sage; and the **sweet** red potpourri of cinnamon, clove, nutmeg and ginger. Bottom line: Vermouth is blissfully accessible. It's got everything wine has but because it's infused, those aromatic notes are obvious. So next time your nose needs a break, pour a Vermouth on the rocks. And don't think; just drink.

EAU DE VIE

While wine made from fruit other than grapes isn't generally very successful, fruit brandy is another story. Occupying an odd space between the bar and the wine cellar, *eau de vie* (water of life) is often offered by the sommelier at the conclusion of the meal. It's also called *alcool blanc* in French, *Schnaps Obstler* in German or *Pálenka* in Czech, but it can be found throughout Europe (and the New World, as well). Here are a few of the key ones to know.

Calvados: French apple brandy from Normandy

Fraise or *Erdbeergeist*: Strawberry brandy

Framboise or *Himbeergeist*: Raspberry brandy

Gratte-Cul: Rose-hip brandy

Houx: Holly-berry brandy (Really? Yes.)

Kajsija: Balkan apricot brandy

Kirsch: Cherry brandy

Mirabelle, *Quetsch*, *Slivovitz* or *Zwetschenwasser*: Plum brandy

Mure: Blackberry brandy

Myrtille: Bilberry/blueberry brandy

Pacharan: Sweetened and spiced sloe berry brandy from Basque country

Poire William: Pear brandy

SECTION 2
BUYING WINE

1 SHOPPING FOR WINE: RESEARCHING

Before you shop for wine, whether for casual enjoyment or to start a major collection, take the time to do your due diligence. Don't make a rookie mistake, like buying a discounted case of something you've never tasted. Instead, read, ask questions and taste. And then taste some more. Here are some good places to start your investigations.

BOOKS

Yes, despite the fact that books are going the way of the Dodo bird, many of them—like this particular volume, I must say—do actually contain lots of very useful information, such as: names of lesser-known estates in top wine-producing regions; vintages to look out for; and underpriced grape varieties.

MAGAZINES, NEWSPAPERS AND NEWSLETTERS

Newspaper wine columnists, wine magazines, newsletters, chat groups and blogs will help you to identify what wine lovers are buzzing about, what you should try, and what's overpriced. Not sure whom you should be reading? Ask your fave somm or wine merchant for recommendations.

AUCTIONS

If you're looking to pick up rare or old wines, an auction house might be the way to go. If you're a numbers person, check out the Liv-Ex web site and peruse some of the data from the international wine market. If you're not, you can still get a feel for the market from wine auction sites like winebid.com and winecommune.com.

HOW TO SAVE AT AUCTION

On auction sites, look for **oddly packaged lots**—unrelated assortments or an odd number of wines—and lesser-known producers. And always remember: Internet shopping might look like a bargain, but once you've paid for shipping, and incurred the risk inherent in shipping wine, you might find it makes more sense to buy locally.

HOW TO SAVE IN STORES

Get to know your local wine merchant and get on the shop's e-mail list so you'll be the first to know when sales come up. And keep an eye out for **bin ends**—those last few bottles of last year's vintage. Also, know that many shops offer discounts—generally of between 10% and 20%—when you buy by the **case** or **half-case** (12 or 6 bottles).

INTERNET

Sites that list prices from multiple vendors—such as wine-searcher, snooth (both *right*) and Vinfolio—can be extremely useful in determining the actual value of a wine you've got your eye on. Be sure to factor in shipping costs as well as local sales taxes, and be wary of price averages that factor in half-bottles, oversized formats and case prices.

SEARCHING ONLINE: TWO TOP SITES

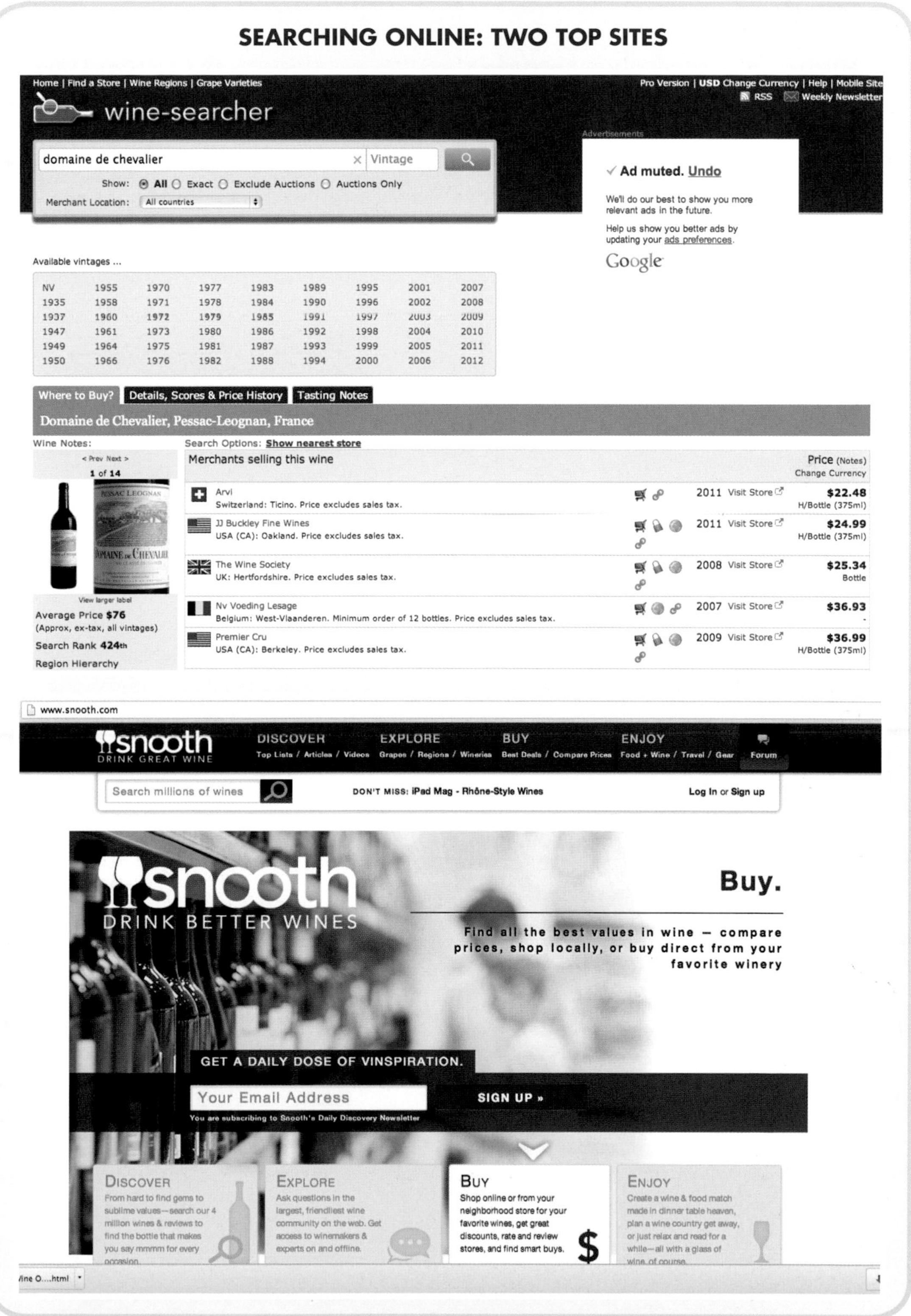

2 SHOPPING FOR WINE: DO VINTAGES MATTER?

You may have noticed that most of the wine recommendations in the first section of this book did not include vintage years. That's because, although each new release does have its own unique character, the grape variety or

varieties, the winemaking techniques and therefore the overall style, don't generally change dramatically from year to year. So: When *do* vintages matter? On the next two pages are eight common scenarios.

1. WHEN PAST VINTAGES ARE STILL READILY AVAILABLE

If you're looking at a closeout price at a wine shop or an inexpensive by-the-glass offering at a restaurant, consider the style of that six-year-old wine. If it's a crisp, lean white, it's probably past its prime. If it's an age-worthy white, such as a Riesling or Chardonnay, you might be looking at a terrific opportunity. Importers and wine buyers must clear their stocks of older vintages every few months to make room for the new stuff, even if the older wines are just hitting their prime.

2. WHEN YOU SEE AN OLDER VINTAGE ON A RESTAURANT WINE LIST

If the savory, earthy, autumnal notes of an older wine sound appealing but you aren't sure how to choose one from the wine list, "The easiest way to select the best wine is to seek advice from the sommelier directly," advises Frédéric Woelfflé, chef sommelier at Hôtel Métropole Monte Carlo. "He might suggest a wine from a less rated vintage but which will be as enjoyable to taste. He might also recommend wines that are showing well but that the client would not have thought of."

3. WHEN THERE ARE TWO OR MORE VINTAGES FROM THE SAME PRODUCER

On the following pages, "Negotiating a Restaurant Wine List," you may well notice two identical wines, both Georges Duboeuf Beaujolais-Villages. Which year is better? Again, as Woelfflé advises, just ask the sommelier which vintage he or she prefers. You might be surprised by his or her honesty.

4. IF YOU'RE ASSEMBLING A VERTICAL OR HORIZONTAL TASTING

A vertical tasting, or vertical flight, is a grouping of bottles of the same wine from the same producer but over multiple vintages. If you see a vertical tasting advertised at a local wine shop, wine bar or restaurant, take advantage of the opportunity. It's a great way to get to know how a region and producer cope with a variety of vintage conditions, and how the wine ages over time. And in case you were wondering, there's also such a thing as a horizontal tasting: This is an array of different producers making the same kind of wine in the same region in the same year.

5. IF YOU'RE BUYING AT AUCTION

Auction houses frequently deal in older vintages. And if it's an auctioneer that specializes in wine, you can be fairly certain that the lot was stored properly. But wading through dated vintages from unknown producers can be a challenge, and auction catalogs may offer little or no guidance other than "scuffed label" or "mid-to-low shoulder" (referring to the level of the wine in the bottle). For situations like these, it helps to have a reference manual. I like *Michael Broadbent's Pocket Vintage Wine Companion*, by a Master of Wine and longtime director of Christie's wine department.

6. IF YOU'RE BUYING IN FUTURES

Highly coveted producers, especially from fashionable regions like Bordeaux or Burgundy, often sell their wines as futures, allocating the entire vintage to buyers before it has ever hit the market. As a consumer, you can place an order through a wine merchant that deals in futures. Or—as is the case with many cult American wineries—you can put your name down on a wait list, and hope that someday you'll earn a spot on the winery's mailing list so that you can, eventually, order your futures directly. Amateur enthusiasts should note that wines sold as futures tend to suffer from price inflation. That said, prices dip when critics declare that a region is having a "bad" vintage. This is a terrific time for you to try a wine from a top producer, since the best vintners have the skill and knowledge to make fine wines even in the worst weather conditions.

7. IF YOU'RE COMMITTED TO A PARTICULAR REGION

Some oenophiles dabble, while others like to make a commitment. If you're in this latter camp—say you've decided that you're a Rioja lover—then it is wise to follow vintage reports. Maybe you like a lighter, more balanced style. If you've read that 2011 was a very hot vintage year in Rioja, resulting in lower acidity and higher alcohol, then you know to avoid it and instead to snap up as much as you can afford of the more balanced 2010s while they're still available.

8. IF YOU'RE A NUMBERS WONK

I'm not a fan of vintage charts, because they make sweeping assessments about wine regions without taking the details into account. But some folks love the idea of looking up vintages while perusing a wine list. If that sounds like your cup of tea (er, glass of wine?), devise a plan before you go out to dine. Invest in a small vintage chart, a pocket vintage guide or a smartphone app, such as *BB&R Wines* from Berry Bros. & Rudd or *WS Wine Ratings* from *Wine Spectator*. *The Wine Advocate* web site also has a handy vintage chart for smart-phone users. Don't waste time Googling the vintage, region and producer in high-end restaurants, where cell-phone use is discouraged and is also rude to your dining companions. And anyway, a Google search doesn't generally turn up the information you're looking for.

3 SHOPPING FOR WINE: BUYING

We may believe the expression "top shelf" really does mean high-quality, but we don't know what sorts of politics went into determining which wine gets displayed at eye level. So, be curious but cautious. Search the middle shelves and the end rows for interesting wines at reduced prices. And frequent small bottle shops that are devoted to a love of wine rather than a love of selling liquor. Here are some more tips:

SUPERMARKET

Some grocery stores—especially in top wine-producing nations—offer surprisingly fine wines. Look for someone bustling around the wine department in an apron, with a pen behind his or her ear. If there's a wine steward on staff, you can be sure the store stocks a solid selection.

BOTTLE SHOP

When the shelf-talkers—small signs, under individual bottles, often with a numeric score from a well-known publication—are hand-written by the shop owner, you know you're in for a treat. Also: Small wine merchants know what's on "post-off," or reduced price from an importer who's bringing in the next vintage, so get to know these people.

WINE CONSULTANT

Many specialty wine shops offer consulting services on the side; or, you can hire your favorite sommelier to come to your house in his or her off-hours to help you get your cellar started or plan that perfect dinner party. Just ask: If you've got a useful skill set, like accounting, web design or dog walking, you may even be able to arrange some kind of trade.

INTERNET

In the United States, where the wine-shipping laws can be byzantine, online wine merchants can be lifesavers. Find an online vendor in your area for the best shipping rates; and be aware that wine can spoil if it's shipped in freezing-cold or hot conditions.

AUCTION

If you find a deal at a small, independent auctioneer that is liquidating an estate, be sure to ask all about how the wine was stored—because the wine could be compromised. Large, reputable houses (Christie's, Sotheby's and many others) guarantee properly stored wines, and most will also allow you to bid as an absentee or online.

DIRECT FROM WINERY

Winery tasting rooms tend to set their per-bottle cost at the highest possible markup so as not to undercut retailers who also sell their wines. So ask your favorite producer if they offer a wine club membership. Members of these clubs receive regular shipments of wines at a slightly discounted price, plus invitations to special tastings and events.

4 SHOPPING FOR WINE: GREATEST WINE STORES

We've tossed our compact disc collections. We put our feet up on the couch to ogle shoes online. We browse magazines on iPads and books on Kindles. And we pick up our food and sundries in brightly lit, sanitized supermarkets.

But the wine shop remains, a vestige of a bygone era. While butchers, bakers and candlestick makers have been subsumed by technological innovations and time-saving takeout joints, bottle boutiques remain and, what's more, prosper.

Archaeologists tell us that the tradition of the wine shop is as ancient as civilization itself. Wine vendors hawked in the central marketplaces of Mesopotamia. Ancient Egyptian merchants stamped the handles of their clay vessels with distinctive seals, forerunners of modern-day labels on bottles. In classical Greece, an amphora filled with wine would cost you 20 drachmae—approximately the same price as one sheep or ten pairs of simple shoes.

Today, the trade is massive and metastatic. Travelers touring wine country ship cases from tasting rooms to their homes overnight, thanks to FedEx. Busy parents pick up their bottles in bulk at megastores. Harried professionals stop at wine-and-spirit warehouses for party supplies and weeknight sustenance. And serious collectors hire consultants to fill their cellars.

But we everyday enthusiasts love our old-fashioned wine shops; perhaps a primal part of us wants to pay our respects at a temple devoted to decadence. In today's ersatz urban environment, the wine store feels like a sacred space, fragrant and hushed. Tracing our fingers along each cool, curved glass vessel, we study the artful labels, traveling vicariously to far-flung locales—South Africa, Argentina, Hungary—and to long-ago eras.

Just ask your wine merchant to tell you about these places and times. He or she will happily explain that the crest on that bottle of Châteuneuf-du-Pape dates back to 1308, when Pope Clement moved the papal castle to Avignon. And that "Zeltinger Sonnenuhr" Riesling? It came from a vineyard where a huge sundial, erected in 1620, still informs passers-by of the time of day.

We hear such stories and can't help ourselves from splurging a bit. "I think it's a fairly small fraction of people who go to wine stores," observes Karl Storchmann, professor of economics at New York University and managing editor of *The Journal of Wine Economics*. "They are wine geeks like you and me. These are people for whom wine is a luxury good, like a piece of art. These people want a wide selection of choices and they are willing to pay more. They go to wine stores to treat themselves."

And so you treat yourself, wherever you are in the world. But you might discover that the citizens of different nations buy their wines in different ways. It might be difficult to locate a proper bottle shop in a Latin country, where tapas and drinks on the plaza are such an important part of life that it's less common to bring bottles home. In India, connoisseurs tend to purchase through membership clubs. In Hong Kong, many importers work hard to develop direct relationships with consumers.

Still, if you're in a locale where wine is served and loved, the chances are good that you'll find a bottle boutique nearby. On the following pages, you'll find an assortment from all over the world. They range from superstores to funky *bars à vin* that sell bottles on the side; what they have in common are expertise, selection and quality. While one or two might require appointments, most are welcoming to walk-in customers who wish to browse, taste and learn.

Opposite: The spiral staircase at L'Intendant in the heart of Bordeaux, where the lower you go, the higher the prices become.

THE AMERICAS (1)

CRUSH WINE & SPIRITS

It's no wonder fashionistas and rock stars—as well as finance types who manage massive Burgundy collections along with their stock portfolios—do their wine shopping here. Celebrity restaurateur Drew Nieporent's swanky Midtown store features a curving, backlit wall of wine (*right*). Other high-design touches: a tasting room that looks like a giant wine barrel, and "The Cube," a sleek, temperature-controlled, steel-and-glass, walk-in vault filled with delicate older vintages. But despite all the glitz, Crush has a cerebral side, too: Germany and Austria, the Jura, the Loire and Sherries all get plenty of play.

153 EAST 57TH STREET, NEW YORK 10022
+1 212 980 9463
WWW.CRUSHWINECO.COM

ACKER MERRALL & CONDIT

This family-run business dates back to 1820 and claims to be "America's oldest." Runs regular fine-wine auctions in New York, Chicago and Hong Kong, plus classes and winemaker tastings.

160 WEST 72ND STREET,
NEW YORK 10023
+1 212 787 1700
WWW.ACKERWINES.COM

ADDY BASSIN'S MACARTHUR BEVERAGES

DC's historic wine merchant imports directly from Europe, employs a cadre of oeno-experts, and hosts an annual California barrel tasting and wine dinner.

4877 MACARTHUR BOULEVARD,
WASHINGTON, DC 20007
+1 317 251 9463
WWW.BASSINS.COM

APPELLATION WINE & SPIRITS

Near the High Line elevated park in New York's West Chelsea Neighborhood, hipsters converge on Appellation for classes, tastings and a wide selection of organic, biodynamic and natural wines.

156 TENTH AVENUE,
NEW YORK 10011
+1 212 741 9474
WWW.APPELLATIONNYC.COM

ASTOR WINE & SPIRITS

Handsomely outfitted Greenwich Village wine destination with tasting bar, refrigerated room for cold wines and custom wood fixtures.

399 LAFAYETTE STREET,
NEW YORK 10003
+1 212 674 7500
WWW.ASTORWINES.COM

BROWN DERBY INTERNATIONAL WINE CENTER

Missouri's source for Bordeaux futures: a 75-plus-year-old institution, publishing a glossy monthly catalog and stocking beers from all over the globe.

2023 SOUTH GLENSTONE AVENUE,
SPRINGFIELD 65804
+1 417 883 4066
WWW.BROWNDERBY.COM

CENTENNIAL WINE & SPIRITS

Texas's wine powerhouse employs six certified sommeliers and boasts 40 stores (some under the name "Majestic" or "Big Daddy's") in the Dallas-Fort Worth region. Spirits, beers and cigars round out the voluminous offerings.

8123 PRESTON ROAD,
DALLAS 75225
+1 214 361 6697
WWW.CENTENNIALWINES.COM

CHAMBERS STREET WINES

Natural-wine proponent, direct importer and champion of the obscure in stylish Tribeca; named "the greatest wine retailer in America" by the prominent blogger Dr. Vino.

148 CHAMBERS STREET,
NEW YORK 10007
+1 212 227 1434
WWW.CHAMBERSSTWINES.COM

EXPAND

Brazil's most influential wine retailer is also a distributor, bringing prominent European producers to its 33 shop locations while supplying supermarkets and restaurants throughout the nation.

EMPÓRIO SANTA MARIA,
790 AVENIDA CIDADE JARDIM,
SÃO PAOLO, BRAZIL
+55 11 2102 7700
WWW.EXPAND.COM.BR

FEDERAL WINE & SPIRITS

It may look like a small, unassuming cellar, but Beantown's financial district merchant is a collector's treasure chest of old and rare European wines, as well as single malts and craft beers.

29 STATE STREET, BOSTON
02109
+1 617 367 8605
WWW.FEDERALWINE.COM

THE AMERICAS (2)

FERRY PLAZA WINE MERCHANT

Four seasoned professionals joined forces to open this dynamic hub of oenological interest in the Embarcadero's historic waterfront Ferry Building. Expect a bustling wine bar, busy event schedule and an ever-changing inventory (including artisan beers and spirits) selected by industry insiders whose tastes run to food-friendly, eclectic wines. After shopping at the Ferry Building's outdoor farmers market or indoor vendors, tipplers are welcome to nibble on their purchases (Cowgirl Creamery cheeses, Acme Bread Company loaves and the like) at the bar, although a light house menu of caviar, pâté and cheeses is certainly enticing.

ONE FERRY BUILDING, SHOP 23, SAN FRANCISCO 94111
+1 415 391 9400 / 866 991 9400
WWW.FPWM.COM

GRAND CRU

It started out as a French importer and distributor in Buenos Aires; now Grand Cru is also a high-end wine boutique, offering collectors' items from the Old World and bargains from Latin America.

RODRÍGUEZ PEÑA 1886,
BUENOS AIRES 1014, ARGENTINA
+54 11 4816 3975
WWW.GRANDCRU.COM.AR

ITALIAN WINE MERCHANTS

Co-owned by über-chef Mario Batali and celebrated restaurateur Joseph Bastianich, this Union Square wine destination offers the broadest selection of Italian wines in the nation.

108 EAST 16TH STREET,
NEW YORK 10003
+1 212 473 2323
WWW.ITALIANWINEMERCHANTS.COM

KERMIT LYNCH WINE MERCHANT

Immerse yourself in the catalog of legendary importer, accomplished author, soulful musician, *chevalier de la légion d'honneur*—and friend of the equally legendary Alice Waters—Kermit Lynch by visiting his Berkeley store.

1605 SAN PABLO AVENUE,
SAN FRANCISCO 94702
+1 510 524 1524
WWW.KERMITLYNCH.COM

K&L WINE MERCHANTS

With two locations in the Bay area and one in Hollywood, this wine-retail institution offers direct imports, auctions, an impressive selection of spirits and a broad but thoughtfully curated assortment of wines.

3005 EL CAMINO REAL,
REDWOOD CITY 94061
+1 650 364 8544
WWW.KLWINES.COM

LE DÛ'S WINES

The West Village man cave of sommelier superstar Jean-Luc Le Dû is a fun place to browse. Find everything from screaming deals (a $9 Tempranillo) to a house Champagne ("Deutz," for $42), as well as the requisite high scorers.

600 WASHINGTON STREET,
NEW YORK 10014
+1 212 924 6999
WWW.LEDUWINES.COM

LIBERTY WINE MERCHANTS

This is British Columbia's largest selection of fine wines, now with seven locations and a wine school. The emphasis is firmly and squarely on French and organic selections, but the range is still wide.

4583 WEST 10TH AVENUE,
VANCOUVER V6R 2J2, CANADA
+1 604 224 8050
WWW.LIBERTYWINEMERCHANTS.COM

LINER & ELSEN

In a grape-obsessed town, L&E stands apart due to its well-heeled clientele and proximity to the Nob Hill restaurant district. An adventurous attitude toward far-flung regions is balanced by strong support of local vintners.

2222 NW QUIMBY STREET,
PORTLAND 97210, U.S.
+1 503 241 9463
WWW.LINERANDELSEN.COM

METROVINO

Classes, wine dinners, obscure offerings and a strong sense of adventure all help to set Alberta's most offbeat bottle shop apart from the rest.

722 11TH AVENUE SW,
CALGARY T2R 0E4, CANADA
+1 403 205 3356
WWW.METROVINO.COM

EL MUNDO DEL VINO

Master Sommelier Héctor Vergara's business plan calls for sharp design and savvy selections. Whether you're shopping for deals or "viñas garage," Vergara's got you covered, in four locations.

ISIDORA GOYENECHEA 3000,
LAS CONDES, SANTIAGO, CHILE
+56 02 584 1173
WWW.ELMUNDODELVINO.CL

THE WINE CELLAR

What to do with all those poker-table winnings? Invest them in wine at this serious subterranean gold mine hidden under the Rio resort's not-so-serious masquerade village (where, let's be honest, the much-hyped "show in the sky" is basically just a bunch of ladies frolicking around in their underwear). Down in the cellar, you can browse a collection of 50,000-some bottles, reportedly worth more than $10 million. $1.2 million of that can be accounted for by an 1855-to-1990 vertical collection of Château d'Yquem. The accompanying wine bar offers more than 100 choices by the glass. Ho, hum.

3700 WEST FLAMINGO ROAD, LAS VEGAS 89103
+1 702 777 7962
WWW.RIOLASVEGAS.COM

MUNDO GOURMET

Distrito federal's source for caviar, foie gras, imported cheeses, wine education, oeno-literature and, yes, a broad selection of wines, including options from Mexican producers.

AVENIDA REVOLUCIÓN NO. 1541,
SAN ÁNGEL, MEXICO CITY
+52 55 5616 2162
WWW.MUNDOGOURMET.COM.MX

PIKE & WESTERN WINE SHOP

A shopping trip to Pike Place isn't complete without a stop at this small but discerning shop, where wines from Washington and around the world are chosen with fresh produce in mind.

1934 PIKE PLACE,
SEATTLE 98101
+1 206 441 1307
WWW.PIKEANDWESTERN.COM

PREMIER CRU

Impressive fine-wine showroom with a "specialty reserve room" and French-tilted, well-priced inventory. First in Oakland, then Emeryville; now in posh Berkeley with well-trained wine-loving staff.

1011 UNIVERSITY AVENUE,
SAN FRANCISCO 94710
+1 510 644 9463
WWW.PREMIERCRU.NET

THE RARE WINE CO.

Pssst! Insiders know importer Mannie Berk as the genius behind the "historic series" Madeiras. His warehouse also sells maps, posters, direct-imported balsamico and olive oil, not to mention Berk's impeccable lineup of table wines.

21481 EIGHTH STREET EAST,
SONOMA 95476
+1 800 999 4342
WWW.RAREWINECO.COM

SHERRY-LEHMANN

The Upper East Side's most distinguished oeno-boutique exudes an aura of luxury, yet there's still plenty of choice in the $20-and-under range. The well-heeled clientele indulge in master classes, dinners and Bordeaux futures.

505 PARK AVENUE,
NEW YORK 10022
+1 212 838 7500
WWW.SHERRY-LEHMANN.COM

67WINE

Since 1941, 67wine's cheery yellow awnings and easy-to-navigate layout have invited Upper West Siders to come in and browse. Buyers work the floor, offering expert advice on every category from kosher to sake.

179 COLUMBUS AVENUE,
NEW YORK 10023
+1 212 724 6767
WWW.67WINE.COM

TWENTY TWENTY WINE MERCHANTS

According to the *LA Times*, this boasts the best inventory of old and rare vintages in the U.S. According to *Food & Wine*, movie stars shop there. Enough said!

2020 COTNER AVENUE,
WEST LOS ANGELES 90025
+1 310 447 2020
WWW.2020WINES.COM

WALLY'S WINE & SPIRITS

A California emporium with more than 130,000 bottles, plus cheeses, cured meats, cookies and more. Over-the-top events include a recent 100-point 2009 Bordeaux dinner at Spago, for $1,500 each.

2107 WESTWOOD BOULEVARD,
LOS ANGELES 90025
+1 310 475 0606
WWW.WALLYWINE.COM

ZACHYS WINE AND LIQUOR

Seven decades in business, this attractive brick shop is also home base for a successful wine-auction house and web site. An Enomatic machine allows for extensive in-store tastings.

16 EAST PARKWAY,
SCARSDALE 10583
+1 800 723 0241
WWW.ZACHYS.COM

EUROPE (1)

LEGRAND FILLES ET FILS

For decades, Lucien Legrand and his daughter Francine discovered then-obscure producers such as Mas de Daumas Gassac, Domaine de Trévallon and Zind-Humbrecht and brought them to international prominence through their Parisian shop, a 19th-century spice warehouse they had converted into a gustatory fantasy ("vinotèque" tasting bar, a gourmet store colorfully festooned with sweets and savories, an annex devoted to wine literature, underground cellars). Today, under new ownership, the place remains a whirlwind of activity, hosting art exhibitions, a wine school, performances and tastings that lure top-tier producers.

1 RUE DE LA BANQUE #12, PARIS 75002, FRANCE
+33 1 42 60 07 12
WWW.CAVES-LEGRAND.COM

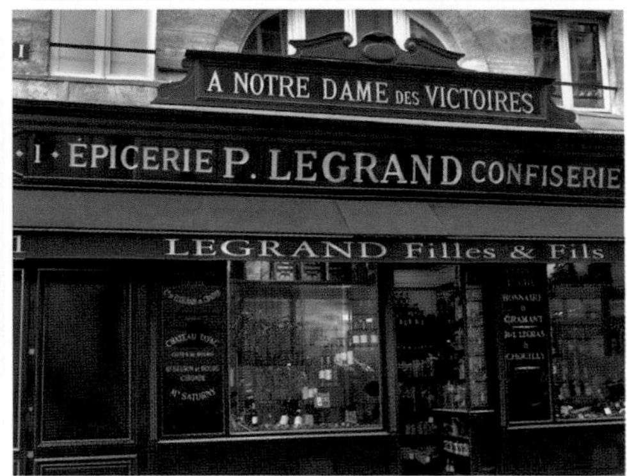

ANTIQUE WINE COMPANY

Whether you need to assemble a seaworthy collection for your yacht, insure your priceless portfolio or build a custom cellar, this oufit has got you covered. Make an appointment to shop where captains of industry do.

53 QUEEN ANNE STREET,
LONDON W1G 9JR, U.K.
+44 20 3219 5588
WWW.ANTIQUE-WINE.COM

LES BABINES

Wine bar offering classes, tastings and a shop offering wines, ciders, spirits and beers. Try a glass before you buy, along with lovingly prepared small plates. Artisan-produced pantry items round out the selection.

25 AVENUE DE LA RÉPUBLIQUE,
PARIS 75011, FRANCE
+33 09 51 87 40 97
WWW.LESBABINES.FR

BERRY BROS & RUDD

BBR employs five Masters of Wine, runs two wine schools and hosts chi-chi events in its townhouse and "Napoleon Cellar." And in case you're feeling intimidated, check out the bargains at the friendly bin-end shop in Basingstoke.

3 ST. JAMES'S STREET,
LONDON SW1A 1EG, U.K.
+44 800 280 2440
WWW.BBR.COM

CAMBRIDGE WINE MERCHANTS

A tasteful independent wine shop that has expanded to seven locations over the past two decades. The earnest oenophiles in charge here like to emphasize family producers in an affordable price range.

42 MILL ROAD,
CAMBRIDGE CB1 2AD, U.K.
+44 12 2356 8993
WWW.CAMBRIDGEWINE.COM

LA CAVE DES PAPILLES

The passionate sommelier-trained staff at Paris's most charming natural wines purveyor claim to offer "authentic and sincere wines, of sensation and emotion." Best of all, the prices are in reach for the bohemian clientele.

35 RUE DAGUERRE,
PARIS 75014, FRANCE
+33 1 43 20 05 74
WWW.LACAVEDESPAPILLES.COM

CAVES AUGÉ

Boutique near the St-Lazare train station crammed with bottles of natural wines you've never heard of. Dating back to 1850 (Proust shopped here), it's famous for its monthly sidewalk tastings and its peevish customer service.

116 BOULEVARD HAUSMANN,
PARIS 75008, FRANCE
+33 1 45 22 16 97
WWW.CAVESAUGE.COM

LES CAVES DU FORUM

Visitors to Champagne know to plunder these 16th-century vaults for their bottled treasures. Geeky finds from regions such as the Jura ensure hours of browsing. The chic upstairs annex hosts tastings and classes.

10 RUE COURMEAUX,
REIMS 51100, FRANCE
+33 3 26 79 15 15
WWW.LESCAVESDUFORUM.COM

CORNEY & BARROW

This 230-year-old firm enjoys exclusive relationships with producers such as DRC, Domaine Leflaive and Salon Champagne. While in London it manages only wine bars, C&B has storefronts in Suffolk and Ayrshire, Scotland.

BELVOIR HOUSE, HIGH STREET,
NEWMARKET CB8 8DH, U.K.
+44 1638 600 000
WWW.CORNEYANDBARROW.COM

CPH GRANDE BOUTIQUE DU VIN

Even in Burgundy, one-stop wine shopping is convenient. On the edge of Beaune, this lovingly curated selection of wines from small-to-medium-sized producers (including non-Burgundians), fits the bill.

AVENUE CHARLES DE GAULLE,
BEAUNE 21200, FRANCE
+33 3 80 24 08 09
WWW.VINSCPH.COM

EUROPE (2)

EATALY

The original outpost of the now-global gastronomic megastore empire, housed in a russet-hued, defunct Carpano Vermouth factory near the Lingotto metro station. A Disney-esque experience for the Slow Food set, its high point (in our opinion) is not its ten trattorias but its Italian wine cellar and reserve room, complete with tasting bar. The jaw-dropping display of 30,000 bottles ranges from the finest Barolos and Champagnes to—yes, it's true!—bulk cuvées priced around $2 per liter. And in the cellars, you'll find barrels of wine aging alongside wheels of Parmigiano.

230/14 VIA NIZZA, TURIN 10126, ITALY
+ OTHER LOCATIONS WORLDWIDE
+39 011 19 50 68 01
WWW.EATALY.IT

DEVINIS ILLUSTRIBUS

A jewel box of a shop leading to dramatically lit 17th-century catacombs near the Panthéon. The stock consists of rare and old bottles, which you can actually dip into by signing up for a guided tasting.

48 RUE DE LA MONTAGNE-STE-GENEVIÈVE, PARIS 75005, FRANCE
+33 1 43 36 12 12
WWW.DEVINIS.COM

ENOTECA BONATTI

Stroll past Piazza Beccaria to reach this friendly bottle shop, owned by the same family since 1934. Euro collector's items join a thoughtfully curated pan-Italian lineup; and they deliver, so stock up for your hotel room.

68 VIA VINCENZO GIOBERTI, FLORENCE 50121, ITALY
+39 055 660050
WWW.ENOTECABONATTI.IT

ENOTECA BUCCONE

A former carriage house near Piazza del Popolo that's been in a few Italian films thanks to its turn-of-the-century antiques, marble-topped tasting tables and vaulted ceilings. Guided tastings include artisanally produced foods.

19-20 VIA DI RIPETTA, ROME 00186, ITALY
+39 06 361 2154
WWW.ENOTECABUCCONE.COM

ENOTECA COSTANTINI

Producer Piero Costanini owns this store as well as the bacchanalian bar, Il Simposio Costanini. Take sommelier courses, browse the sea of bottles, and revel in oddities such as a single-malt whisky from Bangalore, India. When in Rome...

16 PIAZZA CAVOUR, ROME 00193, ITALY
+39 06 320 3575
WWW.PIEROCOSTANTINI.IT

HEDONISM

Who will say this relatively new Mayfair store is not what it claims to be—"the best wine shop there is"? Ancient Madeira, 1811 Yquem, rooms of DRC and Bordeaux first growths, but also hundreds of bottles under $45.

3–7 DAVIES ST, LONDON W1K 3LD, U.K.
+44 207 290 7870
WWW.HEDONISM.CO.UK

L'INTENDANT

While it looks angular and historic from outside, inside this is a modern, spiral-shaped rabbit hole of classed-growth Bordeaux, growing pricier the deeper you descend the twisting stairs (so stick to street level if you're on a budget).

2 ALLÉE DE TOURNY, BORDEAUX 33082, FRANCE
+33 05 56 48 01 29
WWW.CHATEAUPRIMEUR.COM

I PIACERI DEL GUSTO

Truffles and wine? We can't think of a better business plan. Piedmont's palace to all things gustatory boasts four locations, but wine lovers tend to sniff out the strong book and bottle sections in the Alba outlet.

23 VIA VITTORIO EMANUELE, ALBA 12501, ITALY
+39 0173 440166
WWW.IPIACERIDELGUSTO.IT

KADEWE

At this fantasy food bazaar, ensconced in the famed 1907 department store, a dizzying array of gastronomic marvels vie with a gleaming expanse of bottles. Retail and recreation unite in four branded Champagne bars.

21–24 TAUENTZIENSTRASSE, BERLIN 10789, GERMANY
+49 30 21 21 0
WWW.KADEWE.DE

LAVINIA

This gargantuan luxury bottle emporium brings a global perspective to the Madrid wine scene. The sommelier-trained sales staff happily helps bargain hunters and collectors alike. The Paris store may be the world's largest.

16 CALLE DE JOSÉ ORTEGA Y GASSET, MADRID 28006, SPAIN
+34 914 26 06 04
WWW.LAVINIA.ES

LUTTER & WEGNER

Once the favorite hangout of romantic movement author-hero ETA Hoffmann, Lutter & Wegner's wiener schnitzel-centric restaurants are so prolific and popular in Germany and Austria nowadays that one might forget that L&W started out as a wine bar and wine merchant back in 1811. Diners at the elegant Gendarmenmarkt location can browse the floor-to-ceiling, dark-wood shelves to find treasures from Germany and Austria. The word "sekt," for German sparkling wine, apparently entered the lexicon under the roof of Lutter & Wegner; today, the house-label sekt is a screaming deal at around $7 a bottle.

56 CHARLOTTENSTRASSE, BERLIN 10117, GERMANY
+49 030 20 29 54 95
WWW.L-W-BERLIN.DE

LEA & SANDEMAN

London's "most original wine merchants," in five city locations, are friendly and unfussy, offering savvy buys such as a solid house-label Burgundy, and a staff of wine explorers who have actually visited the many producers they stock.

170 FULHAM ROAD,
LONDON SW10 9PR, UK
+44 207 244 0522
WWW.LEAANDSANDEMAN.CO.UK

LA MAISON DU VIN STEINFELS

Zurich's most prominent wine auction house also runs a smart retail store in the Escher Wyss neighborhood, where well-heeled professionals stop by for after-work wine tastings and classes as well as bottles.

PFINGSTWEIDSTRASSE 6,
ZURICH CH-8005, SWITZERLAND
+41 43 444 48 44
WWW.STEINFELSWEINSHOP.CH

MITCHELL & SON

A waterfront warehouse in the international financial services center that once hosted Dublin's legendary Crimean War banquet is now home to this old family-owned retailer. Don't miss the house-blended whiskey.

CHQ BUILDING, IFSC,
DUBLIN 1, REPUBLIC OF IRELAND
+353 01 612 5540
WWW.MITCHELLANDSON.COM

PECK

Milan's four-floor gastronomic paradise near the Duomo. And while the sweets, cured meats, cheeses, prepared foods and pantry items are resplendent, the wine cellar is breathtaking. Deal-seekers should sample the house label.

9 VIA SPADARI,
MILAN 20123, ITALY
+39 02 802 3161
WWW.PECK.IT

RAEBURN FINE WINE

This small Edinburgh wine merchant is an Aladdin's Cave of both classic greats and natural wines, with the exclusive UK rights to several legendary producers, from Gianfranco Soldera's Case Basse, to Josko Gravner.

21/23 COMELY BANK ROAD,
EDINBURGH EH4 1DS, U.K.
+44 131 343 1159
WWW.RAEBURN.CO.UK

THE SAMPLER

A knowledgable and passionate young duo have made their two retail outlets as exciting as any in London, with a broad choice of serious wines to sample from Enomatic machines and a great range of mature and rare wines.

266 UPPER STREET,
LONDON N1 2UQ, U.K.
+44 207 226 9500
WWW.THESAMPLER.CO.UK

SYSTEMBOLAGET

The bad news: the Swedish wine retail trade is controlled by a government monopoly. The good news: Swedes love their wine, and the selection is quite good, particularly at this location near the Kungsträdgården.

REGERINGSGATAN 44,
STOCKHOLM 111 56, SWEDEN
+46 08 796 98 10
WWW.SYSTEMBOLAGET.SE

TERROIRISTEN

Contemporary wine bar and retail store, located on a foodie-focused shopping street in the hopping Noerrebro neighborhood. Specializes in natural wines and direct imports from Italy and Slovenia.

52 JÆGERSBORGGADE,
COPENHAGEN 2200, DENMARK
+45 36 90 60 40
WWW.TERROIRISTEN.DK

UNGER UND KLEIN

In Vienna's textile district, the curving display shelves serve as the wine list for those who choose to linger and dine at this chic wine-bar-cum-bottle shop. Fine choices from Austria and the world, plus a well-priced, juicy house cuvée.

2 GÖLSDORFGASSE,
VIENNA 1010, AUSTRIA
+43 01 532 1323
WWW.UNGERUNDKLEIN.AT

AUSTRALASIA

STEVES FINE WINE & FOOD

More than a half-century in business, but in a thoroughly modern setting, Steves is a must-see for any oenophile in the vicinity of Matilda Bay Reserve. It's a contemporary wine- boutique-eatery-bar, with 35 selections by the glass for sit-down diners and a self-serve Enomatic machine for curious shoppers. The cellar is said to house the largest collection in Australia, and includes marquis European producers—Bordeaux first growths, grand cru Burgundies, Super-Tuscans, top Barolos and the like—along with the best of Australia. In the market, fresh cheeses, preserves, olive oils and other delicacies brighten the shelves.

30 THE AVENUE, NEDLANDS, PERTH, WA 6008, AUSTRALIA
+61 08 9386 5800
WWW.STEVES.COM.AU

BROADWAY CELLARS

Galician José Fernandez imports *jamón iberico*, smoked paprika, saffron and natural ciders, and explores every Spanish wine region to seek out the best bottles, selling both to distributors and to his many customers in Glebe.

96 GLEBE POINT ROAD,
SYDNEY, NSW 2037, AUSTRALIA
+61 2 9817 4564
BROADWAYLIQUOR.COM.AU

CARO'S WINE MERCHANTS

Two oenophilic brothers own this popular Parnell shop and maintain a terrific blog. They team up with winemakers to host popular sit-down tastings, at which the glowing blue fine-wine vault is a scene-stealer.

114 ST GEORGES BAY ROAD,
AUCKLAND, NEW ZEALAND
+64 9 377 9974
WWW.CAROS.CO.NZ

CRYSTAL WINES

Status bottles are proudly on display in this showroom just west of downtown's heart in the Valley Point shopping center. Tastings, wine dinners and cellar storage all help to keep the clientele happy.

491 RIVER VALLEY ROAD,
SINGAPORE, 248371
+65 6737 3540
WWW.CRYSTALWINES.COM

THE MOOMBA WINESHOP

The popular Moomba Australian restaurant and gourmet deli at Boat Quay are accompanied by this bottle boutique, which boasts an unusual and exclusive lineup of Aussie labels. Cellar storage also available.

52A CIRCULAR ROAD,
SINGAPORE 049407
+65 6438 2438
WWW.THEMOOMBA.COM

MONCUR CELLARS

This sleek corner storefront adjoins Bistro Moncur at the Woollahra Hotel. Take home the chef's duck terrine or homemade sausages along with your favorite bottle from France or the southern hemisphere.

60 MONCUR STREET,
SYDNEY, NSW, AUSTRALIA
+61 02 9327 9715
WWW.WOOLLAHRAHOTEL.COM.AU

NICKS WINE MERCHANTS

What began as a rural grocery in 1958 is now East Doncaster's best source for fine bottles. It is also notable for developing the "wine spider" (www.winespider.com)—a rating system for assessing wines.

10–12 JACKSON COURT,
VICTORIA 3109, AUSTRALIA
+61 3 9848 1153
WWW.NICKS.COM.AU

ULTIMO WINE CENTRE

Francophiles flock to this stately brick building near the Powerhouse Museum in the Ultimo district for top-tier Gallic (and global) wines, plus oeno-literature, glassware, tastings and wine dinners.

21/99 JONES STREET,
SYDNEY, NSW 2007, AUSTRALIA
+61 2 9211 2380
WWW.ULTIMOWINECENTRE.COM.AU

THE WINE EMPORIUM

Tastings, classes, special events and a selection of fine wines, beers, ciders and spirits bring residents of the Fortitude Valley / Newstead neighborhoods to the boutique Emporium Hotel building.

SHOP 47, 1000 ANN STREET,
BRISBANE, QLD 4005, AUSTRALIA
+61 07 3252 1117
WWW.THEWINEEMPORIUM.COM.AU

WINE HOUSE

Handsome red Romanesque Revival in Southbank, including a retail component and private function space. WSET courses and a strong selection of Aussie and Kiwi labels make Wine House a true temple to wine.

133 QUEENSBRIDGE STREET,
MELBOURNE 3006, AUSTRALIA
+61 03 9698 8000
WWW.WINEHOUSE.COM.AU

EAST ASIA

BERRYS' FINE WINE RESERVE

While stocking up on ascots and cigars at Alfred Dunhill in the Financial District, why not fill your bags with priceless bottles of first growth Bordeaux and grand cru Burgundy as well? London's St James's-based powerhouse at your service: bespoke wines to go with your bespoke suits. Founded in 1698, BBR is one of the official wine purveyors to the royal family and created Cutty Sark Scotch whisky in 1923. And yet it's also a remarkably forward-thinking firm: it was the world's first online wine retailer and has created a killer iphone and ipad app.

PRINCE'S BUILDING, 10 CHATER ROAD, CENTRAL, HONG KONG
+852 2522 1978
WWW.BBR.COM

CAVE DE RELAX

In Minato near Hibiya Park, a showcase of 100,000 bottles, with sections devoted to both rare wines and global values (including Japanese wines, and no, we don't mean sakes). Step up to the tasting bar to try some by the glass.

1-6-11 NISHIS-SHINBASHI,
TOKYO 105 0003, JAPAN
+81 03 3595 3697
WWW.CAVERELAX.COM

ENOTECA

Importer and wholesaler with 30 shops in Japan, some under the "Les Caves Taillevant" name. Original location is steps from Arisugawa Memorial Park in the Minato district (a healthy walk from the Grand Hyatt).

5-14-15 MINAMIAZABU, ARISUGAWA WEST 1F, TOKYO 106-0047, JAPAN
+81 03 3280 3634
WWW.ENOTECA.CO.JP

EVERWINES

Prolific chain of modern wine boutiques and bars stocking "wines for everyone." A large line-up of greatest hits and sensitivity to scores assure that almost any drinker will walk away happy.

200 TAI ZHOU ROAD,
JING'AN, SHANGHAI, CHINA
+86 021 3208 0293
WWW.EVERWINES.COM

MAJOR CELLAR

Sure, this Kowloon shop stocks almost all of the most coveted French and Italian releases, but it also digs deep into the New World and hosts tastings with top-tier winemakers.

HANKOW CENTRE G6, 5–15
HANKOW ROAD, TSIM SHA TSUI,
HONG KONG
+852 2312 0666
WWW.MAJORCELLAR.COM

RARE AND FINE WINES

Bankers and guests at the Mandarin Oriental might be lured into this Financial District boutique by the Champagne selection, but they stick around for the surprises, from Australia to South Africa.

SHOP L6, THE BANK OF EAST ASIA
BUILDING, 10 DES VOEUX ROAD,
CENTRAL, HONG KONG
+852 2522 9797
WWW.RARENFINEWINES.COM.HK

RED WINE CELLAR

Fine wine retailer with three Hong Kong locations, offering everything from first growth Bordeaux, to New Zealand Sauvignon Blanc. Oh, and yes, they do stock white wines, too.

NICE BUILDING, #3, 6–10 HAU
WONG ROAD KOWLOON CITY,
HONG KONG
+852 2383 4388
WWW.REDWINEHK.COM

TOUR DU VIN

Part of the popular Aligoté Kitchen restaurant group, Tour du Vin is a cozy wine bar/retail store in Seoul's Seorae ("French") Village, with a 500-title list and a clientele that includes Korean music stars.

96-8 BANPOBON-DONG,
SEOCHO-GU, SEOUL,
SOUTH KOREA
+82 02 533 1846
WWW.ALIGOTE.COM

WATSON'S WINE

Part of the multinational AS Watson group, this is a well-organized, temperature-controlled machine, with a wine bar in central Hong Kong and a special fine-wine room in every shop. The original is in the International Finance Centre.

8 FINANCE STREET #3019,
CENTRAL, HONG KONG
+852 2530 5002
WWW.WATSONSWINE.COM

WINE MARKET PARTY

They had us with the name. But the knowledgable sommelier-trained staff at this inviting Shibuya-ku boutique in Yebisu Garden Place can walk you through the broad range, and they sell cheese and gourmet items, too.

YEBISU GARDEN PLACE B1, 4-20-7
EBISU, TOKYO 150 0013, JAPAN
+81 03 5424 2580
WWW.PARTYWINE.COM

5 DINING OUT: NEGOTIATING A RESTAURANT WINE LIST

The sommelier hands you the wine list and you begin to perspire. What to do? 1. Take a deep breath. 2. Get over yourself. 3. Just ask. In wine, there are no stupid questions. So smile at that somm and say, "Could you assist me with a choice?" It's her job, after all, and she'll be happy to help. Here are a few common questions and answers to get you going.

Q CAN I TRUST THE HOUSE WINE?

"If you're at a sandwich shack just off the highway, probably best to stick with beer. But if you're in a restaurant where it's obvious that a wine buyer has put thought into assembling a meaningful wine list, chances are that the "house wine" is good. In some establishments, the house wine changes every week, so ask what it is."

Q I'M TIGHT ON CASH. CAN I JUST ORDER THE SECOND LEAST-EXPENSIVE WINE TO AVOID LOOKING LIKE A TOTAL CHEAPSKATE?

"Here's the problem with this tactic: Many diners have the same idea, so restaurateurs tend to price slow-moving wines accordingly. If you're in a lower price bracket, your best bet is to go for the most ***unusual*** *wine in that range, because sommeliers like to champion their obscure finds by pricing them favorably. And don't be shy about sharing your price constraints with your somm. Remember: Dining professionals tend to be on tight budgets themselves, so they know the bargains. A subtle way to manage this, if you don't want your date to know you're cash-strapped, is to point at a price you can afford and say, "I'm looking for something along the lines of* ***this****." The somm should get the hint."*

Q WHY AREN'T MORE WINES AVAILABLE BY THE GLASS?

"Opened bottles of wine do not keep for long, even if they are resealed and kept refrigerated —up to a week for a big structured red, a couple of days for a delicate white. Rather than serving wine that has lost its freshness, a decent restaurant has to pour unfinished bottles down the drain, which can be costly. Better restaurants tend to have nitrogen preservation systems for open bottles, which is why they can offer more wines by the glass, but these machines are expensive."

Wine List

SPARKLING WINES

Gosset Grande Réserve Brut Champagne NV

La Marca Prosecco di Valdobbiadene NV

WHITE WINES

House white *(by bottle / by glass)*

Bolla Pinot Grigio, Veneto, Italy 2012

au Grüner Veltliner Terrassen, Wachau, Austria 2010

esling, Columbia Valley, Washington State, USA 2012

Dazat Sancerre, Loire Valley, France 2010

ompt Chablis Premier Cru Les Vaillons, Burgundy, France 2010

t Chardonnay, Sanford & Benedict Vineyard, nta Barbara County, California USA 2010

RED WINES

use red *(by bottle / by glass)*

euf Beaujolais-Villages, France 2011

uf Beaujolais-Villages, France 2010

Rioja Crianza, Spain 2008

Chianti Classico, Italy 2008

Hermitage, Rhône Valley, France 2010

r, Central Otago, New Zealand 2010

pa Valley, California 1997

ET WINES

alencia, Spain 2010 *(half bottle / by glass)*

nes, Bordeaux 2007 *(half bottle)*

ED WINES

pain NV *(bottle / by glass)*

, Portugal 1985 *(bottle / by glass)*

Q THERE ARE FOUR OF US EATING TONIGHT. WE'RE ALL HAVING DIFFERENT THINGS, BUT WE WANT ONLY ONE BOTTLE OF WINE—WHAT SHOULD I DO?

"First, ask your dining companions what style of wine they like, regardless of what they're eating. You may discover that the one person who has ordered pork is a big fan of chardonnay, which would work with everyone else's fish, as well. Also, don't be shy about discussing a price range you can all agree on; if you are going to be splitting the bill, better to discuss this now than to deal with disgruntled looks later. Finally, give your sommelier or server all the information you've gathered and ask for help in choosing something."

Q I'VE SEEN THIS WINE AT MY LOCAL BOTTLE SHOP. WHY IS IT SO MUCH MORE EXPENSIVE HERE?

"Restaurants buy wines wholesale just like shops do, but because restaurants are providing glassware, service and food-pairing expertise, their markups are much higher than retail. You can get around this by bringing your own bottle, but you'll be charged a corkage fee (in the U.S., this can run from $10 to $30), so it's often less expensive to pay the restaurant price."

Q I'VE NEVER HEARD OF CHÂTEAU SUDUIRAUT. WHAT DOES IT TASTE LIKE? CAN I TRY IT FIRST?

"If the wine is available by the glass, most restaurants will allow you to taste it before ordering it. But if it's a by-the-bottle selection, it's less likely that you'll be allowed an advance taste, since once it's open, the wine can spoil, and it would be difficult to re-sell since customers like to see their bottle opened at the table."

6 DINING OUT: TOP CHEFS & SOMMS SPILL THEIR WINE-PAIRING SECRETS

Just how far can food-and-wine pairing go? We've asked some of the world's most exciting chefs to share their tastiest morsels of vinous wisdom, and—along with some of our fave somms—to recall their most memorable matching experiences. You'll see every wine style represented here, and paired in unusual ways with some of the planet's best food. Perhaps you'll be inspired to try your own outrageous match-ups. *Bon appétit*!

THE CHEF: GUY SAVOY

PARIS + LAS VEGAS + SINGAPORE

THE RESTAURANTS: Guy Savoy + Atelier Maitre Albert + Le Bouquinistes + Le Chiberta.

WINE WEAKNESSES: Savennières; white wines from Anjou; Champagne.

THE WISDOM: "The first rule is *no rules*... The most important rule is to wonder with whom we should drink a wine, not what dish we should eat with it."

THE MATCH: "A *lièvre à la Royale* (traditional hare stew) with a Château d'Yquem 1943; or caviar with Pommard Rugiens."

THE STYLES: Lusciously sweet white; light, refreshing red.

THE CHEF(S): MASSIMILIANO AND RAFFAELE ALAJMO

PADUA + VENICE

THE RESTAURANTS: Le Calandre + Quadri.

WINE WEAKNESSES: Champagne; white or red from Burgundy; native varieties from Piedmont or Tuscany; Trebbiano or Ribolla.

THE WISDOM: "I like contrast and balance." – Max. "I pair wine with the situation, not the food." – Raf.

THE MATCH: "A 2010 Josko Gravner Ribolla Anfora with whole-wheat panettone, made with extra-virgin olive oil and prunes." – Max.

"Château Musar 2003 with chicken liver, sage and lemon-zest risotto." – Raf.

THE STYLES: Orange wine (see unit on rosés); structured, medium-bodied reds.

THE CHEF: ADAM BYATT

LONDON

THE RESTAURANTS: Trinity + Bistro Union.

WINE WEAKNESSES: Rhône Valley; older Bordeaux; new-world Chardonnay without food, white Burgundy with food.

THE WISDOM: "The wine has to act as a balance for the food. If the dish is sweet, I will look for wine with high tannin and acidity. If the dish has richness and fat, I'm looking for more fruit and mineral content to balance those out."

THE MATCH: "Back in 2002, I did a dish of cod, poached in Banyuls, then pressed in a terrine with foie gras and served with a reduction of Banyuls. We served this with a glass of slightly warmed Banyuls. I thought it was great! But then, those were heady days..."

THE STYLE: Fortified wine.

PRIVÉE
GUY SAVOY

THE CHEF: CARLO CRACCO

MILAN

THE RESTAURANT: Ristorante Cracco.

WINE WEAKNESSES: Organic and biodynamic wines.

THE WISDOM: "Sometimes the best thing to do is to be totally free and work with the mind, senses and emotions."

THE MATCH: "I paired not a wine, but Fentimans tonic water from the UK, with my new creation called 'Acids,' which is a composition of different acidic ingredients such as green tomato pulp, tuna eggs, yogurt, baby cucumber, basil seeds, goat mascarpone cream, lemon skin, glacialis... and it matched just perfectly."

THE STYLE: No wine!

THE CHEF: ALEXANDRE GAUTHIER

MONTREUIL-SUR-MER

THE RESTAURANT: La Grenouillère.

WINE WEAKNESSES: Whites and reds from the Jura.

THE WISDOM: "Stop believing in prejudgments. Pairing food and beverages is an infinite route full of discovery, happiness and disappointment. To discover those moments of happiness, we need to get off the beaten path."

THE MATCH: "Praline and Jerusalem artichoke ice cream with a tannic red Bordeaux. The freshness and delicacy of the dessert goes perfectly with the strength of the wine. It is a pairing that is very contemporary and at the same time very classical."

THE STYLE: Rich, full red.

THE CHEF: ANNA HANSEN

LONDON

THE RESTAURANT: The Modern Pantry.

WINE WEAKNESSES: Greco di Tufo or Falanghina from Campania; Pinot Noir from New Zealand.

THE WISDOM: "If I have a special bottle, I'll cook food to suit the wine, rather than the other way around. If you think about the wine as a sauce to balance the food, you won't go far wrong."

THE MATCH: "Garlicky snails with chorizo mash swamps almost any wine you could imagine. One day—more or less by accident—I tried it with Gonzalez Byass's Apostoles, a Palo Cortado Sherry, and it worked brilliantly because it had enough character to cut through a really strongly-flavored, palate-coating dish: bone-dry, but rich and nutty, with a terrific lemony acidity and great length."

THE STYLE: Fortified wine.

THE CHEF: ENRICO CRIPPA

ALBA

THE RESTAURANT: Piazzo Duomo.

WINE WEAKNESSES: Champagne and Franciacorta; Barolo and Barbaresco.

THE WISDOM: "Wines should be paired with intelligence and good taste. That's it!"

THE MATCH: "My 'Salad 21, 31, 41' (seasonal, fresh vegetables with dashi marinade) with Riesling Auslese from Mosel, Germany... outstanding!"

THE STYLE: Lively, aromatic white.

THE SOMM: GERARD BASSET

HAMPSHIRE, U.K.

THE RESTAURANT: Hotel TerraVina.

THE MATCH: Chilled Pinotage + sushi.

THE STYLE: Rich, full-bodied red.

THE SOMM: ANTOINE PETRUS

PARIS

THE RESTAURANT: Restaurant Lasserre.

THE MATCH: 48-month-old Comté from Fromagerie Antony + Madeira flight of Sercial 1910, Bual 1864, and "a magic solera from 1748."

THE STYLE: Fortified wines.

THE SOMM: ADRIEN FALCON

NEW YORK

THE RESTAURANT: Bouley.

THE MATCH: Miso, razor clams, scallops and orange paste + 1989 Beerenauslese Riesling.

THE STYLE: Lusciously sweet white.

THE SOMM: YVONNE CHEUNG

HONG KONG

THE RESTAURANTS: Upper House + Café Gray Deluxe.

THE MATCH: 2001 Domaine Huët Demi-Sec Vouvray + artichoke potage with elderflower and chrysanthemum.

THE STYLE: Lively, aromatic white.

THE SOMM: FRÉDÉRIC WOELFFLE

MONTE CARLO

THE RESTAURANT: Hotel Métropole Monte-Carlo.

THE MATCH: A sweet, egg-based dessert + an old Colheita Port.

THE STYLE: Fortified wine.

THE SOMM: FERRAN CENTELLES

BARCELONA

THE RESTAURANT: elBulli (–2011).

THE MATCH: Mussels steamed in Riesling + Georg Breuer Schlossberg.

THE STYLE: Lively, aromatic white.

THE SOMM: RAJAT PARR

SAN FRANCISCO

THE RESTAURANTS: RN74 (+ Mina Group restaurants, U.S.)

THE MATCH: Domaine Jamet Côte-Rôtie + lamb vindalhoo.

THE STYLE: Rich, full-bodied red.

THE SOMM: PAZ LEVINSON

BUENOS AIRES

THE RESTAURANT: Nectarine.

THE MATCH: Grilled artichokes with roasted walnuts and *jamón Iberico* + Bodegas Lopez "Jerez" Fortified Wine, Argentina.

THE STYLE: Fortified wine.

THE SOMM: YANNIS KHÉRACHI

MONTPELLIER

THE RESTAURANT: Le Jardin des Sens.

THE MATCH: Roasted Breton lobster with spices and sautéed wild mushrooms + 2001 Château Rayas Châteauneuf-du-Pape.

THE STYLE: Rich, full-bodied red.

THE SOMM: NICOLAS BOISE

SAN SEBASTIÁN

THE RESTAURANT: Mugaritz.

THE MATCH: Steamed sea anemone, served over bone marrow + Equipo Navazos La Bota de Fino Marcharnudo Alto No. 27.

THE STYLE: Fortified wine.

7 DINING OUT: WAITER, THERE'S A FLAW IN MY GLASS

The wine is poured. We swirl and sniff. And it smells…funny. But what if it's *supposed* to smell that way? Any time you purchase a faulty wine, you should be able to exchange it for a replacement. That said, one person's off-putting aroma might be another's olfactory bliss. So: Did you get a bum bottle, or not? Here's a list of red flags that will alert you to the most common wine flaws…and non-flaws, with tips on how to identify them.

FLAWED

Buttered Popcorn: **Diacetyl**, a naturally occurring byproduct of malolactic fermentation, smells and tastes like butterscotch or buttered popcorn. While it's permissible (to an extent) in an intentionally buttery Chardonnay, it should not be noticeable in red wines or most other whites.

Dank Swimming Pool, Wet Cardboard, Damp Basement: This odor is caused by the chemical compound 2, 4, 6-trichloroanisole (TCA) and is known as **cork taint**. Since it's usually just an individual bottle that's **corked**, a duplicate from the same producer should be just fine.

Madeira or Stewed Vegetables: Madeira, of course, should smell like Madeira. Any other wine that smells this way has been in an excessively warm environment. You might be able to identify a **cooked** bottle before you open it, because the expansion of warm air will have caused the cork to protrude a bit; it also may look suspiciously brownish.

Rubber, Burnt Match: When **sulfur dioxide**, used as a preservative, reacts adversely with wine, **reductive** aromas result. If you stir the wine with a silver spoon, toss a penny into the glass, or let it aerate for half an hour, you might find that the **bottle stink** has **blown off.**

Skunk, Rotten Eggs, Cabbage: Sulfur, in various forms, is both friend and foe of the winemaker. It can act as a preservative and a fungicide, but too much of it can be a nasty thing...and if the overexposure didn't happen during the bottling process, a silver spoon probably won't help you out. Sorry about that.

Vinegar, Nail Polish Remover: **Volatile acidity**, as **acetic acid**, makes wine smell like vinegar and might have happened in handling or storage. In the form of ethyl acetate, it's responsible for the delightful aroma of rubber cement or nail polish remover. In this case, the fault occurred at the winery, so a duplicate bottle will be just as nasty.

NOT FLAWED... OR...?

Barnyard, Cow Manure, Stinky Cheese: ***Brettanomyces***, or **brett**, is a yeast that commonly crops up in wineries. Some enthusiasts love the **funk** notes of a rustic, bretty wine. Brett-haters claim it's a flaw, the result of unsanitary conditions in the winery. An overwhelming odor of it is a fault.

Crystals: **Tartaric acids** coat the insides of wine barrels and look like tiny shards of glass. Many producers **cold-stabilize** their wines to get rid of them, but if you find these **tartrates** in your glass or on your cork, rest assured that they are totally harmless natural deposits.

Decrepit Cork: As we now know, a "corked" wine has been exposed to TCA, (which is ironically introduced by chlorine *cleansers*, used on the cork or in the winery). But if the cork *looks* rotten, the wine is probably fine—so long as the seal has remained airtight. Some producers occasionally **recork** old bottles for customers to ensure their longevity.

Moth-Eaten Label: Wine should be stored in humid cellar conditions so that the cork won't dry out and allow air into the bottle. So if the label on that older wine looks like it's been sitting in a rainforest, possibly collecting moss, all the better. Drink up!

Sherry: This is tricky, because many wines—including, of course, Sherry—are intentionally made in an **oxidative** style. An **oxidized** wine, on the other hand, has been overexposed to oxygen, either in the winery or in a bottle with a faulty cork. There's no harm in asking your sommelier, "Is this *supposed* to smell like Sherry?"

Spritz: Vintners add carbon dioxide to many light whites and rosés at bottling to keep them fresh and lively. But a glass of *still* red wine that's spritzy may have finished off its fermentation in the bottle, unbeknownst to the winemaker (usually a small producer whose cellar is naturally chilly). If you aerate a spritzy red, the fizz may flatten out.

SECTION 3
SERVING AND DRINKING WINE

1 TOOLS OF THE TRADE: WHAT TO STOCK UP ON

Sure, you can get by with a corkscrew and a couple of glasses. But if you plan to delve deeply into wine appreciation, you'll want to be armed with the proper equipment. Here are some of the devices you'll find in the cellars of serious oenophiles.

WINE BAG

The pros wheel around town with nylon rollerbags (approximately $65 to $350) built specially for bottles, but I prefer my nine-bottle Reisenthal Bottlebag (approximately $15), made from indestructible polyester (better than those flimsy freebies from wine shops), for traveling to dinner parties.

TRAVEL PROTECTOR

For air travel, you can purchase expensive foam-lined titanium wine cases, but the Wine Skin ($3 each, *top right*), a leak-proof, lined plastic bag, works fine when stuffed into the middle of your suitcase. Or, devise something with bubble wrap; just remember that wine must always be checked and can't be carried into the cabin of the airplane, however much you might want to coddle it there, and however special the wine might be.

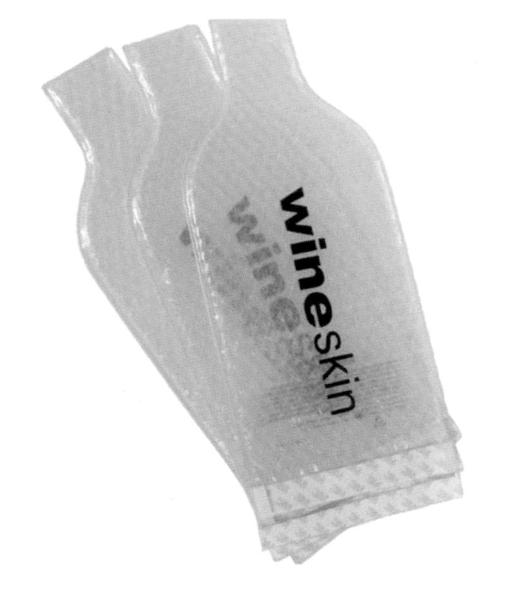

ICE BUCKET

Glass or crystal ice buckets are accidents waiting to happen; go for a basic stainless-steel model instead. Handles can be helpful, so long as they aren't attached with flimsy screws or joints that could rust or fall off with frequent use. And anyway, hold your bucket from the bottom, please.

CHOOSING A DECANTER

Grandma's antique cut-crystal decanter is lovely to look at, but impractical—heavy and probably rather too high in lead, too. Invest in a simple decanter with a wide bottom, gently curving neck and flared top. Even better: A "duck"-shaped decanter, which is tilted on its side and includes a handle for easy pouring. (These sell for anywhere from $25 to $300.)

WHAT'S IN YOUR DOCTOR'S KIT?

"When I do outside events, like private tastings for collectors, I come to their houses with a doctor's bag of tools," says Michael Madrigale, the smooth-serving Head Sommelier and Wine Buyer for Bar Boulud, Épicerie Boulud and Boulud Sud in New York City. What's in Madrigale's "doctor's bag"? For starters, a cradle: "It's as basic as the wheel, and just as essential. It looks antiquated, like this little wicker Easter basket," Madrigale observes. "But it's super-duper functional, especially if you don't want to decant the bottle."

WHEN TO USE A CRADLE

"There are certain wines, like hundred-year-old Bordeaux, that you don't want to decant because it's going to fall off the cliff very quickly. So stand the bottle straight up for a day, then set it in a cradle (approximately $25) and pour it from the cradle," advises Madrigale. This way, the sediment stays in the bottle, and doesn't end up in your glass.

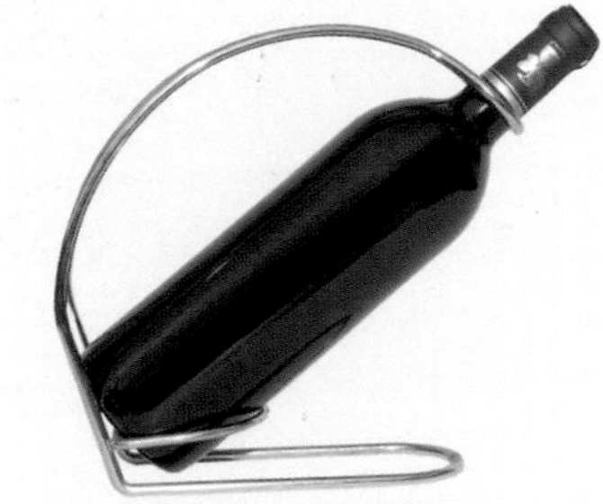

CORK RETRIEVER

"Every good sommelier should have one," Madrigale tells me. "It's kind of like that machine at carnivals that you use to clamp on a fuzzy stuffed animal and pull it out of the bin." Use this inexpensive tool (approximately $5 to $15) to fish out a broken cork that's aggravatingly floating around in your bottle.

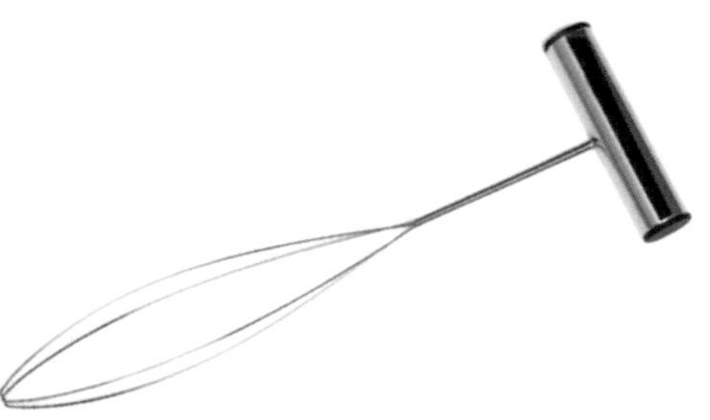

COLOR-CODING LABELS

"As the evening progresses, you can quite easily forget which glass is which, and perish the thought that you might pour the wrong wine in the wrong glass," says Madrigale. "I just use those little color-coding stickers that are sold at office-supply stores to mark the foot of each glass. It's classy, and it's a cool way of keeping track."

WAITER'S WINE KEY

Fancy devices can break, and they don't fit in your pocket. I have about ten Pulltap's waiter's wine keys stashed throughout my house, in various kitchen drawers, my cellar, my wine bag, and maybe even my bike and my car, come to think of it. Costing only about $5 to $20, the double-hinged "waiter's friend" model won't let you down.

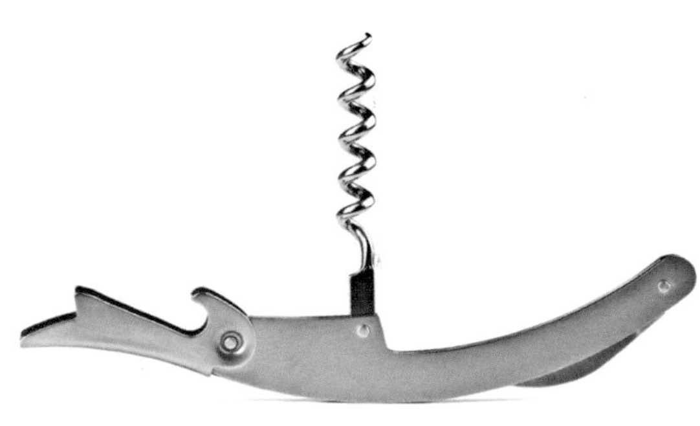

HIGHER-END CORKSCREW

If you'd like to invest in something more substantial, check out the handsome and compact wood-handled corkscrews from the French brand Laguiole, which have a nice heft when held in your palm (prices start at around $120) and curved blades. Whichever wine key you choose, make sure it has a serrated blade for cutting through foil capsules.

THE DURAND

"This thing is the bomb; it's really good," swears Madrigale. "It's this thing that's like the love child of a corkscrew and an Ah-So. First, twist the coil (also known as the "worm") into the cork. Then, stick the Ah-So prongs in on top and connect the two parts." Give the whole thing a gentle twist, and that fragile cork is out in one piece. ($125)

2 TOOLS OF THE TRADE: STEMWARE

I'd hate for anyone to think that they couldn't properly enjoy wine without purchasing 15 different shapes and sizes of sommelier-grade crystal stemware. At the same time, if you're reading this book, you're probably looking to take your involvement with wine from casual to passionate. In which case, you should invest in at least a few key pieces.

THE BASICS: MATERIAL AND SHAPE

Let's begin by deconstructing the form, to deepen your understanding of the essentials, and then explore a few shapes that will cover a lot of vinous territory. For starters, consider raw materials. Crystal may be pricier than ordinary glass, but it's much better for wine appreciation; made with barium, potassium, zinc (or, decreasingly, lead) instead of calcium, it's clearer, shinier and denser. Its strength allows it to take more daring shapes, and it conducts aromas more fluidly than simple glass does.

Sip wine out of a cheapie goblet and you'll get a mouthful of nothing but glass (yes, glass does have a distinct aroma and flavor). Crystal's strength allows for a construction of thin walls and a clean-cut—rather than rounded—rim, delivering wine directly to your alimentary canal without getting in the way. As for that classic tulip shape, the rounded bowl brings the wine's maximum surface area in contact with oxygen, then funnels the resulting aromas through the tapered top toward your proboscis. And the stem serves three purposes: It allows you to hold your glass without warming it up; it elevates your view, so that you can admire the wine from every angle; and it underscores the elegance of the sipping experience. Of course, long, thin stems are fragile. If you can find a quality crystal glass with a fairly short stem, you're in luck.

ON STEMS AND DISHWASHERS

I find stemless wine glasses to be as graceless as decapitated tulips. For starters, that Vinho Verde won't stay ice-cold for long when you're gripping the bowl with your 98.6° F metacarpus. Forget about serving finger foods, unless you don't mind the sight of greasy prints sullying those crystal-clear globes. Good luck assessing clarity and color when your wine is down amid the jumble of the tabletop; and if you're the sort who swirls overzealously, prepare for more wayward drips of *rouge*. Finally, I've heard the argument that the stemless glass is less likely to break during washing, but I don't buy it. Of all the stemware I've broken over the years, it has always been the bowl that has shattered.

Speaking of washing: Restaurants use automatic dishwashers, and so do I, and so can you. The two greatest risks to your glassware are your two hands at the end of a wine-soaked evening. But if you are determined to hand-wash, follow these steps: 1) Rinse the glass. If some wine residue sticks to the bottom, pour warm water in the bowl and allow it to soak a few minutes. 2) Remove lipstick marks and germs by gently wiping a damp, barely soapy sponge or cloth around the rim. Hold the bowl, not the base! 3) Rinse the glass again with warm water and allow to air-dry. Important: Keep soap out of the bowl, unless you want your next glass of wine to smell like shampoo.

A GOOD HOME TRUTH

The old adage that stemware should be hand-washed is bunk. Older dishwashers used powdered soaps that created an unsightly film on glassware, but modern dishwashers take liquid soap and rinse agents, waste less water than hand-washing does, and leave your crystal looking crystal-clear.

SHOPPING FOR THE BASICS

Now it's time to shop. We'll look below at six basic pieces that should meet all of your stemware needs. They're arranged in such a way that you can start out by purchasing the first shape, then transition onto additional shapes as your vinous curiosity and budget allow. You should consider your investment in glassware to be as important—and also as risky—as an investment in fine wine: Wait until you can afford the highest quality possible, and be prepared for the occasional disappointment along the way (the corked wine or, in this case, the glass that is knocked to the floor with a crash). The most important thing is to buy your crystal from a producer that has designed pieces with serious wine-tasting in mind.

FIRST: AN ALL-PURPOSE AND A FLUTE

An inexpensive 12-to-14-ounce goblet will go a long way. Don't worry about what it's called; if it's got a nice round bowl and thin rim, it will accommodate reds, whites, bubbles and dessert wines. Beer, too! Insider tip: You may be able to find a good basic crystal glass at a restaurant-supply store in boxes of twelve or 24. Buy a case, or two...or three. Entertaining is oh-so-much more fun if you can put an elegant stem in every guest's hand at that cocktail party for 30. Once you've built up your collection of fine crystal stemware, you can always relegate these all-around glasses to the kitchen cupboard for nightly use and save the expensive stuff for special dinner parties. And don't think twice about slipping these puppies into the dishwasher.

Now we must shift our attention to bubbly. Although quite a few wine professionals prefer to sip Champagne from large wine glasses, the flute remains the most elegant shape, and the best way to view those endlessly mesmerizing lines of bubbles. Also, its limited size allows for a bottle of expensive Champers to last a bit longer. So get yourself a set of at least eight 8-ounce Champagne flutes. These should be narrower at the lip than the bowl to better channel the delicate aromatics of sparkling wine. If Champagne isn't on the agenda, pour sweet or fortified wines into your flutes. It's a pretty way to serve these pigment-rich wines, and the 8-ounce size limits the volume to the amount of Madeira you might actually want to consume in one sitting.

SECOND: A SNIFTER

Your grandfather drank Scotch out of a heavy, cut-crystal, old-fashioned glass. But that doesn't mean that you have to do so as well. Instead, go for a squat glass with a rounded bowl that will accommodate a couple of ice cubes—just in case you or your guests like your brown liquor on the rocks. A short or nonexistent stem means you'll warm your whiskey or brandy with your hand, opening it up. And while this style of glass works best for Scotch, brandy or bourbon, it does double duty for Port, Madeira or dessert wines.

As for which manufacturer to look out for, the big name in the game is Riedel, the Austrian crystal company that pioneered the practice of designing lots of specific shapes to best suit the diverse array of vinous varieties and styles. Far-fetched as the idea might seem, these shapes really do work—I've tested them numerous times—to emphasize the best characteristics of each particular wine. That said, your senses won't be woefully deprived if you sip out of a more standard-shaped glass. Riedel also owns one of its direct competitors, Spiegelau, which tends to be a bit more affordable; other good brands to look for are Rosenthal, Schott Zwiesel, Stötlzle and Zalto. If you're registering for wedding gifts, better department and specialty stores (like Tiffany & Co.) will all offer wine-minded selections of crystal.

AND A GIANT

Ready to relegate your all-around glasses to aperitif hour? Your starter glasses are great for that moment when you're cooking and everyone else is standing around the kitchen, snacking on hors d'oeuvres. But the next step is to make a statement on the dinner table with a set of oversized Bordeaux glasses, with a capacity of 20 to 30 ounces. Of course, you won't be pouring 30 ounces of wine into each one—a standard wine bottle only holds 25 ounces of fluid! Instead, carefully pour red wine into the bottom of the bowl until you reach the widest part. (That's only about a quarter of the way up.) This way, you won't empty the bottle before you've reached everyone's place setting. And, more important, you'll be aerating that rich red for maximum enjoyment.

LAST: A WHITE AND A RED BURGUNDY

Your guests have sipped white wine or Champagne during cocktail hour. But now it's time to sit down to dinner, and you're planning on serving that fabulous magnum of Montrachet. A small-to-medium-sized stem, holding 12 to 20 ounces, will look elegant next to your larger Bordeaux glasses, and there won't be any confusion about which wine goes where. Some aficionados swear by a wider, balloon-like bowl for aerating Chardonnay and fine white Burgundies, but if you're not a committed Chard drinker, go for the more standard U shape, which will suit Riesling, Chenin Blanc and any other fine white you've got up your sleeve as well.

Finally, if you've fallen in love with Pinot Noir, it really is worthwhile to invest in a Burgundy glass, ridiculous as it may look. At its most awesome—i.e., the Riedel Sommelier Series model (*below*), at $125 a pop—this ungainly thing holds 37 ounces, or more than a liter, of liquid. And while a Bordeaux-style glass cartoonish-ly over-accentuates the delicate fruit and bright acidity in Pinot, a good Burgundy glass shows this wine's subtle shades. The large bowl aerates, the narrow top focuses aromas, and the flared lip smooths out the mouthfeel. Because this glass is so ungainly, it isn't an ideal candidate for large dinner parties, where it will take up too much table space. So just purchase two or four, and bring them out for special bottles to be shared among close family and friends.

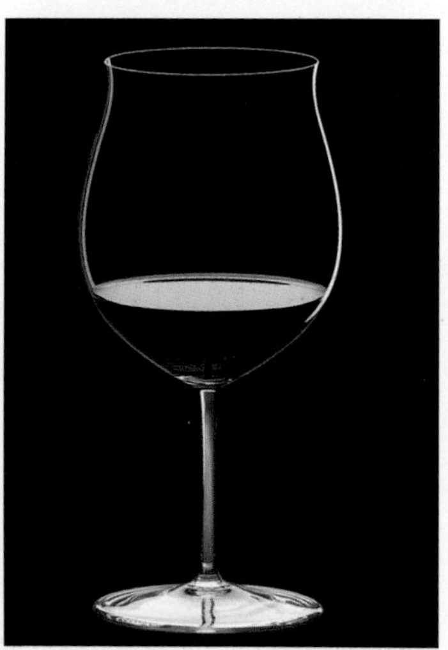

3 TOOLS OF THE TRADE: WINE STORAGE & PRESERVATION

Most wine is consumed within a few hours of purchase. But perhaps you're ready to buy a few special cases to put down for some years. Protect your investment by storing that special wine properly. Here's how.

KNOW THY ENEMIES

Here are the foes of wine: Light. Agitation. Heat. Fluctuating temperature. Dryness. (That's LAHFD for short—ha!) Here are some of the worst places to store your wine: Over the refrigerator or next to the radiator (hot/dry). Next to a drafty window (light/fluctuating temperature). In an apartment that's next to train tracks (agitation).

YOUR KITCHEN FRIDGE IS NOT YOUR FRIEND

It's fine for chilling a bottle for tonight, but don't keep your wine in your regular refrigerator long-term—it's too dry in there. If you open a white or a red, and recork it, you can keep it fresh in your fridge (not on the counter!) for a few days, but be aware that if there's something stinky, like fish, in there, your wine will be compromised.

YOUR CAR IS A DEATH TRAP (FOR WINE)

It's never a good idea to leave wine in your car. If you're driving to a summer getaway with some special bottles, devise a chest or box, equipped with ice packs, and padded with towels, to keep your wine cool, dark and stable. If the weather is cold, insulate your bottles so they don't freeze.

ABOUT THAT AUNT OF YOURS...

Say a family member has a magnificent wine cellar setup. Why not stash your treasures with Aunt Eloise? Here are three reasons, for starters: You can't be sure that the conditions will always be ideal; Auntie may forget the wine is yours and drink it; and what if she goes out of town and you need your wine? Better to find your own solution.

BEDDING DOWN AT A BOTTLE SHOP

Some bottle shops offer professional storage services to their customers, for a fee. This can work well if you always plan to order wine through this particular merchant, but it can be awkward if you decide you'd prefer to shop elsewhere. Also, it can be inconvenient if you need to get to your wine in off-hours when the shop is closed.

GOING WITH THE PROS

Most major cities have professional wine-storage, where you can keep your wine in a secure, humidity-and temperature-controlled unit for a fee. The best facilities are constantly staffed, allow you 24-hour secure access, include monthly gatherings for members, and are pretty great!

ARE YOU VERY OLD? BECAUSE YOU'VE GOT LINES ON YOUR NECK

In theory, a wine cork creates an airtight seal. In practice, cork is a somewhat porous substance that allows for a tiny bit of evaporation each year. Over time, older wines—even in the best storage conditions—will lose volume. When assessing old wines for auction or resale, experts measure the liquid level in the bottle, or the ***ullage****. In young wines, the ullage should be in the* ***neck****. If it's at the mid-shoulder or lower in an older wine, cork deterioration is suspected and the wine's value is downgraded.*

MAKING YOUR SPACE WORK

Provided you don't live directly over a subway line, on a bobbing sailboat or in a sauna, there may be a good spot in your home to stash a case or two: the back of a cool, dark closet, or in the crawl space under the stairs. Just be sure to store your wine on its side, unless it's Champagne or Madeira, which like to be upright.

MAKE IT A SAFE ROOM

If you've got a spare storage room or empty corner in a nice cool basement—or if you're contemplating building a cellar—consider taking a few additional steps to secure your wine. A lock on the door isn't a bad idea, especially if you've got wiley teenagers around.

WINE COOLERS

As I've explained, the refrigeration process is drying. So what about those special wine coolers? It's worthwhile to invest in a high-end model that includes humidity and precise temperature control. Beware of the lower-end "beverage fridge," which is fine for chilling wines, but over the long term will dry out those corks.

RACKS

As you consider racks or shelving for your cellar, choose a design that's flexible enough to hold oversized and undersized bottles. Avoid those with small square openings and go for big X or diamond shapes instead. And be sure the rack can be secured to the wall, so it won't tip over.

TYPE IT OR TAG IT?

Congratulations: You've installed a cellar! Now, are you planning to amass thousands of bottles, to resell at auction? If your answer is no, don't waste your time on wine-cataloging software. Instead, check out online wine-specialty stores for simple single-bottle tags. You can write on these tags with an extraordinary device. It's called a pen.

TEMPERATURE CONTROL

If you live in a warm region, or if you might resell your wine, you should invest in a specialized, programmable cellar-cooling system. It should include an evaporator, to keep the humidity level high. Typical home air conditioning, like refrigeration, is drying; and you need to ensure that your wine will stay cool even when you're out.

4 HOW TO SERVE WINE: OPENING AND DECANTING

Now that you've bought that beautiful decanter, let's put it to use. I've asked Gerard Basset, the owner of Hotel Terravina in the United Kingdom and the first person on the planet to have achieved both the Master of Wine and Master Sommelier distinctions (oh, and he was also crowned the "World's Best Sommelier" in 2010) to help me out in offering some advice on opening and decanting wines.

DECANT MOST REDS

"I decant most red wines, unless it is a very old bottle and I am worried about giving it too much air, because that could damage it," says Basset. "But a two-, three-, 10- or 15-year-old wine? Decanting will ensure you don't have any sediment. And a little bit of air doesn't do any harm."

TIMING YOUR DECANTING

Decant most white wines and very old red wines just prior to serving. Serious red wines, including Vintage Ports, can benefit from an hour or two of aeration in a decanter. Decant dense Barolos and Barbarescos around lunchtime—especially if they're less than 20 years old—if you're preparing for a dinner party later in the evening.

PREPARING AND OPENING A BOTTLE

An older bottle that has been stored on its side should sit upright for at least 24 hours so that the sediment will drop to the bottom. Then, Basset recommends leaning it into a cradle: "Keeping the bottle as horizontal as possible, put the basket around the bottle, hardly moving the bottle."

If you're using a waiter's wine key, flip out the serrated blade and run it around the second lip of the bottle. (That's where there's a little ledge in the glass.) Pros typically don't tear all the foil off; they just neatly remove the top portion.

Twist the corkscrew coil in and use the metal arm to lever the cork out of the bottle. If you've got a hinged-arm corkscrew, clamp the middle ledge onto the lip of the bottle first, pull the cork out a bit, then clamp the lower ledge, and finish gently pulling out the cork.

LIGHT A CANDLE AND DECANT

"Take the bottle out of the basket, and, keeping it as horizontal as possible, hold it in front of a lit candle or small lamp (so that you can see the sediment) and decant it in one go," says Basset. Stop pouring when you see the sediment getting close to the neck of the bottle. This applies even to the very fine, smoky sediment, which can often taste quite bitter if it makes it into your glass.

PREPARING A CHAMPAGNE BOTTLE

Peel the foil from the top of the bottle with your fingers and, holding your thumb over the top of the cork, twist the wire fastener loose. Remove the wire cage while keeping a thumb over the top of the cork. An explosive "pop" is a great way to lose a lot of wine. Instead, grip the cork and, maintaining a bit of downward pressure, slowly twist it. Try to remove the cork silently, or with the faintest hiss—"a nun passing gas," as a sommelier once described it to me.

THE INDISPENSIBLE TOWEL

Sommeliers call them serviettes; we call them tea towels. Either way, they're essential for wine service. Put a towel under a bottle of wine to avoid scratching or staining marble kitchen countertops. And always have one on hand when you're opening Champagne in case of an eruption. Use your towel to wipe off the top of the cork after you've removed the foil, then again to dab the lip of the bottle after you've removed the cork. And if you're a sloppy pourer (who isn't, other than sommeliers?), you can wipe dribbles of wine off the side of the wine bottle or the foot of a guest's glass.

YOU CAN DECANT WHITES, TOO

Decanting is an insurance policy for lighter whites—if they stink of sulfur, that smell should "blow off" if you open and decant the wine in advance. And whites made in an oxygen-friendly style, such as many white Burgundies, will open up in a decanter. You can even decant Champagne!

QUICKIE DECANTING ALTERNATIVE

Don't have the time or patience to decant? Simply pour the wine a half-hour before your guests arrive. Each glass will benefit from the oxygen exposure, and the wine remaining in the half-full bottle will also get a bit of breathing time. "If it is a new wine and you know that there is no sediment, you can be more relaxed about it," says Basset.

FILL THE GLASSES

"Fill" is really the wrong verb here, because you should pour only to the widest part of the glass, for maximum oxygen exposure. "If you have filled the glass to one-third or even one-quarter, the wine will open up very quickly," says Basset.

EXTRA CREDIT: DOUBLE DECANT

If you want to be a total pro about it, you can rinse the sediment out of the bottle, allow it to dry, and then pour or siphon the decanted wine back into the bottle for presentation's sake—especially if you have a special bottle or several special bottles, when this technique can help make sure you know which wine is which. I've never done this at home, though...I'm too eager to taste the wine!

5 HOW TO SERVE WINE: HOST'S CHECKLIST

Whether you're hosting a wine-focused dinner party or a blind tasting, it's the worst if you get to the big moment and realize you've forgotten something. As far as I'm concerned, a wine tasting where there aren't any napkins is just as bad as a pool party with no towels. Here's the basic checklist that I run through in my head every time I'm getting ready to host.

TEMPERATURE

A few hours before you plan to open your wine, make sure you've got it chilling or warming up to room temperature, depending on what style of wine you'll be serving. (If you flip ahead a couple of pages, you'll find a handy guide to appropriate serving temperatures for each wine style.)

STEMWARE

If your plan involves a rustic bottle of Valpolicella and a pizza, your guests can sip their wine out of tumblers. But if you've sprung for a magnum of Champagne, make sure you have enough flutes or small wine glasses to serve everyone properly. We've already seen the importance of having suitable stemware.

WATER TUMBLERS

Spare your guests the morning-after headaches by keeping them hydrated while they drink wine. Put a couple of ice cubes in each glass and fill them in advance, and they'll be the perfect temperature by the time you sit down to dinner.

PAPER CUPS & PAPER BAGS

If you're planning a formal blind tasting, ask your local wine merchant for some single-bottle-sized paper bags in which to hide the bottles. (Or, simply wrap the bottles in paper or foil.) And provide a disposable paper "spit cup" for each guest.

BUCKETS

Keep Champagne chilled in a bucket of ice at a party (be sure to put a towel under it, for splashes), or use an old ice bucket as a "dump bucket" if you plan to taste through a number of wines. Guests can pour their spit cups or half-empty glasses in here if they want to try something different.

HALF-BOTTLE

The next time you see a 375ml bottle of wine, buy it, drink it and keep the bottle. Then, the next time you can't finish a bottle, pour it in the half-bottle, recork it and store it in the fridge. The low temperature and decreased oxygen exposure will help to keep the wine tasting fresh.

PAPER NAPKINS

They're so basic, and yet so often absent. Even if you're planning a wine tasting that doesn't revolve around food, napkins are essential. And I apologize for this hard truth, but here goes: If you'll be tasting and spitting, be prepared to be splashed.

DRESS FOR SUCCESS

Wine pros know to wear dark colors, preferably black, which won't show wine stains. And we embrace polyester and rayon blends, which ward off wine spots much more effectively than cotton. (Ladies, I have three words for you: Diane von Fürstenberg.)

WHITE TABLECLOTH

I know, I've been warning you about stains and now I must admit that I use a white (cotton!) damask cloth for tastings, because it's the best backdrop for assessing a wine's color. Sure, it has a few faint marks, but I just cover them up with glasses, bottles, spit bucket and the rest.

MEAT, CHEESE, BREAD

Slices of hard cheese, beef carpaccio or almonds are ideal for wine tastings, because the proteins in these foods break down mouth-coating tannins. Plain slices of bread or water crackers also neutralize the palate. And I like the cleansing sensation of carbonated, rather than still, water.

NOTEPADS AND PENS

If you're hosting a serious tasting, provide your guests with writing utensils, so that you can all discuss your impressions later. If you've got a number of bottles lined up, and guests milling about, it's easy to lose track of which wine is which.

CLEANING WINE STAINS

I've tested a number of household products and found the best solutions to your stain problems. First, know that different fabrics require different cleansers. Second, always place a napkin or towel ***under*** *the fabric before applying the cleanser. On wool blends and silk ties, dab hydrogen peroxide or rubbing alcohol. (In a pinch, use vodka or gin!) On cotton, apply boiling-hot milk or salt. (Later, you can apply pre-wash spot cleaner and launder the cotton in warm water.) And for upholstery, make a paste from baking soda and water (three parts to one), then gently wipe it off once it has dried.*

6 HOW TO SERVE WINE: TEMPERATURE

If you have a beverage refrigerator, you can calibrate it to the style of wine you plan to serve. If you don't, don't worry—you needn't dunk a thermometer into every bottle. Just keep these numbers in mind: Room temperature is approximately 68°F–73°F (20°C–23°C); standard refrigerator temperature is 35°F–40°F (1.5°C–4.5°C). And cellar temperature is, well, it depends on your cellar, but let's say 55°F–60°F (13°C–16°C).

THE RIGHT TEMPERATURE

CRISP, LEAN WHITES

We tend to drink this style of wine in the summertime, when the balmy weather warms it up quickly, wilting the crisp mouthfeel and turning those linear aromas of mineral and citrus tinny.

40°F–45°F 4.5°C–7°C

LIVELY, AROMATIC WHITES

The fruity and floral notes in these whites unfurl with a soupçon of warmth. If you remove them from the refrigerator and allow them to sit on the counter while you serve and refill, they will reveal layers of fragrance as they open up.

45°F–50°F 7°C–10°C

RICH, FULL-BODIED WHITES

Serve the heartiest whites chilled but not ice-cold. If you allow them to thaw too much, the alcohol will be overtly obvious. But if they're too cold, barrel-fermented whites can taste bitter. So aim for the temperature of a brisk autumn day.

50°F–55°F 10°C–13°C

CHILLING IN A PINCH

Darnit! It's time to uncork that bottle of Muscadet, and you've forgotten to chill it. What to do? If you've got an ice bucket or a wide, deep bowl, fill it half with ice, half with cold water, then plunge the bottle in this ice-cold soup. It will be nice and chilly within 20 minutes. Or, put the bottle in your freezer for 10 minutes. If you're throwing a party, your fridge is full, and you need to keep multiple bottles cold, set up a service table outside—provided it's cold. Or, purchase some corrugated-metal bins and stock them with ice. And here's a good trick: Fill your bathtub with ice and chill down your bottles there.

LUSCIOUSLY SWEET WHITES

A luscious sweet wine that's too warm tastes saccharine. But if a fine dessert wine is served ice-cold, you can't enjoy the full effect of the nose. So, clutch the bowl in your palm to warm the glass and reveal its gorgeous aromatics.

SPARKLING WINES

A chilled flute of Prosecco can be so refreshing, and there's nothing more festive than Champagne on ice. That said, if you allow your bubbly to warm in your glass for a few minutes, you'll get more out of the bouquet.

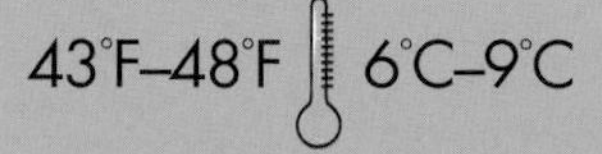

ROSÉS

Like crisp and lean whites, rosés are most often served during the summer months or else in Mediterranean climates. So, chill them down, but know that as the atmosphere warms them up, they'll reveal more of their berry and stone-fruit notes.

47°F–52°F 8°C–11°C

THE RIGHT TEMPERATURE

LIGHT, REFRESHING REDS

The greatest error in wine-service temperature is made in the category of lighter reds. When properly cooled, the nuances and subtle minerality of this style come into focus. Allowed to warm up, they quickly tend toward flimsy fruit and more awkward tannins.

MEDIUM-BODIED REDS

Yes, we're still in cold territory here. If you've ever tasted in a subterranean winery cellar, you'll have noticed how the different structural pieces—minerality, spice, acidity and tannin—just stack up so neatly down there. So, chill these wines a bit.

RICH, FULL-BODIED REDS

Even the richest reds benefit from a cooling-off period. Then, there's the pleasure of tracking their progress as they warm up. That velvety mouthfeel! That opulent fruit! You'll enjoy these elements more if you follow their evolution in the glass.

FINO SHERRY AND DRY MADEIRA

The featherweight mouthfeel of this wine style just falls apart if it's allowed to warm up. And bone-dry fortified wines aren't about fruit; they're about tang and brine. So, treat them like raw oysters and put them on ice.

TAWNY PORT AND SWEET SHERRY

As with dessert wines, serve the sweeter styles of the fortified category cold, then warm the glass with your hand as you sip from it and enjoy the progression of the aromatics, from cigar box, to cinnamon stick, to maple syrup.

SWEET MADEIRA AND VINTAGE PORT

Serve these wines too cold and you lose out on their baroque spices and extravagant fruit. But a mouthful of tepid sugar and alcohol just doesn't appeal. So cool these just a bit, and they'll shine like polished brass.

SECTION 4
THE WORLD OF WINE MADE SIMPLE

WINEMAKING

We all romanticize the idea of winemaking, but in truth, it's toil. Harvest season is a blur of picking, sorting and processing fruit, followed by more sleepless hours spent supervising percolating fermenters. The rest of the year is devoted to racking, filtering, tasting, blending, assessing lab samples, bottling, labeling, filling out reams and reams of paperwork, guiding cellar tours, cleaning, hosing down and then cleaning some more. Then there's the truly hard work: Once you've made the wine, you've got to sell it.

Vignerons are cerebral types, interested in subjects like geology and horticulture. At oenology school, they aren't taught how to charm the pants off of merchants, restaurateurs, wholesalers, importers and consumers. But during the dormant months, folksy winemakers, with their dirt-and-grape-stained hands, quickly learn charisma. Because no matter how ethereal you think your own wine is, there are thousands of others out there that taste just as sublime. And so the winemaker's winter is spent chasing sales. Possible side effects: weight gain, homesickness and an addiction to antacid.

Oh, and if you're still thinking about buying a vineyard and starting up your own winery, plan on adding anti-anxiety drugs, antidepressants and sleep aids to your medicine cabinet, as well. Despite a recent dip in worldwide real-estate prices, the price of entry into the profession is higher than ever. Thanks to a rising demand for wine—and wine-country tourism—land is at a premium, which means that once you've bought a vineyard, the pressure to turn a profit is high. And don't try to explain the financials of grape growing to an accountant: "Dropping fruit," or letting perfectly good clusters drop to the ground and wither, looks like sheer lunacy. But the *quality* of the fruit improves as the *quantity* per vine dwindles. And quality is what it's all about.

Today's up-and-coming vintners don't start out by purchasing estates (unless, of course, they're the lucky offspring of a titan of industry). It's easiest to begin as a small négociant, buying fruit and barrels of finished wine from other producers and creating a custom blend. The next step is to secure a few exclusive vineyard contracts, borrowing or renting space and equipment from another winery—perhaps the same winery where they work their day jobs—at night or on the weekend.

Sounds exhausting, doesn't it? But visit wine country anywhere in the world and you'll see a surprising number of young faces. There's a fresh generation of idealists out there who have chosen the life of the cellar rat over that of the rat race. They're in wellington boots, tramping down muddy vine rows in the rain, repairing trellis wires with ice-cold pliers. They're in thick rubber gloves, lugging buckets, pushing down fermenting must, and moving heavy hoses. Their eyes are rimmed with dark circles, their arms are aching, and they exhale puffs of steam in the dank cellar air. You can find these young people, in the evenings, drinking beer together. But they aren't commiserating about their shared misery. They're rhapsodizing about the most beautiful wines they've ever tasted, and how, one day, they plan to make something just as transcendent themselves.

If you've read through the "Masterclass" and "What's Trending" sections of this book, you may have picked up a few vine-tending techniques and winemaking tricks. Now it's time to put all of those puzzle pieces together and look at the big picture. Let's look at grape growing and winemaking through the eyes of the laborers who turn unassuming plots of land into bottled poetry.

Opposite: While there is a festive and romantic side to the annual harvest, gathering in the grapes is also back-breaking work.

1 THE VINEYARD YEAR

Most crops grow on flat land and rich, soft, moist soil. Wine grapes thrive on steep slopes and poor, rocky soil. Because the more the vines struggle to survive, the more complex the fruit—and thus, the finished wine—will be. And so, every month of the year, the winegrower works to maintain the balance between health and hardship for the vines.

WINTER

EARLY WINTER WEATHERING THE STORM

In continental climates, snowfalls covering the vineyard act as blankets, protecting the vines from the elements. In temperate climates, **cover crops** that were planted in late summer now flourish between and below the vines, minimizing soil erosion during rainstorms.

WINTER UPKEEP

It is the dead of winter and the vines are dormant. Vine tenders take advantage of this break in the growing season to repair their vineyard infrastructure. They brave the cold temperatures to clear brush and repair broken **trellis wires** and fence posts.

LATE WINTER CANE PRUNING

It's time to prune the vine trunks, leaving just one or two healthy **canes** for the next growing season. Pruning encourages each plant to focus on fruit development rather than vegetative growth (leaves and stalks) and continues throughout the year.

SPRING

EARLY SPRING EARLY SPRING

Buds on each cane burst open, revealing petite, pink-and-green rosettes—primordial stems, **leaves** and **clusters**, layered like petals on a flower. Frost, hail, rain, wind or snow could damage or destroy these tender buds, so vineyard managers watch the weather.

SPRING SHOOT MAINTENANCE

The buds quickly stretch out into green **shoots**, adorned with nascent flower clusters and baby leaves. Vine tenders check the undersides of these leaves for **mildew**, and spray a **fungicide** such as sulfur if they see white spots or black lesions.

LATE SPRING REVISIONS

It's time to plant new vines, reconfigure the trellising system, or convert established roots to grow different grapes. To **graft** a new variety onto existing rootstock, workers prune the trunks down and insert **scions**, or healthy new canes.

> *"We farm totally naturally,"* the vigneron says humbly. *"The grapes just grow themselves."* Sounds idyllic, but it isn't true. Left to their own devices, grapes grow from seed, and climb up the trunks of trees.

SUMMER

EARLY SUMMER BLOOM

Vine tenders mark their calendars on the day that the delicate, white, sweet-smelling **flowers** blossom in the vineyard. Three months—approximately—from this day, the fruit will be ready to harvest.

MID SUMMER FRUIT SET & CANOPY MANAGEMENT

Thanks to the miracle of **pollination,** the flowers are now small, hard, green and tart **berries.** If they are concerned that the fruit isn't getting enough sunlight or air flow, vineyard workers might selectively prune leaves, exposing the grape **clusters.**

SUMMER THINNING

Field hands reduce yields by clipping and discarding grape bunches. This accelerates the ripening process, develops more complex flavors in the fruit that remains, and reduces the risk of **rot** spreading.

AUTUMN

AUTUMN PREPARING FOR HARVEST

As birds, rodents and other **pests** eye the ripening fruit hungrily, vine tenders may protect it with netting. When conditions are humid, they may also need to protect the vines against mildew and rot.

AUTUMN HARVEST

Finally: It's time to pick. Workers move quickly and carefully down each vine row, clipping the grape bunches, dropping them into baskets or buckets and then dumping them into **bins** to be hauled to the winery.

LATE AUTUMN DÉNOUEMENT

Photosynthesis is done. The green vine shoots are now woody canes; the leaves turn gold and red and drop to the ground. *Vignerons* prepare for the next growing season by building compost piles from vineyard debris and winemaking waste.

2 HOW RED WINE IS MADE

Winemaking is like a complex flow chart: Every small decision made during harvest and fermentation determines the options and outcomes that will arise later. Here's an illustrated guide to the most common path taken by red grapes as they journey from harvest bin to bottle. Once you're familiar with these standard steps, you'll enjoy exploring wines that have taken the side roads.

1 SORTING

A bin tips fresh-picked grapes into a **hopper,** which slowly sifts the fruit onto the **sorting table.** Cellar workers stand over this conveyor belt, picking through the clusters and removing and discarding debris (leaves, twigs, bugs) and rotten or raisined bunches.

2 CRUSHING

A **destemmer** separates the individual grapes from the stems. (Some winemakers then return to the sorting table for a second, individual **berry sort.**) Then, a **crusher** gently smashes the fruit without cracking the bitter seeds.

3 COLD SOAK

The juice macerates in a chilled (or not) vat, soaking up color and tannin from the grape skins. Then the **grape must** warms up and the winemaker either adds yeast or else waits for **ambient yeasts** to start fermentation spontaneously.

4 FERMENTATION

Workers either **pump over** or **punch down** the **cap** of skins that floats to the top, using a plunger-type device. When fermentation is done, the winemaker drains the tank and **presses** the remaining skins to extract the last drops of juice.

5 SECONDARY FERMENTATION

Next comes secondary, or **malolactic,** fermentation, which converts astringent malic acid into soft lactic acid. If it doesn't happen spontaneously, the winemaker can **inoculate** the wine with bacteria to kick-start the process.

THE THIEF IN THE CELLAR

It conjures up the image of a deadbeat in a ski mask, tiptoeing through a cellar, but actually, a **barrel thief** is a banal glass pipette. The winemaker removes the **bung,** or plug, from the top of the barrel, and dips the thief in to gather a sample of the maturing wine. The winemaker examines the **barrel sample** to calculate the alcohol percentage, determine whether to **fine** or **filter,** contemplate blending possibilities, and decide when to bottle. If you've ever been to a **barrel tasting,** you've had the chance to try a barrel sample of unfinished wine. Did you like it?

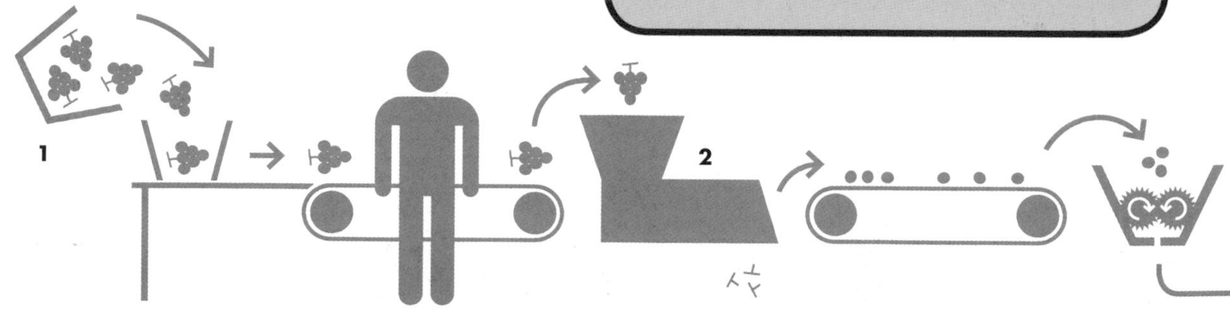

6 RACKING

Draining the fermentation tank—or, moving the wine from barrel to barrel—the vintner takes care to leave the creamy-colored **lees** behind. Repeated **racking** keeps the wine clean of sediment, and the oxygen exposure aids in maturation.

7 BARREL AGING

The juice then rests in barrels for months or even years. Exposure to wood softens the texture, smooths out the **tannins**, and brings layers of flavor to the wine. The barrels are typically stored on their sides, on racks, and are often stacked ceiling-high.

8 TOPPING OFF & BLENDING

Cellar hands regularly **top off** any wine that has evaporated from the barrel to keep oxygen exposure to a minimum. The vintner tastes through the barrels to decide which ones should be **blended** together, and at what proportions.

9 BOTTLING

It's time to bottle. In some wine regions, **mobile bottling lines** travel from winery to winery, with all the necessary equipment on a trailer or large truck. The winemaker adds a small amount of **sulfur dioxide** at bottling to prevent spoilage.

10 LABELING + SEALING

Bottles are sealed different ways: With a **cork** (natural, plastic or composite), often topped by foil or wax, with an aluminum **screwcap**, or with a glass **stopper**. The words and images on the label must be approved by regional and federal authorities.

11 TO MARKET

It's time for the new vintage to ferment in the barrel, but the cellar is getting crowded. Many wineries send **new releases** out to the marketplace in late autumn to free up storage space.

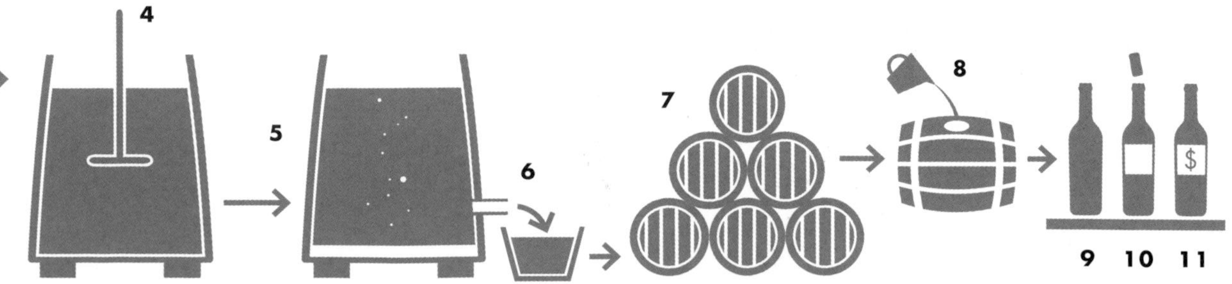

3 HOW WHITE WINE IS MADE

Red wine juice lazily soaks up color and tannins from the skins, then indolently wallows in oak barrels. Most white grapes shed their skins immediately, then require painstaking care in airtight tanks, for quick turnaround and fresh, clean flavors. Who are the type-A personalities in wine country? The vintners who specialize in whites.

1 CHILLING + SORTING

The just-harvested grapes might go to a **cold room** to chill until they've reached about 55°F (13°C), to deter **microbial activity** and preserve fresh flavors. Cellar hands may then pick through the bunches, discarding debris, bugs and moldy or rotten fruit.

2 DESTEMMING + PRESSING

The winemaker calibrates the **crusher-destemmer** so that it will destem but not crush the grapes. The destemmed berries fall into the **press**. In the pneumatic presses commonly used today, a **bladder** squeezes them against the inside of a giant sieve, releasing the juice and trapping the skins.

3 SETTLING + CLARIFICATION

The juice that comes out of the press is cloudy, like apple cider. The particulates floating in the **must** (juice) can impart pungent flavors to the wine, so the vintner allows them to **settle** and **racks** the wine off its "gross lees" to **clarify** it.

WHY A WINE PRESS WON'T WORK WITHOUT TASTE BUDS

The moment they fall into the press, the grapes begin leaking pale **free-run** juice into the tank below. As the bladder begins squeezing the pulp against the inside of the press, the richer **press-run** juice flows out. Toward the end of the press run, as the bladder squeezes the last drops of juice from the **cake** of skins and seeds, the juice becomes increasingly bitter. To minimize this astringency, the winemaker runs the press lightly and slowly, tasting the **run-off** frequently, until her taste buds tell her to stop.

4 FINING

By adding a coagulating material such as **bentonite** (clay) or **gelatin**, the winemaker further clarifies, or **fines**, the juice to prevent browning, remove bitterness, and ensure heat stability during fermentation.

5 TESTING + ADJUSTING

It's time to do a quick check to test the **brix** (sugar), total **acidity** and **pH** of the wine. If anything is off, now is the time to adjust it. Some winemakers add **enzymes** at this stage to deter browning, prevent malolactic fermentation, or enhance mouthfeel.

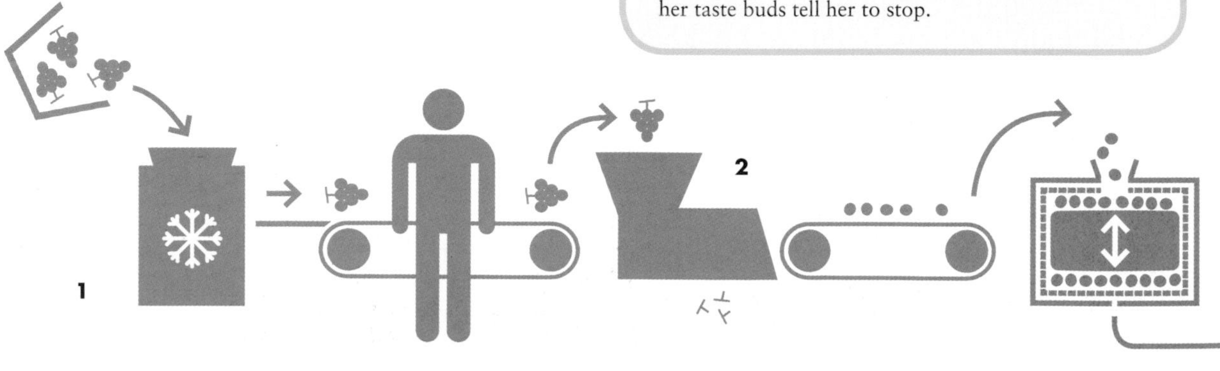

6 FERMENTATION

Fermentation proceeds in wooden barrels or stainless-steel tanks, via either cultivated or indigenous ("natural" or "wild") yeast. Cellar hands stir the fermenting must frequently, to keep the yeast moving through the liquid and release unwanted gases and odors. Fruity, off-dry wines are fermented in cool tanks, then chilled down further to **halt fermentation** and retain sugar.

7 *SUR LIE* OR NOT *SUR LIE*

The fermented wine is cloudy with yeast particles, or "fine lees," which fall to the bottom of the barrel or tank. If some or all of this sediment is allowed to remain, it will impart a creamy texture, which the winemaker can amplify by ***stirring the lees*** (***bâtonnage***).

8 SKIPPING MALOLACTIC

To avoid the creamy, buttery effect of malolactic fermentation in favor of a fresher style of white wine, the vintner chills the fermentation tank, adds an **enzyme** and/or **sulfur dioxide** to discourage the process, and/or racks the wine off the lees.

9 FILTERING

White wines are nearly always **filtered**, for clarity and also for stability. A filter with the tightest possible pores will remove unwelcome bacteria and yeasts, in effect neutralizing many possible **flaws**.

10 COLD STABILIZATION

The vintner often chills the wine down to almost-freezing, then removes the crystals, or **tartrates**, that drop to the bottom of the tank. If **cold stabilization** doesn't happen in the winery, it happens in your refrigerator—and you find tiny crystals in your wine glass. These are completely harmless, and should not be mistaken for shards of glass.

11 TO MARKET

After bottling, sealing and labeling, white wines typically hit the market in the spring. This frees up **cellar space** and brings in cash to cover the costs of the summer and fall seasons of vine tending and winemaking.

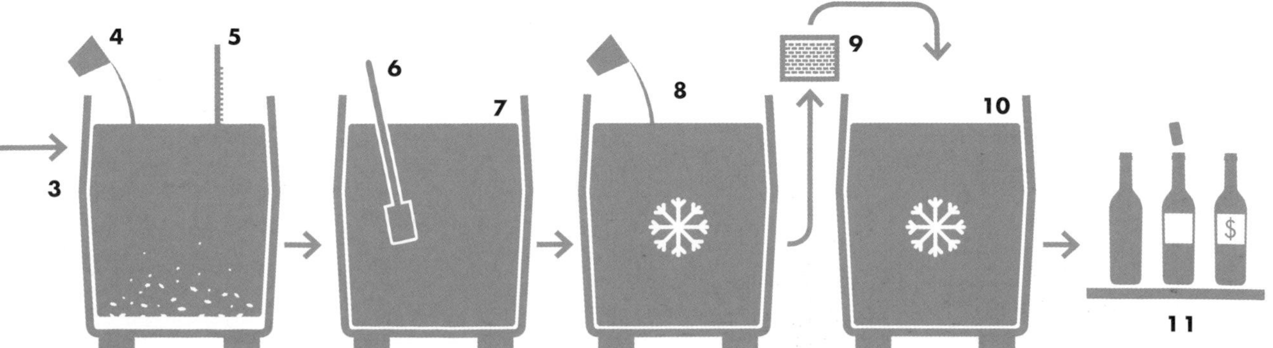

4 HOW SPARKLING WINE IS MADE

It's challenging enough to make still wines. But to induce an additional fermentation cycle in *every individual bottle*, then train the yeast to perform a circus trick, well, that's quite a feat. But if you're the kind of person who can't help but smile when someone hands you a flute of Champagne, then you'll agree that all the extra effort is worthwhile.

1 EARLY HARVEST

Where still wines are made from ripe fruit, sparkling wine is best made from grapes that are lower in sugar and higher in acidity. So harvest happens early, and always by hand (not machine), because any broken skins could color the wine.

2 MULTIPLE SITES

Large Champagne houses with big brands (***grandes marques***) source their fruit from many different vineyards all over the Champagne region. As far as possible, vintners keep these lots separate in the winery, so that they'll have more flexibility for blending later on.

3 PRESSING

The fruit is not destemmed, to limit exposure to oxygen. The bunches go into the press immediately and are **pressed off the skins**, so that no color is extracted. This way, a red grape like Pinot Noir or Pinot Meunier can become a white sparkling wine.

4 FIRST FERMENTATION

The fresh juice sits in a stainless-steel tank—or, in some cases, large oak **casks**—to settle and clarify. Then, most producers add commercial yeast to start fermentation and make a still white wine (the *vin clair*).

5 *ASSEMBLAGE*

Most Champagnes are made in a Non-Vintage (NV) house style that stays more or less the same from year to year. To maintain this consistency, the cellar master blends different lots of still wines (*vins clairs*) from the various vineyard sites with reserves from prior vintages. Vintage Champagne is all from one year.

6 *TIRAGE* + BOTTLE AGE

The blended wine is bottled with a mixture of sugar and yeast, called ***liqueur de tirage***, then topped with a cork or **crown cap** (like those on beer bottles) and set horizontally in a cool, dark cellar to **bottle-age** for a minimum of 16 months for Non-Vintage Champagne, 36 months for Vintage Champagne.

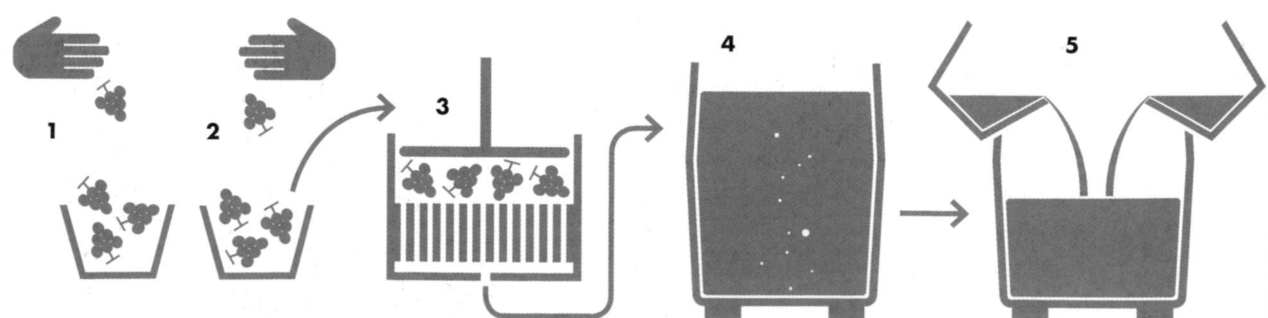

THE CHARM OF *CHARMAT*

Outlined here is the ***méthode traditionnelle*** of producing sparkling wine. Even if you've got machines like **gyropalettes** to speed things along, it's a slow and labor-intensive process. For lighter, fresher-style sparkling wines, such as Italian Prosecco, the ***charmat*** method is used. In Champagne, the additional fermentation happens in each bottle. In Friuli, this second fermentation takes place in a large tank that's chilled and pressurized. While they might lack the sumptuous yeastiness of bottle-fermented Champagne, ***charmat*** wines have their own charm—and are cheaper, too.

7 SECOND FERMENTATION

The sweetened wine, with its additional yeast, ferments again, this time inside the bottle. The **carbon dioxide** that's released from this process is trapped inside the bottle, in effect carbonating the wine and making it sparkle.

8 *SUR LIE*

The yeast is also trapped inside the bottle, and as it decays it imparts—by the process of **autolysis**—a creamy texture and distinctly **yeasty** aroma to the wine. Because it's happening in a sealed bottle and over such a long period of time, the effect is pronounced.

9 RIDDLING

Cellar workers called ***rémueurs***—or, machines called **gyropalettes**—slowly **riddle**, or rotate and tip, the bottles each day so that the yeast begins to accumulate in the necks. By the time the bottles are upside-down, the necks are full of the white yeast sediment.

10 DISGORGEMENT + *DOSAGE*

The *rémueur* plunges the neck of the bottle into frozen brine, then removes the cap. The yeasty **"ice cork"** pops out and the *rémueur* tops up the bottle with sweetened wine (***liqueur d'expédition***). ***Dosage*** refers to the sweetness of the finished Champagne. The range begins at **natural** (no sugar added) and rises through **extra brut, brut, extra dry, sec, demi-sec** and **doux.**

11 SEALING

On the bottling line, a compressed cork is crammed partway into the neck of the bottle. The top is squashed over the lip of the bottle, making a mushroom shape, and secured with a **wire cage.** A foil **capsule** goes over the top.

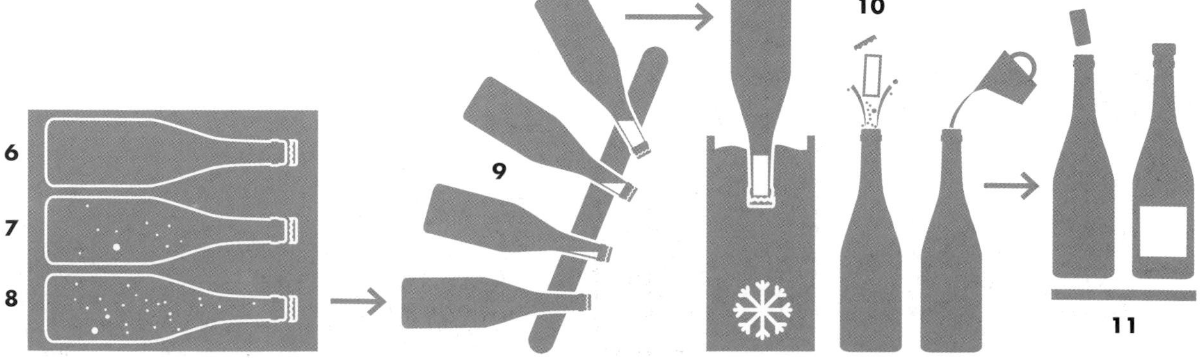

5 HOW FORTIFIED WINE IS MADE

Take everything you know about oenology and throw it out the window: That's how to make the world's most decadent beverages, fortified wines. Blended vintages, yeast colonies gone wild, oxidation and even heat are all part of the fortified winemaker's toolkit. The flamboyant aromas and flavors in the resulting wines stretch our palates and spark our imaginations.

1 SHERRY HARVEST

In Andalusia, southwestern Spain, **Pedro Ximénez** grapes are laid out in the sun to dry. **Palomino** grapes are pressed immediately after harvest. This wine settles and clarifies; the winemaker might adjust the acidity.

2 FERMENTATION

Fermentation, in large oak barrels (**butts**) or (more common now) stainless-steel tanks, is allowed to **run hot**; the heat and oxygen of fermentation begin to build those distinct Sherry aromas and flavors. The finer, free-run juice from better vineyards is **fortified** up to about 15.5% ABV, while the more robust press run from lesser vineyards is fortified to 18% ABV.

3 BIOLOGICALLY AGED FINO/MANZANILLA

The finer, free-run juice, destined to become Fino (or Manzanilla in Salúcar de Barrameda) is stored in butts with some air space, at the ideal temperature to develop *flor*—a layer of yeast that imparts distinctive aromas and flavors as well as keeping the wine pale by protecting it from further oxidation.

4 OXIDATIVELY AGED OLOROSO

Flor can't develop in the press-run wines due to their higher alcohol; these also age in butts exposed to the air and become cola-colored **Oloroso**. The sweet wine made from the dried Pedro Ximénez grapes becomes maple syrupy **PX Sherry**; Oloroso blended and sweetened with PX is commercial "Amontillado," sweet Oloroso, or **Cream Sherry**.

5 SOLERA AGING/FRACTIONAL BLENDING

A **solera** is a barrel-aging system in which vintages are blended for consistency of style. A Fino that has aged in solera for several years and loses its *flor* becomes a "true" **Amontillado**; if it loses its *flor* earlier it develops as a **Palo Cortado**, which in style is half way between an Amontillado and an Oloroso (and commercial versions may be a blend of the two).

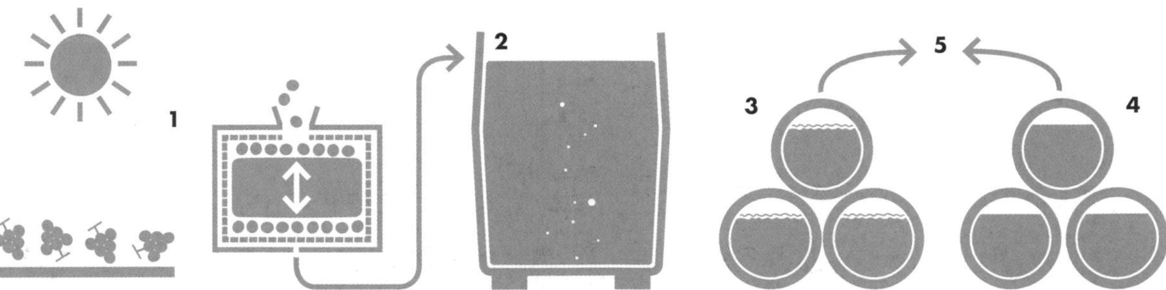

DARING TO EXPLAIN MADEIRA

The weird wine award goes to Madeira. For a start, it's not even really from Europe: The tropical Portuguese island by the same name is actually closer to Africa. But the truly crazy part? It's intentionally heated—artificially (by ***estufagem***) or more naturally, by the heat of the sun (***canteiro***). The result is a salty, nutty, mouthwatering and often sweet wine that can age almost indefinitely and doesn't deteriorate when exposed to oxygen, movement or heat. So go ahead: Bring a bottle of Madeira along on that Sahara Desert motorcycle tour you've always wanted to do.

1 PORT CRUSH

To extract as much color and flavor from the skins as possible without splitting the bitter seeds, workers still occasionally tread the grapes by foot in a giant granite or cement trough (***lagar***). But it is far more common nowadays for the grapes to be crushed in **robotic *lagares*** or percolator-like **autovinifiers**.

2 FERMENTATION + FORTIFICATION

Fermentation happens during crush; when the alcohol reaches 6% to 8% ABV, the juice is transferred to large vats and fortified with brandy at 77% ABV, which stops the fermentation process and preserves the sweet fruity character of the wine.

3 TANK AGING

Ruby Port gets its bright saturated color and pronounced fruitiness from aging in tank and bottling after only two or three years. Higher-quality rubies are called **Premium Ruby** or **Reserve.** These wines are all filtered for stability.

4 SHORT-TERM BARREL AGING

The Port remains in the quinta until the springtime, when it is moved down-river to warehouses in Vila Nova de Gaia, opposite Oporto, to age in barrels called **pipes.** Here, oxygen reacts with the wine, which becomes lighter in color. After a few years, some are bottled as **Tawny Port.**

5 SINGLE VINTAGE AGING

A single vintage left in barrel for four to six years prior to release is a **Late Bottled Vintage.** Top wines from the best—**declared**—vintages are wood-aged for two or three years prior to release as **Vintage Port,** when it may be drunk or left to age in bottle for 10 to 20 years. **Single-Quinta** (single-estate) Ports are bottled in good, but not great, vintages.

6 LONG-TERM BARREL AGING

Some of the best Tawnies age in a solera-type system and are labeled according to the average number of years (10, 20, 30 or over 40) spent in barrel. Others are set aside as single-vintage wines for many years and then bottled as vintage-dated **Colheita.**

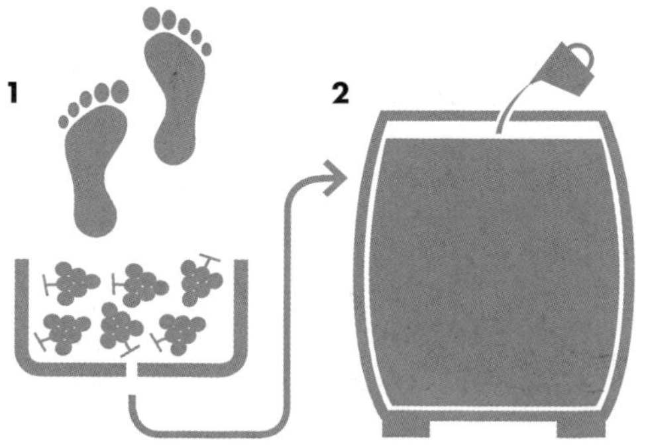

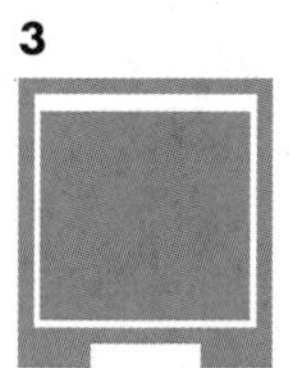

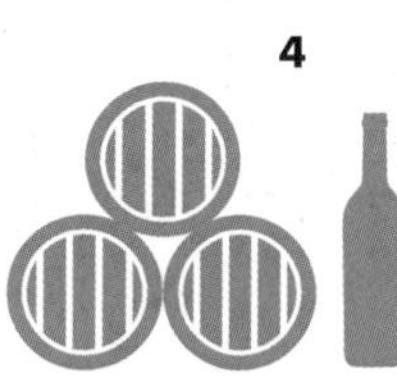

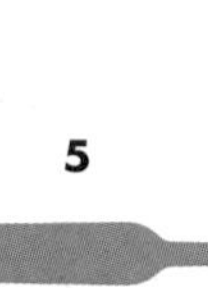

SECTION 5
RULES TO REMEMBER

FOOD AND WINE PAIRINGS BY STYLE

	CRISP, LEAN WHITES	LIVELY, AROMATIC WHITES	RICH, FULL-BODIED WHITES	LUSCIOUSLY SWEET WHITES
CINNAMON, SAFFRON, PAPRIKA, CUMIN, CORIANDER, CLOVES			●	
BEANS, LENTILS	●		●	
BEEF, VENISON				
CHEESE, CREAM SAUCES		●	●	●
CHILIES (HOT)		●	●	●
CHOCOLATE				●
COOKIES, BISCUITS, CAKES, TARTS				●
FISH & SHELLFISH	●	●	●	
LAMB, PORK, VEAL		●		
POTATOES (MASHED, CHIPS, FRENCH FRIES)	●		●	
POULTRY	●	●	●	
SALADS, FRESH HERBS, CITRUS	●	●		
SMOKED FISH, BARBEQUE			●	
SPRING & SUMMER VEGETABLES (ASPARAGUS, TOMATOES)	●	●		
WINTER VEGGIES (SQUASH, ROOT VEGETABLES, MUSHROOMS)			●	●

SPARKLING WHITES & ROSÉS	ROSÉS	LIGHT, REFRESHING REDS	FIRM, MEDIUM-BODIED REDS	RICH, FULL-BODIED REDS	FORTIFIED WINES
	●		●	●	●
●	●	●	●	●	
		●	●	●	●
●	●				●
			●	●	
				●	●
●					●
●	●	●			
●	●	●	●		
●	●				
●	●	●	●		
●	●	●			
	●			●	
●	●	●	●		
●		●	●	●	

COUNTRIES AND GRAPE VARIETIES BY STYLE

CRISP, LEAN WHITES	LIVELY, AROMATIC WHITES	RICH, FULL-BODIED WHITES	LUSCIOUSLY SWEET WHITES	SPARKLING WHITES & ROSÉS
SPAIN ALBARIÑO	**NEW ZEALAND** SAUVIGNON BLANC	**AUSTRALIA** CHARDONNAY	**GERMANY** RIESLING	**UNITED STATES** SPARKLING (CHARDONNAY, PINOT NOIR)
ITALY SOAVE (GARGANEGA)	**AUSTRIA** GRÜNER VELTLINER	**FRANCE** RHÔNE (MARSANNE)	**FRANCE** SAUTERNES (SÉMILLON, SAUVIGNON BLANC)	**FRANCE** CHAMPAGNE (CHARDONNAY, PINOT NOIR, PINOT MEUNIER)
FRANCE MUSCADET (MELON DE BOURGOGNE)	**GERMANY** RIESLING	**UNITED STATES** VIOGNIER	**HUNGARY** TOKAJI ASZÚ (FURMINT)	**ITALY** PROSECCO (GLERA)
GERMANY SILVANER	**FRANCE** GEWURZTRAMINER	**ARGENTINA** TORRONTÉS	**ITALY** MOSCATO	**SPAIN** CAVA (BLEND)
PORTUGAL VINHO VERDE (BLEND)	**SOUTH AFRICA** CHENIN BLANC	**SOUTH AFRICA** SÉMILLON	**GREECE** MUSCAT	**GERMANY** SEKT (VARIOUS)
GREECE RODITIS	**UNITED STATES** PINOT GRIS	**ITALY** FALANGHINA	**CANADA** ICEWINE (VIDAL, RIESLING)	**PORTUGAL** ESPUMANTE (BLEND)

ROSÉS	LIGHT, REFRESHING REDS	FIRM, MEDIUM-BODIED REDS	RICH, FULL-BODIED REDS	FORTIFIED WINES
FRANCE CORSICAN ROSÉ	**FRANCE** BURGUNDY (PINOT NOIR)	**ITALY** CHIANTI, BRUNELLO (SANGIOVESE)	**ARGENTINA** MALBEC	**PORTUGAL** PORT (BLENDS)
SPAIN ROSADO DE GARNACHA	**AUSTRIA** ZWEIGELT	**SPAIN** RIOJA, RIBERA DEL DUERO (TEMPRANILLO)	**UNITED STATES** ZINFANDEL	**SPAIN** SHERRY (PALOMINO, PEDRO XIMÉNEZ)
ITALY CERASUOLO	**ITALY** LAMBRUSCO	**PORTUGAL** DÃO, DOURO VINHO TINTO (BLENDS)	**FRANCE** BORDEAUX (MERLOT)	**FRANCE** BANYULS (GRENACHE BLENDS)
FRANCE TAVEL, BANDOL (GRENACHE BLENDS)	**UNITED STATES** GAMAY NOIR	**GREECE** AGIORGITIKO	**ITALY** BAROLO, BARBARESCO (NEBBIOLO)	**ITALY** MARSALA (BLEND)
AUSTRIA ROSÉ (BLAUFRÄNKISCH, ETC.)	**CANADA** CABERNET FRANC	**AUSTRIA** BLAUFRÄNKISCH	**CHILE** CABERNET SAUVIGNON	**AUSTRALIA** LIQUEUR MUSCAT
UNITED STATES ROSÉ (PINOT NOIR)	**FRANCE** TROUSSEAU	**GEORGIA** SAPERAVI	**SPAIN** MONASTRELL	**PORTUGAL** MADEIRA (VARIOUS)

COMMON GRAPE VARIETIES

CABERNET SAUVIGNON

FRANCE	ITALY	U.S.	AUSTRALIA
Bordeaux	Tuscany	California	Barossa Valley
Red Blend	Super-Tuscan Red Blend	Napa Valley Cabernet	Cabernet / Shiraz

MERLOT

FRANCE	ITALY	U.S.	U.S.
Bordeaux	Tuscany	California	Washington
St.-Émilion, Pomerol, Médoc, Entre-Deux-Mers	Super-Tuscan	Napa Valley Merlot	Columbia Valley, Walla Walla, Red Mountain

PINOT NOIR / SPÄTBURGUNDER

FRANCE	U.S.	NEW ZEALAND	GERMANY
Burgundy, Champagne, Loire	Oregon, California	Central Otago, Marlborough, Martinborough	Ahr, Baden, Franken, Pfalz, Rheingau, Württemburg
	Willamette Valley, Russian River Valley, Sta. Rita Hills		

SYRAH / SHIRAZ

AUSTRALIA	FRANCE	SOUTH AFRICA	U.S.
Barossa Valley, McLaren Vale, South Australia	Rhône	Stellenbosch, Western Cape	California
	Hermitage, Côte-Rôtie, St.-Joseph, Cornas		Paso Robles, Sonoma County, Central Coast, Santa Barbara

CHARDONNAY

FRANCE	AUSTRALIA	U.S.	FRANCE
Burgundy Chablis, Côte d'Or, Mâconnais, Châlonnais	Adelaide Hills, Hunter Valley, Margaret River	California Russian River, Sonoma County	Champagne Blanc de Blancs

CHENIN BLANC

FRANCE	SOUTH AFRICA	FRANCE	U.S.
Loire Vouvray, Savennières, Montlouis, Crémant de Loire (sparkling)	Stellenbosch, Swartland, Western Cape Steen	Loire Vouvray, Coteaux du Layon, Quarts de Chaume moelleux (sweet)	California, Washington Napa Valley, Columbia Valley, Columbia Gorge

RIESLING

GERMANY	FRANCE	AUSTRALIA	AUSTRIA
Mosel, Nahe, Pfalz, Rheingau, Rheinhessen	Alsace	Clare Valley, Eden Valley, Tasmania, Victoria	Wachau Kabinett, Spätlese, Auslese, Beerenauslese in Austria & Germany

SAUVIGNON BLANC

NEW ZEALAND	FRANCE	CHILE	FRANCE
Marlborough, Hawke's Bay	Loire Valley, Sancerre, Pouilly-Fumé	Casablanca Valley, Central Valley, Colchagua Valley, Leyda Valley, Maule	Bordeaux Graves, Sauternes, Barsac (the latter two sweet blends with Sémillon)

GLOSSARY

ACIDITY Essential element in wine, noticeable on the palate as a mouthwatering sensation rather than a flavor. In finished wine, measured as TOTAL ACIDITY (TA).

ALCOHOL Noted on wine labels as alcohol by volume (ABV). The higher the alcohol, the greater the sensation of sweetness.

AMPHORA Ancient fermentation and aging vessel, now back in vogue among natural winemakers.

APPELLATION Officially designated grape-growing and winemaking region. Known in France as an *appellation d'origine contrôlée* (AOC) and in the USA as an American Viticultural Area (AVA).

BARREL Also called a *barrique* (France), *botte* (Italy), butt, pipe or tun. Gently roasted over a flame by expert barrel-makers, this vessel can impart caramel aromas and spicy notes to wine, depending on its size, age and degree of TOAST.

BIODYNAMIC Semi-spiritual, ultra-natural farming method that goes one step beyond ORGANIC in its reliance on organic composts and natural tinctures to achieve plant health.

BODY The texture of a wine, usually correlative with the alcohol level, ranging from LIGHT to MEDIUM to FULL.

BOTRYTIS A fungus that, as NOBLE ROT, shrivels white grapes, concentrating their sugars; and as GRAY ROT, turns red grapes moldy and mushy.

BRUT Means "dry," in reference to sparkling wines, although there are drier styles: BRUT NATURE or BRUT ZERO. These are made without any *dosage*, or added sugar, after the second fermentation. EXTRA BRUT gets a small *dosage*; BRUT a bit more. Confusingly, EXTRA DRY or EXTRA SEC, and DRY or SEC, are slightly sweeter. DEMI-SEC is sweeter still, and finally, DOUX, or SWEET, actually delivers what it promises.

CARBONIC MACERATION A whole-grape fermentation executed in a sealed, airtight tank. In this oxygen-free environment, each grape begins to ferment inside its own skin; the resulting wine is relatively light in color and low in tannins. Used to make fruit-punchy Beaujolais Nouveau.

CLASSICO A classic sub-region within a traditional Italian grape-growing appellation.

CLONE Viticultural term for a cultivar, strain or vine selection of a specific grape variety.

COOPERAGE The art of barrel-making. Winemakers consider the forest, the type of oak, and the cooper when choosing barrels.

COPITA Glass used in Spain for sipping Sherry.

CRUSH The act of crushing grapes; also, the term for the busy winemaking period directly following HARVEST.

D.O. *Denominación de Origen*, or official Spanish winegrowing appellation.

D.O.(C.)(G.) *Denominazione di Origine (Controllata) (e Garantita)*, the three quality levels for Italian appellations.

DECANTING The practice of pouring wine from bottle to a DECANTER, either to aerate a young wine or to remove the SEDIMENT from an old wine.

DRY According to the International Riesling Foundation's Riesling Taste Profile, a wine in which the sugar level is lower than, or equal to, the acidity level.

ÉLEVAGE The aging or finishing of wine, in oak barrels, steel tanks, bottles or some other vessel.

FERMENTATION The conversion of sugar to alcohol that occurs when crushed grapes come in contact with YEAST.

FIELD BLEND Random assortment of grape varieties from the same vineyard.

FINING/FILTERING The removal of sediment and impurities.

FINISH The sensations that linger following a sip of wine.

FORTIFICATION The process of blending wine with brandy to make a FORTIFIED WINE.

FOUDRES Large, upright, oak casks; the more traditional alternative to stainless-steel FERMENTATION TANKS.

GRANDES MARQUES Large-scale Champagne producers, or *négociant-manipulants*, who purchase fruit from numerous vineyards then blend the wines from different vineyards and vintages to create a cuvée that upholds a consistent house style from year to year. At the other end of the spectrum is the GROWER, or *récoltant-manipulant*, who makes a unique sparkling wine from his or her own vineyards each year.

GROSSES GEWÄCHS German term for the country's best SINGLE-VINEYARD wines.

HEAD SPACE The air space created by the evaporation of wine through the slightly porous barrel staves. Winemakers keep their wines from oxidizing by TOPPING UP the head space, as well as injecting a bit of sulfur dioxide, nitrogen or carbon dioxide, to displace the air.

HOT Term for a wine that, due to its high alcohol content, creates a burning sensation on the tongue and throat.

IGT *Indicazione Geografica Tipica*, an Italian designation for wines that do not fall within the traditional geographic boundaries or specified grape varieties specified by the DO, DOC or DOCG designations.

INOCULATION The act of adding a CULTURED yeast to control the fermentation processs, rather than allowing WILD yeast to start fermentation spontaneously.

IVDP *Instituto do Vinho do Porto*, or quality-assurance bureau in Portugal, responsible for the certification stamp of "*Vinho do Porto Garantia.*"

LAGAR Cement trough, used in traditional Port houses, to foot-tread grapes.

LATE HARVEST *Vendange tardive,* a term for sweet wines made from grapes that have been allowed to hang on the vine past ripeness, even to the point of becoming raisins. Even sweeter is *sélection de grains nobles*, from the most botrytized, shriveled and sugary late-harvest grapes.

LEGS The drips that slide down inside a glass after swirling.

MALOLACTIC FERMENTATION Process whereby sharp malic acids are converted into smoother lactic acids. Common in red wines, less common in whites.

MICRO-OX Micro-oxygenation is the controversial act of

softening a red wine in the cellar by pumping small amounts of oxygen through it.

MINERALITY An imprecise term for the aroma, flavor and sensation of minerals or stones in wine. Most famously, oenophiles ascribe a chalk note to Chablis, gunflint to Sancerre, oyster shells to Muscadet and slate to Mosel Riesling.

MOUSSE The foam of bubbles, or *PERLAGE*, in sparkling wine.

MOUTHFEEL Texture.

MUST Crushed grapes: skins, seeds, stems, pulp and juice.

NOSE The aroma of a wine; to smell a wine.

NV NON-VINTAGE wines, such as many sparkling wines, in which multiple vintages are blended together.

NATURAL WINE An amorphous, unregulated term to describe wine made by all or most of the following procedures: ecologically sensitive (such as organic or biodynamic) farming, hand harvesting, fermentation in a natural vessel (such as a cement or oak cask), spontaneous fermentation, no fining or filtering and no additives (including sulfur dioxide).

NÉGOCIANT A merchant or producer who purchases fruit, juice and/or finished wine from other growers and producers to sell under their own label.

NEUTRAL The term for oak barrels that have been used previously and no longer impart smoky or woody notes to the wines maturing in them.

OXIDATIVE A style of wine that has been deliberately exposed to oxygen, rendering it more mellow and soft; an unintentionally OXIDIZED wine may be yellow and smell like Sherry or vinegar.

PASSITO A sweet wine made from dried grapes.

PET NAT *Pétillant naturel*: sparkling wine produced in the most traditional manner, with no added sugar or yeast. Also called, *méthode ancestrale, méthode rurale* or *pétillant original*.

PHYLLOXERA A pernicious root louse that wiped out many of the world's vineyards until it was discovered that vines could survive if GRAFTED onto phylloxera-resistant American rootstock. Not present in grape-growing regions with markedly sandy soils.

PRÄDIKAT German (and Austrian) wine classifications, mostly in reference to Riesling: kabinett is reserve-quality; spätlese is fully ripe, harvested later; auslese is late-harvest; beerenauslese is ultra-ripe and may include some NOBLE ROT; and trockenbeerenauslese refers to the most shriveled of the Noble Rot lot. A Qualitätswein mit Prädikat (QMP) is a top-quality wine.

PROPRIETARY NAME A unique name bestowed on a wine by the producer. Particularly popular with reserve-level Ports, such as Graham's Six Grapes or Warre's Warrior, and with prestige cuvée Champagnes, such as Moët & Chandon's Dom Pérignon or Louis Roederer's Cristal.

PUTTONYOS An indication of the sweetness level of Tokaji Aszú, on a scale of 3 to 6.

QUINTA Vineyard estate in Portugal.

REDUCTIVE A modern winemaking process and wine style that uses cool stainless-steel tanks to preserve freshness by excluding oxygen. Not to be confused with REDUCTIVE FLAWS, in which REDUCED NOTES of sulfur affect the aroma of a wine.

RESIDUAL SUGAR (RS) The sugar remaining in a wine after fermentation, measured as grams of sugar per liter of wine.

SAIGNÉE The practice of siphoning juice off a tank of recently crushed red grapes, to make a more concentrated red wine and/or to produce a rosé.

SCREWCAP Aluminum bottle closure, believed to be best for fresh, younger wines due to its lack of porosity.

SEC "Dry" in French. Off-dry is DEMI-SEC; MOELLEUX is sweet; DOUX is sweeter; LIQUOREUX is sweetest of all.

SÉLECTION MASSALE A method of planting a new vineyard block by selecting cuttings from the very best existing vines.

SHIPPER Term for exporting merchant, especially in Portugal.

SKIN CONTACT The act of allowing skins to macerate in juice, bringing color and texture to wine. Most whites are pressed off the skins, with no contact.

SOLERA A method of FRACTIONAL BLENDING—used most notably in Jerez, but also in other fortified winemaking regions such as the Douro—whereby incremental amounts of older vintages are blended with newer vintages. Fractionally blended fortified wines are also made in Australia, Greece, Cyprus, France, Italy and elsewhere.

SPRITZ The pinprick sensation that results when carbon dioxide is trapped in wine. Also called *pétillance* or *spritzig*.

SULFITES Sulfur dioxide is used as a fungicide in the vineyard and to prevent spoilage in winemaking. In the U.S., any finished wine containing more than 10 parts per million of sulfur dioxide is labeled with the words "contains sulfites."

SUR LIE Time spent "on the lees" (spent yeast cells) imparts a creamy texture to white wines, particularly if the lees are stirred.

TANNIN The compound that comes from grape skins, seeds and stems, as well as from oak barrels, contributing astringency and dryness of texture, most noticeably in red wines.

TECH SHEET A page of technical data relating to the vintage, vineyard site, harvest conditions, winemaking procedures and the finished wine.

TERROIR The notion that the location and setting of a vineyard can be perceived through the aroma and flavor of a wine.

TRADITIONAL METHOD *Méthode traditionnelle*, the labor-intensive process of producing sparkling wines such as Champagnes, Crémants, Cavas, Blanquettes, Franciacortas and the like, which acquire their fizz through a second fermentation in the bottle.

VIN DE PAYS A simple French country wine, higher in quality than a VIN DE TABLE.

WHOLE-CLUSTER FERMENTATION A process that—if managed correctly—captures fresh fruit flavors, increases savory and spicy aromas and smooths out tannins. Also called WHOLE-BUNCH FERMENTATION.

VIGNERON Grape-grower.

WINE THIEF Glass pipette used to remove a sample of wine from a barrel or cask. Also: a person who steals wine.

INDEX

AUTHOR'S ACKNOWLEDGMENTS

Thanks to Neil Beckett, Johanna Wilson and the *World of Fine Wine* team for making *Complete Wine Selector* happen. Also: colossal gratitude to my family for putting up with me during the production of this book.

PHOTOGRAPHIC CREDITS

All interior photography of Katherine Cole © Jon Wyand.

Pages 6, 7, 18, 55 © Jon Wyand
Page 82 © Inglenook Winery
Page 106 © Ambassadeurs des Vins Jaunes
Page 107 © Josko Gravner
Page 119 © Richard Mayson / Quinta do Centro / Sonho Lusitano Vinhos
Page 130 © Castello d'Albola / Casa Vinicola Zonin
Page 151 © Marchesi di Grésy
Page 155 © Gil Lempert-Schwarz
Page 162 © Quinta do Vesuvio / Symington Family Estates
Page 167 © Jesús Barquín
Page 184 © Crush Wine and Spirits
Page 186 © Ferry Plaza Wine Merchant
Page 187 © The Wine Cellar
Page 188 © Legrand Filles & Fils
Page 190 © Eataly
Page 191 © Lutter and Wegner
Page 192 © Steve's Fine Wine & Food
Page 194 © Berry Bros & Rudd
Page 199 © Guy Savoy
Page 201 © Gerard Basset OBE
Page 206 © Riesenthal Bottlebag
Page 206 © Wine Skin
Page 209 © Laguiole
Page 209 © The Durand
Pages 212–13 © Riedel